READING LISTS FOR COLLEGE-BOUND STUDENTS

DOUG ESTELL
MICHELE L. SATCHWELL
PATRICIA S. WRIGHT

Prentice Hall
New York • London • Toronto • Sydney • Tokyo • Singapore

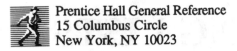 Prentice Hall General Reference
15 Columbus Circle
New York, NY 10023

Copyright © 1993, 1990 by Doug Estell,
Michele L. Satchwell and Patricia S. Wright
All rights reserved
including the right of reproduction
in whole or in part in any form

An Arco Book

Arco, Prentice Hall, and colophons are
registered trademarks of Simon & Schuster, Inc.

Library of Congress Cataloging-in-Publication Data

Estell, Doug
    Reading lists for college-bound students / Doug Estell,
Michele L. Satchwell, Patricia S. Wright.—2nd ed.
        p.   cm.
        ISBN 0-671-84712-0
        1. College students—Books and reading. 2. Universities and
colleges—United States—Entrance requirements. 3. High school
libraries—Book lists. 4. Bibliography—Best books. I. Satchwell,
Michele L. II. Wright, Patricia S. III. Title.
    Z1039.C65E88   1993
    028.5'35—dc20   92-10227
                                                           CIP

Manufactured in the United States of America

1   2   3   4   5   6   7   8   9   10

We dedicate this book to
Jodi Estell
Russ Satchwell
Lloyd Wright

CONTENTS

Preface to the Second Edition

In the new and improved Second Edition of *Reading Lists for College-Bound Students,* you'll find not only revised lists from your favorite colleges, but some brand-new lists as well.

In response to the BIG question "Who *are* the Top 10 authors?":

1. **William Shakespeare**
2. **William Faulkner**
3. **Charles Dickens**
4. **Ernest Hemingway**
5. **Jane Austen**
6. **Homer**
7. **Mark Twain**
8. **Sophocles**
9. **Nathaniel Hawthorne**
10. **F. Scott Fitzgerald**

CHAPTER 1

WHY YOU NEED THIS BOOK

"How can I best prepare for college?" is a question that students often ask themselves.

"I'm scared to death of freshman English."

"Is there any way I can have an edge?"

"What should I read to prepare for my first year?"

Here finally is a book that answers these questions. If you plan to go to college, this book will give you:

- suggested reading lists from representative American colleges

- a reading list of the 100 most-often-recommended books from these college lists

- a plan for making your personal reading list

- a chart for keeping a reading diary

- tips for better reading skills

Why Reading is Essential in College Preparation

Your success in college depends on your reading:

- It improves your vocabulary.

- It makes you a better writer.

- It helps you understand yourself and others, as well as the past and present societies you will be studying.

- It provides you with the background to succeed in college.

Let's look at each of these ideas.

Improve Your Vocabulary

Have you ever talked with a person whose way of speaking is very different from your own? Some examples might be a Southerner if you are from the North, an Easterner if you are from the West, or a person from a social class different enough from yours that his or her choice of words sounds strange to you. If you are around people from other environments long enough, you will pick up some of their words, their patterns of speech.

That's how you began to accumulate your vocabulary, isn't it? For your first few years your words—*mama, cookie, baby*, etc.—came mainly from those who raised you. You weren't born with these words in your mind. You heard them. Books can have the same effect on you. If you live for a while with authors such as Dickens or Shakespeare or Melville, you will begin to add their words to your vocabulary—and you won't have to look up each new word you encounter. When you hear words in your mind often enough, you begin to understand them and finally to use them—just as you did when you were a child.

Let's spend a moment reading a passage from Herman Melville's *Moby-Dick*. If you're not familiar with the book, it's a story about a mad sea captain, Ahab, and his enemy, the white whale Moby-Dick.

> But at this critical instant a sudden exclamation was heard that took every eye from the whale. With a start all glared at dark Ahab, who was surrounded by five dusky phantoms that seemed fresh formed out of air. The phantoms, for so they then seemed, were flitting on the other side of the deck, and, with a noiseless celerity, were casting loose the tackles and bands of the boat which swung there. This boat had always been deemed one of the spare boats, though technically called the captain's, on account of its hanging from the starboard quarter. The figure that now stood by its bows was tall and swart, with one white tooth evilly protruding from its steel-like lips. A rumpled Chinese jacket of black cotton funereally invested him, with wide black trousers of the same dark stuff. But strangely crowning this ebonness was a glistening white plaited turban, the living hair braided and coiled round and round upon his head. Less swart in aspect, the companions of this figure were of that vivid, tiger-yellow complexion peculiar to some of the aboriginal natives of the Manillas;—a race notorious for a certain diabolism of subtlety.

Weren't you able to feel the rising fear in this passage? Yet perhaps some of the words were new to you. In the middle of an exciting scene, you don't always need to turn to a dictionary to understand the meaning of a word. You can use context clues: the emotion in the passage, the meaning of the words around the unknown word, or the subject matter of the passage. If you encounter new words often enough in reading, they become part of your vocabulary. Knowing them will help you perform better on college entrance tests, in college courses, and on the job later in life.

Become a Better Writer

As you apply to colleges, you may find you're required to write a college application essay. Often these essays ask you to discuss something from your reading. Recently one of Notre Dame's questions asked for a discussion of Martin Luther King's famous "I Have a Dream" speech. Frequently the University of Pennsylvania has prospective students list four or five of their favorite books and discuss one of them. Stanford University often asks applicants to choose a favorite quotation and comment on its significance. Barnard College has its applicants list the books they have read during high school, saying, "the most diverse lists are the most attractive on an application." If colleges do not ask specific literary questions, they may instead ask you to "describe yourself." Your essay will be stronger if you can support your ideas with examples from your reading.

Once you get to college, the list of writing assignments will be almost endless. Reading can help you become a better writer with an enlarged vocabulary, more complex sentence patterns, and expanded ideas.

Obviously if you understand and use more words, you can communicate more effectively in writing as well as in speaking. But reading also can make your sentence patterns more sophisticated and more effective. Professor Martha Rainbolt of DePauw University says that works of 19th-century British fiction help show readers "the 'right' way to write sentences." How does this work?

As a child you began by imitating other people's sentence patterns. At first it was just one word: *bye-bye, cookie, mama.* Gradually you advanced to simple sentences: "Go bye-bye." "Want cookie." And then to more complex structures: "Please give me a cookie." "May I go to the store with you?" Finally you became as communicative as your desire and your environment allowed you.

Has your mom ever embarrassed you by showing your elementary school papers to your high school friends? Have you ever run across any of your old junior high book reports? Were you surprised at how simple they sound to you now? As you have experienced more sophisticated reading, your writing style has also become more sophisticated. As you read for college you will be building a foundation for the kind of expression expected by university professors. Unconsciously you absorb the patterns in what you read and you become a better writer.

No matter how elegant your sentences are, your writing will not impress your professors unless you have good ideas. The more you read, the more information you will have to write about.

According to the Temple University English Department, one reason writing is emphasized in college is that "industry, business, and government place high value on communications skills." From your reading you will strengthen these skills. You will acquire broader ideas and attitudes. You will learn to make value judgments. And therefore, you will develop improved critical thinking skills that will be reflected in your writing.

Better Understand Yourself and Others

You grew up in an alien world. We all do. When we are small, almost everyone is bigger and stronger and smarter than we. We spend our lives adapting to a world that is different from our inner world. Books can help here. They can help you understand your own feelings, ideas, opinions and those of others.

You've probably already experienced this. Did you read *A Separate Peace* or *The Catcher in the Rye*? Haven't you had some of the problems those young people faced? Experienced some of their feelings? Shared some of their opinions? Isn't it nice to know that someone out there is a little like you? The more you read, the more you will find this is true, and the more help you will get in thinking through your own ideas and emotions. Now and then you may even change your mind or your heart. Books on the college and university lists such as Hesse's *Siddhartha*, Sophocles' *Antigone*, and Twain's *The Adventures of Huckleberry Finn* are about some of the problems young people face.

Wide reading will also make you better able to understand the people you will be learning about in your other classes—history, sociology, psychology, education, and the rest. When you have read Harper Lee's *To Kill a Mockingbird*, you can begin to understand the emotions of those involved in the civil rights movement of the 1960s. After reading *The Pearl* by John Steinbeck, you come to understand how greed can corrupt people in a society. From Victor

Hugo's *Les Misérables* you learn about the poverty and despair that bred revolt in 19th-century France. The list of the 100 most-often-recommended works in Chapter 4 covers societies from ancient times to the present day. As you read you will learn of the successes and failures of particular nations and cultures.

Succeed in College

Most colleges will either give you credit or exempt you from classes on the basis of tests you take that demonstrate your mastery of the subject. You may be familiar with Advanced Placement programs, which offer such tests while you are in high school. When you have selected your college, you need to contact the admissions officer to find out if that university offers the College-Level Examination Program (CLEP) or similar programs. These programs can save you (and your parents) lots of money and time. How can you best prepare for these tests? READ.

Whether or not you will be able to test out of classes, reading will help you get the most out of the classes you do take. Let's look into your future. It is the second semester of your freshman year. You have three chapters to read in sociology, two in world history, two in trigonometry (plus the problems at the end of the chapters), and your freshman lit teacher wants you to read *The Iliad* by Friday. Can you feel the panic rising? If you had already read *The Iliad* last year and were familiar with it, all you would have to do is review it, not start from scratch. And if your world history professor assigns an essay asking you to discuss the Trojan War, well, you'd have it made. There are so many demands on your time when you are in college that reading now can give you the head start you may need to survive.

More than anywhere else, college is the place to share and explore ideas. If you have read lots of books before you get there, you will have more to share—both with your professors and with your friends.

CHAPTER 2

HOW TO USE THIS BOOK

You say you don't have time to read 100 books before you go to college? You may surprise yourself. If you read a few books at a time, you'll soon have made a sizeable dent in your reading list.

The most important thing is to be realistic about yourself, your reading ability, and your time limitations. In this chapter we'll look at

- the lists in this book
- a prototype of a personal reading list
- making a personal reading list

The Lists in This Book

In Chapter 4 is the list of the 100 most-often-recommended books compiled from individual college lists. Each book is annotated so you can have an idea of what it is about, when it was written, and the nationality of the author. In addition, you are given an affordable edition and the number of pages in that edition. Obviously this is a good list to choose from if you want to know what many colleges suggest.

In Chapter 5 are lists from 103 representative colleges and universities across the nation. Some have pre-college reading lists; others include selections from their freshman-sophomore syllabi or required core programs. As you scan this section, don't limit yourself only to the colleges you recognize. Professors from many institutions have given interesting tips on what to read and how to read.

Making a Personal Reading List

If you're like many students and your time is limited, start your reading with the ten or twenty books that sound most interesting. Choosing what you are going to read is like filling your plate at a Thanksgiving buffet. Like Thanksgiving food, all the books listed are good—some are filling and nutritious and others are delicious and fattening. It doesn't matter which you pick. Vonnegut's *Slaughterhouse Five* and Orwell's *Animal Farm*, even though they satirize serious matters, are delicious and fattening. Conrad's *Heart of Darkness* and Thoreau's *Walden* are filling and nutritious. The first leads you on an increasingly frightening river journey into the heart of Africa, and the second gives you ideas on being an individual—"marching to a different drummer."

Read as many kinds of books as possible. Don't limit yourself to one particular style, country, or time period, or to only male or female authors. The most important thing is that you have lots of variety in your reading.

If you think the book listed for a particular writer is too long or too difficult for the moment, choose another of his or her titles. If wading into Melville's *Moby-Dick* seems to be more than your schedule can handle right now, try one of his other classics such as *Billy Budd*.

On the following pages you will find a sample reading list and a blank list that you may use.

Notice that in the sample every category is filled with at least one work. When you have completed your reading, make sure that you, too, have read something from each category.

Have fun with this list. Remember to tailor it to fit your needs, your interests, and your busy schedule.

Personal Reading List: Sample

FICTION

American Novel
Fitzgerald, Great
  Gatsby
Updike, Rabbit, Run

British Novel
Orwell, Animal
  Farm
Austen, Pride and
  Prejudice

World Novel
Camus, The
  Stranger
Flaubert, Madame
  Bovary

Male Author
Hemingway, The Sun Also Rises
Crane, Red Badge of Courage

Female Author
Brontë, Jane Eyre
Cather, My Antonia

Pre-18th C. Works
Bible: "Job," "Genesis"
Chaucer, Canterbury Tales
  (Prologue & Wife of Bath's
  Tale)

18th C. Novel
Swift, Gulliver's Travels
Fielding, Tom Jones

19th C. Novel
Twain, Huckleberry Finn
Dickens, Great Expectations

20th C. Novel
Morrison, Sula
Salinger, Catcher in the Rye

Short Stories (American)
Faulkner, "The Bear"
Poe, "Fall of the House of
  Usher"

Short Stories (World)
Kafka, "Metamorphosis"
O'Connor, "A Good
  Man is Hard to Find"

DRAMA

Classical Drama

Sophocles, Antigone

Aristophanes, Lysistrata

American Drama

Miller, Death of a Salesman

Williams, Glass Menagerie

British Drama

Shakespeare, Hamlet

Shaw, Pygmalion

World Drama

Ibsen, A Doll's House

POETRY

Lyrical

Emily Dickinson

Walt Whitman

Robert Frost

Epic

Homer, The Odyssey

Dante, Inferno

NONFICTION

Biography

Franklin, Autobiography

History

Thoreau, Civil Disobedience

Philosophy/Religion

Plato, Apology

Science

Darwin, Origin of Species

Personal Reading List

FICTION

American Novel

_____
_____
_____
_____

British Novel

_____
_____
_____
_____

World Novel

_____
_____
_____
_____

Male Author

_____
_____

Female Author

_____
_____

Pre-18th C. Works

_____
_____
_____
_____

18th C. Novel

_____
_____
_____
_____

19th C. Novel

_____
_____
_____

20th C. Novel

_____
_____
_____

Short Stories (American)

_____
_____
_____

Short Stories (World)

_____
_____
_____

DRAMA

Classical Drama

_____

_____

_____

British Drama

_____

_____

_____

American Drama

_____

_____

_____

World Drama

_____

_____

_____

POETRY

Lyrical

_____

_____

_____

Epic

_____

_____

_____

NONFICTION

Biography

_____

_____

History

_____

_____

Philosophy/Religion

_____

_____

Science

_____

_____

Caution: Reader's Guides

Once you have made your personal reading list, you may be tempted to skip the books and invest in a complete set of *Cliff's Notes, Monarch Notes,* or some other type of reader's guides. DON'T! There is no substitute for the real thing. You cannot get a feel for the author's use of language, the speech patterns of the characters, or the vividness of the descriptive passages from reading ABOUT the book. Just as hearsay is not admissible as evidence in a court of law, knowing a book only through secondhand information from a reader's guide is not admissible in the college classroom.

Reader's guides can, however, help you if you are experiencing difficulty in understanding a particular book. If you have trouble understanding the main idea, isolating the theme, or interpreting the characters, the reader's guide can sometimes point you in the right direction, or at least give you a point of departure. Your librarian can help you find literary criticism that gives profiles of the authors' lives and synopses and critiques of their works. This is a better alternative.

CHAPTER **3**

WHAT TO LOOK FOR WHEN YOU READ

You've scanned the lists of the 100 most-often-recommended books and the lists from the colleges. You've made your personal reading list. And you've gone to the library and found one of the books from the lists. Maybe you've brought home four or five possible books. Not a bad idea. Give yourself some choice. Books are like people. Our moods often determine the company we keep.

Finally, you've decided what you are going to begin reading. Now what? Now you need to adopt what Coleridge called "a willing suspension of disbelief." WHAT? Relax. That simply means that while you're reading you have to accept the world the author presents to you, no matter how strange it seems to you. Don't decide that world is impossible or impossibly boring until you've given the book a good chance. Every book is like meeting a new person. It isn't fair to decide you don't like that person just because his hair is purple and orange. Sometimes the most eccentric people are the most interesting. And that is so for books. So read a few chapters before you reach a conclusion about any book. The more of it you read, the better you may like it.

When you've found a book that seems interesting, the secret is to relax and enjoy. Some day you may have to take a test on the particular book you are reading. But you'll have a chance to read it again before that test. At this point your only need is to get from the book what you can for your own enjoyment—and for enlightenment—because most of the books on these lists are not pure escape reading. From them you can get insights into your self and your world.

One way to keep track of what you've read is to keep a reading diary. What should it include?

No matter what you read, it helps to find some information about the author—when and where he or she was writing and any other interesting personal information. Books are not written in a vacuum. They reflect the influence of the author's surroundings on his or her particular thoughts, attitudes, and emotions.

It is also important to be aware of the main idea of the work itself. If you're reading fiction, you may want to jot down the main elements: character, plot, setting. If your book is nonfiction, be sure to list the support for the author's main idea. In poetry you should note the word pictures that are most vivid.

After you've finished your reading, be sure to note what was unforgettable about the work. Write down your evaluations. Often writing will help you crystallize your impressions of the work.

On the following page you will find a sample format for a reading diary. Just remember to adapt it to fit your needs.

Reading Diary

TITLE_____When written:_____

AUTHOR_____Nationality:_____

_____

_____

_____

_____

TYPE OF WORK (Fiction, nonfiction, poetry, etc.)_____

_____

_____

MAIN IDEA_____

_____

_____

_____

_____

_____

_____

_____

IMPORTANT ELEMENTS_____

_____

_____

_____

_____

_____

_____

_____

EVALUATION_____

_____

_____

_____

_____

_____

_____

_____

_____

_____

_____

CHAPTER **4**

THE 100 MOST-OFTEN-RECOMMENDED WORKS

This list of the 100 works most frequently recommended by the colleges and universities is compiled from the pre-college reading lists, freshmen syllabi, and core programs detailed in Chapter 5. The annotations will help you decide which books you'd like to read first.

The author's nationality and the date of publication are in parentheses before each annotation. Most of these books are available in many editions. At the end of each annotation you are given a selected edition, identified by publisher, with the number of pages in that particular edition. If you are interested in other works by the same author, alternate suggestions that were consistently mentioned by the colleges appear in parentheses. A key to the abbreviations for the publishers and the authors' nationalities is included at the end of the chapter.

Novels and Short Stories

Austen, Jane, *Pride and Prejudice* (BR, 1813): A novel about love and marriage among the English country gentry of Austen's day. The hero's pride in his social class conflicts with the heroine's prejudice against him based on first impression. WSP 464 pp. (*Emma*)

Baldwin, James, *Go Tell It on the Mountain* (AM, 1953): This semi-autobiographical novel about a 14-year-old black youth's religious conversion is based on Baldwin's experience as a young storefront preacher in Harlem. DP 224 pp. (*Notes of a Native Son*)

Bellow, Saul, *Seize the Day* (AM, 1956): In this novella, a son grapples with his love and hate for an unworthy father. When he won the Nobel Prize in 1976, Bellow was cited for "the human understanding and the analysis of contemporary culture that are combined in his work." VKP 107 pp. (*Henderson the Rain King*)

Brontë, Charlotte, *Jane Eyre* (BR, 1847): This romantic novel introduced a new type of heroine to English fiction. Jane Eyre is an intelligent, passionate, and not especially beautiful young woman who falls in love with a strange moody man tormented by dark secrets. SC 461 pp.

Brontë, Emily, *Wuthering Heights* (BR, 1847): One of the masterpieces of English romanticism, this is a novel of love and revenge. The demonic passion of the hero-villain Heathcliff destroys his beloved Catherine, her family, and eventually himself. WSP 460 pp.

Camus, Albert, *The Stranger* (FR, 1942): An existential novel in which a young man, observing rather than participating in life, commits a senseless murder. While in prison awaiting execution, he comes to value life. Camus won the Nobel Prize in 1957. VIN 154 pp.

Carroll, Lewis, *Alice's Adventures in Wonderland* (BR, 1865): A fantasy in which Alice follows the White Rabbit to a dream world. The characters she encounters (the Mad Hatter, the Queen of Hearts, and others) are part of the adult world she must deal with. Sir John Tenniel's illustrations have become as classic as Lewis Carroll's story. NAL 143 pp. with annotations. (*Through the Looking Glass*)

Cather, Willa, *My Antonia* (AM, 1918): A realistic novel about immigrant pioneers as they strive to adapt to the Nebraska prairies. It is the story of the struggles of Antonia and other women who are strengthened by the harsh realities of life. HM 238 pp. (*Death Comes for the Archbishop*)

Cervantes, Miguel de, *Don Quixote* (SP, 1605, 1617): A novel in which an eccentric old gentleman setting out as a knight goes "tilting at windmills" to right the wrongs of the world. This work, made up of twelve stories, "has been translated into more languages than any other book except the Bible." (L.H. Hornstein) VKP 653 pp.

Chopin, Kate, *The Awakening* (AM, 1899): This is the story of a New Orleans woman who abandons her husband and children to search for love and self-understanding. A controversial book when it was published because of the character's extramarital affair, the book was virtually ignored for 50 years. BC 208 pp.

Conrad, Joseph, *Heart of Darkness* (BR, 1902): A probing psychological novel that explores the darkness in the soul of each man. Conrad's narrator Marlow makes a journey into the depths of the Congo where he discovers the extent to which greed can corrupt a good man. SC 93 pp. (bound with *The Secret Sharer*). (*Lord Jim*)

Crane, Stephen, *The Red Badge of Courage* (AM, 1895): This Civil War novel, which Crane called "a psychological portrayal of fear," reveals the grim aspects of war in the life of an ordinary soldier. Henry Fleming joins the army full of romantic visions of battle which are shattered by combat. WSP 224 pp.

Defoe, Daniel, *Robinson Crusoe* (BR, 1719): Based on the true story of Alexander Selkirk's sea experiences, this novel is about the adventures of a man who spends 24 years on an isolated island. With the help of an islander whom he names Friday, Crusoe shows courage and ingenuity in meeting the challenges of his predicament. BC 288 pp.

Dickens, Charles, *Great Expectations* (BR, 1860–61): A novel about Pip, a poor boy, who is made rich by a mysterious benefactor, sets out to realize his "great expectations," and finally becomes a man of worth and character. As in all his works, Dickens populates this novel with memorable and eccentric characters. WSP 466 pp.

Dostoevski, Feodor, *Crime and Punishment* (RU, 1866): A psychological novel about a poor student who murders an old woman pawnbroker and her sister. After the crime, his conscience bothers him until he confesses. He is sent to Siberia, and finally becomes truly repentent. BC 496 pp. (*The Brothers Karamazov*)

Eliot, George, *The Mill on the Floss* (BR, 1860): The Victorian world of male supremacy is the background for this novel of a stormy relationship between a brother and sister. Maggie Tulliver's life is miserable because her brother Tom disapproves of her choices of romances. BC 474 pp. (*Middlemarch*)

Ellison, Ralph, *Invisible Man* (AM, 1947): "I am an invisible man," begins this novel of an unnamed black man's search for identity as an individual and as a member of his race and his society. This story goes beyond one man's search and chronicles every man's struggle to find himself. VIN 568 pp.

Faulkner, William, *The Sound and the Fury* (AM, 1929): The theme for this Nobel Prize–winning author's novel is the decline of the Southern family. Presented through four points of view, it examines the deterioration of the Compson family. VIN 371 pp. ("The Bear")

Fielding, Henry, *Tom Jones* (BR, 1749): A humorous novel about the adventures of an amorous young man whose impulsiveness often leads him into difficult situations. PC 874 pp. (*Joseph Andrews*)

Fitzgerald, F. Scott, *The Great Gatsby* (AM, 1925): A novel in which a young man corrupts himself and the American Dream in order to regain a lost love. *The Great Gatsby* "belongs not only to American but to

world literature . . . to the tragic predicament of humanity as a whole."
(A. E. Dyson) S 182 pp.

Flaubert, Gustave, *Madame Bovary* (FR, 1857): A realistic novel in
which a young wife is bored with her husband. In her extramarital affairs, she seeks unsuccessfully to find the emotional experiences she has
read about in romantic novels. PC 361 pp.

Forster, E. M., *A Passage to India* (BR, 1924): A pessimistic novel about
man's inhumanity to man. A young English woman in British-ruled India accuses an Indian doctor of a sexual assault; her accusation causes
racial tension between the British and Indian communities and destroys the young man's career. HBJ 322 pp.

García Márquez, Gabriel, *One Hundred Years of Solitude* (CO, 1967):
This Latin American novel portrays seven generations in the lives of
the Buendia family. Garcia Marquez employs a technique called magic
realism—the use of magic, myth, and religion to intensify reality. AV
383 pp.

Golding, William, *Lord of the Flies* (BR, 1954): In this novel a group of
English schoolboys who are stranded on an island without adults become savages. This moral fable implies that defects in society are
caused in part by defects in individuals. PU 190 pp.

Hardy, Thomas, *Tess of the D'Urbervilles* (BR, 1891): A Victorian novel
in which the happiness and marriage of Tess and her husband are destroyed because she confesses to him that she bore a child as the result
of a forced sexual relationship with her employer's son. BC 414 pp.
(*The Return of the Native*)

Hawthorne, Nathaniel, *The Scarlet Letter* (AM, 1850): A novel about an
adulterous Puritan woman who keeps secret the identity of the father
of her illegitimate child. Her sin and the secret sin of the father are
dwarfed by the vengefulness of her husband. WSP 276 pp.

Hemingway, Ernest, *A Farewell to Arms* (AM, 1929): In this semiautobiographical novel that takes place during World War I, an American
lieutenant falls in love and runs away with the woman who nurses him
to health. Hemingway, winner of the 1954 Nobel Prize, is known for
his journalistic style. S 336 pp. (*The Sun Also Rises*)

Hurston, Zora Neale, *Their Eyes Were Watching God* (AM, 1937): A
novel about a woman's search for a happy life. "The image of the black
woman as the mule of the world becomes a metaphor for the roles that
Janie repudiates in her quest for self-fulfillment. . ." (Sherley Williams)
UIP 286 pp.

Huxley, Aldous, *Brave New World* (BR, 1932): In this bitter satire about the future, Nobel prize–winner Huxley conceives a world controlled by advances in science and social changes. Individuals are no longer important and their lives are planned out for them. BC 177 pp.

James, Henry, *The Turn of the Screw* (AM, 1898): This novella is a study of good and evil in which the children are "the arena and the victim" (Hortense Calisher). A governess in charge of two children discovers they are under the evil influence of ghosts and attempts to save them. BC 103 pp. (*Portrait of a Lady*)

Joyce, James, *A Portrait of the Artist as a Young Man* (IR, 1916): A novel about a young man growing up in Ireland and rebelling against family, country, and religion to become an artist. Joyce's use of stream-of-consciousness has influenced many modern writers. P 253 pp.

Kafka, Franz, *The Trial* (CZ, 1925): In this novel a man is tried for a crime he knows nothing about, yet he feels guilty and is executed. W. H. Auden described Kafka as "the author who comes nearest to bearing the same kind of relation to our age [that] Dante, Shakespeare, and Goethe bore to theirs. . ." SCN 288 pp. (*Metamorphosis*)

Lawrence, D. H., *Sons and Lovers* (BR, 1913): An autobiographical novel about a youth who is torn between a dominant working-class father and a possessive genteel mother. "Lawrence has been one of the most influential figures in Anglo-American literature and life of this century." (Martin Seymour-Smith) SI 406 pp. (*Women in Love*)

Lewis, Sinclair, *Babbitt* (AM, 1922): A satirical novel about a middle-class businessman in an average midwestern city. Babbitt becomes a pathetic yet comical character because of his exaggerated sense of his importance. Lewis was the first American to win the Nobel Prize. SC 319 pp. (*Main Street*)

Malamud, Bernard, *The Assistant* (AM, 1957): A novel in which a Gentile hoodlum 'out of a compelling pity' goes to work for a Jewish grocer whom he has robbed. Finally taking the grocer's place, he becomes a Jew himself and accepts all that is Jewish. AV 304 pp.

Mann, Thomas, *Death in Venice* (GE, 1912): In this novella an author becomes aware of a darker side of himself when he visits Venice and fantasizes a love for a young boy he sees there. This story alludes frequently to Greek literature and mythology. BC 68 pp.

Melville, Herman, *Moby-Dick* (AM, 1851): A complex novel about a mad sea captain's pursuit of the White Whale. To Clifton Fadiman, "as we turn the pages, our hands close about an imaginary harpoon . . . in our ears rings the cry: 'There she blows!' " WSP 466 pp.

Morrison, Toni, *Sula* (AM, 1973): A novel about the lifelong friend-ship of two vastly different women who become estranged when one causes the other's husband to abandon her. "Its humor is earthy and delightful, and its dialogue is especially sharp." (Jonathan Yardley) NAL 176 pp. (*Beloved*)

O'Connor, Flannery, *A Good Man Is Hard to Find* (AM, 1955): A triad of short stories set in Georgia. The title story is about the deadly con-frontation between a religious grandmother and a mad murderer. O'Connor's characters "hold their fears at bay with a rustic religiosity that is as functional as their speech or dress." (James Greene) HBJ 251 pp.

Olsen, Tillie, *Tell Me a Riddle* (AM, 1956–60): A group of short stories including a novella about the problems of aging. An old man and woman quarrel bitterly about whether to stay in their own home or to move to the Haven, a retirement home. DP 125 pp.

Orwell, George, *Animal Farm* (BR, 1945): The classic satire of commu-nism in which the pigs lead the other farm animals in a revolution against the humans, setting up their own government where "All ani-mals are equal, but some animals are more equal than others." SC 128 pp. (*1984*)

Paton, Alan, *Cry, the Beloved Country* (SA, 1948): A novel about a black minister in South Africa who goes in search of his children and finds them corrupted and destroyed by white society. The roots of both the generational and racial conflicts of black South Africans are explored in this story. S 283 pp.

Poe, Edgar Allan, *Great Tales and Poems* (AM, 1839–45): Poe is consid-ered the father of detective stories and a master of supernatural tales. The stories most often recommended are: "The Fall of the House of Usher," "The Purloined Letter," "The Cask of Amontillado," "The Pit and the Pendulum," and "The Tell-Tale Heart." WSP 373 pp.

Salinger, J. D., *The Catcher in the Rye* (AM, 1951): A novel in which a prep school dropout rejects the "phoniness" he sees all about him. *Catcher* is "one of those rare books that influenced one generation after another, causing each to claim it as its own." (Adam Moss) BC 212 pp.

Scott, Sir Walter, *Ivanhoe* (BR, 1820): A story of chivalry in which the Norman hero Wilfred finally wins his true love, the Saxon Rowena, with the help of the Black Knight (Richard the Lion-Hearted in dis-guise) and brings about a temporary peace between the Normans and the Saxons. SC 467 pp. (*Heart of Midlothian*)

Shelley, Mary, *Frankenstein* (BR, 1818): A gothic tale of terror in which Frankenstein creates a monster from corpses. Because everyone who sees him fears him, the monster despairs and turns on his creator. BC 206 pp.

Steinbeck, John, *The Grapes of Wrath* (AM, 1939): A historical novel by the 1962 Nobel Prize–winner about the desperate flight of tenant farmers from the Midwest during the Depression. The Joad family struggles to retain their humanity and dignity in the face of the hostility they find in California. P 581 pp.

Swift, Jonathan, *Gulliver's Travels* (BR, 1726): A satire on mankind in which an 18th-century Englishman visits foreign lands populated by bizarre creatures who illuminate many of the vices and weaknesses of his society. BC 217 pp.

Thackeray, William Makepeace, *Vanity Fair* (BR, 1847–48): A novel of 19th-century upper-middle-class British society that portrays 20 years in the lives of two young women very opposite in character: gentle, sentimental Amelia and lively, cunning Becky. P 797 pp.

Tolstoy, Leo, *War and Peace* (RU, 1865–69): A historical novel of the Napoleonic Wars that celebrates the Russian spirit and shows the effect of war and peace on every social class in Russian society. SC 1,453 pp.

Turgenev, Ivan, *Fathers and Sons* (RU, 1862): In this novel two young men experience difficulty in their relationships with their parents and with their women friends. "The aspirations of Russia's liberal youth are pitted against those of the conservative landowning gentry. . ." (R. Freedman) BC 203 pp.

Twain, Mark, *The Adventures of Huckleberry Finn* (AM, 1886): In this novel Huck takes a trip down the river with a runaway slave and learns the worth of life. According to Ernest Hemingway, "All modern American literature comes from one book by Mark Twain called *Huckleberry Finn*." BC 292 pp.

Updike, John, *Rabbit, Run* (AM, 1961): The first of the Rabbit Angstrom novels in which an immature young man still longing for the lost glory of his youth runs away from his responsibilities and abandons his wife and child. FA 284 pp.

Voltaire, *Candide* (FR, 1759): A satire against those who complacently accept life's disasters. This bitter criticism is disguised as a rollicking travel story in which Candide is puzzled because everything bad happens to him in this "best of all possible worlds." BC 128 pp.

Vonnegut, Kurt, *Slaughterhouse Five* (AM, 1969): A semiautobiographical novel about the firebombing of Dresden in World War II. In the story a time traveller, Billy Pilgrim, finds peace in a future world where he is "grateful that so many of those moments are nice." DP 205 pp. (*Cat's Cradle*)

Walker, Alice, *The Color Purple* (AM, 1982): A novel that focuses on "the role of male domination in the frustration of the black woman's struggle for independence." (Mel Watkins) In this story a young black girl sees herself as property until another woman teaches her to value herself. WSP 295 pp.

Welty, Eudora, *Thirteen Stories* (AM, 1965): A collection of short stories about people and life in the deep South. Most often mentioned by colleges are "Why I Live at the PO," "The Worn Path," and "The Petrified Man." HBJ 243 pp.

Wharton, Edith, *The Age of Innocence* (AM, 1920): A novel about a couple condemned to a loveless marriage by the conventions of their social class. "Wharton's work formed a bridge from the 19th-century novel to the magazine fiction of the present." (Louise Brogan) S 384 pp. (*The House of Mirth*)

Woolf, Virginia, *To the Lighthouse* (BR, 1927): Written in stream-of-consciousness, this semiautobiographical novel describes the Ramsey family's life in their country home. The lighthouse they see from the window is a symbolic goal for them all. HBJ 310 pp. (*A Room of One's Own*)

Wright, Richard, *Native Son* (AM, 1940): In this novel Bigger Thomas, a young black man from the Chicago slums, lashes out against a hostile society by committing two murders. The book is based partly on Wright's experiences, partly on an actual murder case. H&R 398 pp.

Drama

Aeschylus, *Orestia* (GR, 458 BC): A triad of plays in which a son seeks revenge against his mother for the murder of his father. In the final play he is exonerated for killing his mother by a tribunal of Athenian judges and the goddess Athena. P 182 pp.

Aristophanes, *Lysistrata* (GR, 411 BC): In this comedy the women of warring Athens and Sparta go on a marital strike until their men end their fighting. "Aristophanes made in this play a last appeal, half farcical, half serious, for peace." (Sir Paul Harvey) BC 42 pp. (in *The Complete Works of Aristophanes*)

Beckett, Samuel, *Waiting for Godot* (IR, 1952): A Theater of the Absurd play in which two tramps sit endlessly waiting for someone named Godot who never arrives. GRO 68 pp.

Brecht, Bertolt, *Mother Courage and Her Children* (GE, 1941): In this antiwar play set during the Thirty Years War, Mother Courage moves her wagon from battlefront to battlefront peddling her wares. One by one her three children are killed even though she seeks to profit from war, not become personally involved in it. GRO 129 pp.

Chekhov, Anton, *The Cherry Orchard* (RU, 1904): The members of an aristocratic family in this play are unwilling and unable to face the loss of their property. Their plight depicts the decline of the powerful Russian landowners following the end of the feudal system in 1861. HE 67 pp. (*The Three Sisters*)

Euripides, *Medea* (GR, 431 BC): In this tragedy of vengeance, Medea is a passionate woman whose love turns to hate when her husband deserts her. It climaxes with her killing their two sons. P 85 pp. (*The Bacchae*)

Goethe, Johann von, *Faust, Part I* (GE, 1808): A play about the legendary scholar who sells his soul to the devil. In this poetic drama, Faust is attracted to a young peasant girl. The devil's plans for his soul are temporarily defeated because Faust's lust for her turns to love. AN 355 pp.

Ibsen, Henrik, *A Doll's House* (NO, 1879): In this drama the main character slams the door and walks out on a marriage based on inequality. Her revolt against her marriage to a selfish, hypocritical man who treats her as a doll rather than an individual gave impetus to the fight for women's rights. P 231 pp.

Marlowe, Christopher, *Doctor Faustus* (BR, 1604): In this play, Faust is torn between his lust for knowledge as a means to power and his awareness of the sinfulness of his desires. Because the legend of Faust appears so frequently in the arts, the term *Faustian* has come to mean a willingness to sacrifice spiritual values in return for knowledge or power. WSP 208 pp.

Miller, Arthur, *Death of a Salesman* (AM, 1949): A Pulitzer prize–winning play in which a travelling salesman "riding on a smile and a shoeshine" realizes that his dreams will never be real and, unable to cope with the failures of his life, commits suicide. P 138 pp.

Molière, *The Misanthrope* (FR, 1666): Alceste, the leading character in this comedy, is admirable in hating the hypocrisy in his society. In his zeal for complete honesty, however, he succeeds in becoming a complete fool. P 75 pp. (*Tartuffe*)

O'Neill, Eugene, *Desire Under the Elms* (AM, 1924): A naturalistic drama about love, lust, and greed that contrasts a sensitive, emotional son with his severe, puritannical father. VIN 55 pp. (*The Emperor Jones*)

Shakespeare, William, *Hamlet* (BR, 1600): A great tragedy in which a prince is troubled by his inability to act to avenge the "murder most foul" of his father. William Hazlett says the play "abounds most in striking reflections on human life. . ." WSP 174 pp. (Many colleges urge students to read as much Shakespeare as possible: at least one tragedy, one comedy, and one history.)

Shaw, George Bernard, *Pygmalion* (BR, 1913): A play in which a professor of phonetics interferes with the social order by teaching a Cockney girl to act and speak like a duchess. WSP 176 pp. (*Saint Joan*)

Sophocles, *Oedipus Rex* (GR, 430 BC): The tragedy of a king who unwittingly has killed his father and married his mother. When he discovers what he has done, he blinds himself for "there is nothing beautiful left to see in this world." WSP 108 pp.

Wilde, Oscar, *The Importance of Being Earnest* (BR, 1895): A worldly and cynical farce about a confusion of identities that ends happily when the real Earnest turns out to be a long-lost infant whose nurse had absentmindedly misplaced him. AV 83 pp. (*Lady Windermere's Fan*)

Wilder, Thornton, *Our Town* (AM, 1938): In this Pulitzer Prize–winning play the stage manager speaks directly to the audience from a set bare of props. The play tells the story of two families as they experience daily life, love and marriage, and death. H&R 103 pp.

Williams, Tennessee, *The Glass Menagerie* (AM, 1945): The mother in this play dwells on the past and longs to find "a gentleman caller" for her crippled daughter who has withdrawn into the world of her glass animals. As in many of Williams's plays, the characters live in a world of unfulfilled dreams. NDB 115 pp. (*A Streetcar Named Desire*)

Poetry

Allison, Alexander, Ed., *Norton Anthology of Poetry* (Shorter Edition): A collection of poetry by American and British poets. The poets most frequently recommended by the colleges are: William Blake ("Songs of Innocence and Experience"); Robert Browning; Emily Dickinson; T. S. Eliot ("The Love Song of J. Alfred Prufrock"); Robert Frost; John Keats; William Shakespeare (the sonnets); Alfred, Lord Tennyson; William Wordsworth; and William Butler Yeats. NO 628 pp.

Anonymous, *Beowulf* (BR, *c* 700 AD): In this adventurous Old English epic poem, Beowulf overcomes monsters and slays a fire-breathing dragon. The poem is based on Norse legends and historical events of the sixth century. ME 121 pp.

Anonymous, *Sir Gawain and the Green Knight* (BR, *c* 1350–1400): "The jewel of medieval English literature" (M. Gaston Paris), this Arthurian tale is about the ordeals an ideal knight undergoes to prove his courage and his virtue. The two main episodes are Gawain's beheading of the terrible Green Knight and his efforts to resist the advances of a beautiful lady. P 176 pp.

Chaucer, Geoffrey, *Canterbury Tales* (BR, *c* 1387–1400): In this poetic narrative, Chaucer presents a colorful group of medieval travellers on their way to a religious shrine. On their journey they tell each other tales: some amusing, some serious, some ribald. WSP 525 pp. (Many colleges suggest reading only the prologue and one or two tales.)

Dante, *Inferno* (IT, *c* 1320): In this first book of *The Divine Comedy*, Dante's journey through Hell reveals the medieval view of sin. As he travels through the different levels of the Underworld, he witnesses the punishments for sin. BC 400 pp.

Homer, *The Odyssey* (GR, *c* 9th century BC): The epic of Odysseus' ordeals after the Trojan War as he tries for ten years to return home to Ithaca. On his journey he faces the dangers of the Cyclops, the Sirens, Circe, and others. Many other writers have used the character and the journey of Odysseus (Ulysses) in their works. WSP 352 pp. (*The Iliad*)

Milton, John, *Paradise Lost* (BR, 1667): Considered the greatest epic in any modern language, this poem tells of Satan's temptation of Adam and Eve, their expulsion from the Garden of Eden (Paradise), and the promise of their eventual salvation by the Son of God. ME 344 pp.

Vergil, *The Aeneid* (IT, *c*18 BC): This epic poem recounts the troubled journey of Aeneas as he leads the survivors of Troy to Italy where they become the founders of Rome. P 361 pp.

Whitman, Walt, *Leaves of Grass* (AM, 1855): In his use of free verse and his emphasis on the importance of the individual, Whitman was a forerunner of modern poetry. In these twelve untitled poems he wanted to "elevate, enlarge, purify, deepen, and make happy the attributes of the body and soul of man." BC 440 pp.

Miscellaneous

Aristotle, *Poetics* (GR, 4th cent. BC): A treatise on literary principles. The theories of tragedy in this work still influence Western drama. Called by Dante "the master of those who know," Aristotle is one of the world's greatest philosophers. UNC 70 pp.

Augustine, Saint, *Confessions* (IT, 397–401): A spiritual autobiography of St. Augustine's early life and his conversion to Christianity. His is "the only detailed account of the childhood of a great man which antiquity has left us." (Maynard Mack) ME 350 pp.

Bible: A collection of the sacred literature of Judaism and Christianity. Much of our Western writing alludes to the language and the stories in the Bible. Many colleges suggest the King James Version for literary study. NAL 972 pp.

Darwin, Charles, *Origin of Species* (BR, 1859): Darwin's book on his theories of natural selection and of evolution was a sellout the day it was issued and caused a storm of controversy that still continues today. ME 476 pp. (*The Voyage of the Beagle*)

Emerson, Ralph Waldo, "The American Scholar" in *Essays* (AM, 1837): An address at Harvard in which Emerson urged Americans to declare intellectual independence from Europe, to be thinkers and "not parrots of other men's thought." WSP 21 pp. ("Self-Reliance")

Franklin, Benjamin, *Autobiography* (AM, 1867): An account of Franklin's life and achievements during the first 51 years of his life. In it Franklin appears "as a universal genius . . . the embodiment of what we like to call the American spirit." (S. E. Morrison) COL 156 pp.

Freud, Sigmund, *Civilization and Its Discontents* (GE, 1930): A book about the conflict between the human desire for personal freedom and the demands of society. Freud writes that "The price we pay for our advance in civilization is a loss of happiness through the heightening of the sense of guilt." NO 109 pp. (*Dora*)

Hamilton, Edith, *Mythology* (AM 1940): A collection of Greek, Roman, and Norse myths and legends that are often alluded to in the language and literature of the Western world. NAL 355 pp.

Machiavelli, Niccolò, *The Prince* (IT, 1532): A treatise giving the absolute ruler practical advice on ways to maintain a strong central government. The term *Machiavellian* has for generations meant "ruthless and deceitful," because Machiavelli theorized that politics are above moral law. OUP 99 pp.

Marx, Karl, *Communist Manifesto* (GE, 1848): Written with Friedrich Engels as the official platform of the International Communist League, this short book expresses Marx's belief in the inevitability of conflict between social classes and calls on the workers of the world to unite and revolt. WSP 143 pp.

Montaigne, Michel de, *Selected Essays* (FR, 1580): The creator of the personal essay, Montaigne wrote about many subjects—cannibals, friendship, women, books, prayer. Though the entire work is a self-portrait, this book about one man is "really a book about all men." (Walter Kerr) MUP 344 pp.

Plato, *Republic* (GR, *c* 370 BC): In this dialogue Plato creates an ideal society where justice is equated with health and happiness in the state and in the individual. Echoing Omar about the Koran, Ralph Waldo Emerson said of the *Republic*, "Burn the libraries, for their value is in this book." H 288 pp. (*Apology*)

Thoreau, Henry David, *Walden* (AM, 1854): In this book Thoreau, an extreme individualist, advised "a man is rich in proportion to the number of things he can afford to let alone." *Walden* is about the 26 months he spent alone in the woods to "front the essential facts of life." SC 221 pp. (*Civil Disobedience*)

Publisher Abbreviations

AN	Anchor Publishing Company
AV	Avon Books
BC	Bantam Classics
COL	Collier Books
DP	Dell Publishing Company, Inc.
FA	Fawcett Crest Books
GRO	Grove Press
H	Hacket Publishing Company, Inc.
H&R	Harper & Row, Publishers
HBJ	Harcourt Brace Jovanovich
HE	James H. Heinemann, Inc.
HM	Houghton-Mifflin Company
ME	Mentor Books
MUP	Manchester University Press
NAL	New American Library
NDB	New Directions Books
NO	W. W. Norton & Company, Inc.
OUP	Oxford University Press
P	Penguin Books

PC	Penguin Classics
PU	G. P. Putnam's Sons
S	Charles Scribner's Sons
SC	Signet Classics
SCH	Schocken Books, Inc.
SI	Signet Books
UIP	University of Illinois Press
UNC	University of North Carolina Press
VIN	Vintage Books
VKP	Viking Paperbound Portables
WSP	Washington Square Press

Nationalities of the Authors

AM	American
BR	British
CO	Colombian
CZ	Czechoslovakian
FR	French
GE	German
GR	Greek
IR	Irish
IT	Italian
NO	Norwegian
RU	Russian
SA	South African
SP	Spanish

CHAPTER **5**

THE COLLEGE AND UNIVERSITY LISTS

Alaska Pacific University
4104 University Drive
Anchorage, AK 99508
(907) 564-8288

According to Professor Aubrey Nixon, Assistant to the Chair and Faculty of Humanities, Arts, and Communication, the following is a general list of the texts required in several of Alaska Pacific's introductory English courses.

APPROACHES TO LITERATURE

Diyanni, Robert	*Literature: Reading Literature, Poetry, Drama, the Essay*

WORLD LITERATURE

	Exodus from the Bible
	Gilgamesh (Herbert Mason, tr.)
	Mahabharata (William Buck, tr.)
Aeschylus	*Oresteia*
Dante	*The Inferno (Alan Mandelbaum, tr.)*
Shikibu, Murasaki	*The Tale of Genji*

BRITISH LITERATURE

Blake, William	*The Marriage of Heaven and Hell*
Butler, Samuel	*Erewhon*
Shakespeare, William	*The Tempest*
Swift, Jonathan	*Gulliver's Travels*

Genres in Literature: The Novel

Mack, Maynard, et al., eds.	*Norton Anthology of World Masterpieces,* Vol.1, 5th ed.
Brontë, Emily	*Wuthering Heights*
Burgess, Anthony	*A Clockwork Orange*
Conrad, Joseph	*Heart of Darkness*
Flaubert, Gustave	*Madame Bovary*
Hardy, Thomas	*Tess of the D'Urbervilles*
Hemingway, Ernest	*A Farewell to Arms*
Lawrence, D. H.	*Women in Love*
Tolstoy, Leo	*Kreutzer Sonata*

Medieval Literature

Beowulf (Raffel, tr.)
The Maginogi (Ford, tr.)
Parzifal (Hatto, tr.)

Genres in Literature: The European Novel

Austen, Jane	*Pride and Prejudice*
Balzac, Honoré De	*Lost Illusions*
Dickens, Charles	*Oliver Twist*
Flaubert, Gustave	*A Sentimental Education*
Stendhal (Henri Beyle)	*The Red and the Black*
Thackeray, William Makepeace	*Vanity Fair*

Themes In Literature: Northern Literature

Carter, Marilyn	*Legends, Tales & Totems of Alaska*
Cornberg, David	*Liquid Mirrors*
McPhee, John	*Coming into the Country*

Amherst College
Amherst, MA 01002
(413) 542-2328

Amherst's course *Writing about Reading* is primarily intended for freshmen and sophomores. It is an introduction to a variety of texts and the reading problems they pose. Writing is frequent—at least one short paper every week. The course includes the following works:

Bender, Robert & Charles Squier, eds.	*Sonnet: An Anthology*
Jacobs, Harriet	*Incidents in the Life of a Slave Girl*
Middleton, Thomas	*The Changeling* (Patricia Thomson, ed.)
Morrison, Toni	*Beloved*
Omang, Joanne, ed.	*Psychological Operations in Guerrilla Warfare*
Pynchon, Thomas	*The Crying of Lot 49*

The supplemental texts that might be included are:

Barthes, Roland	*Camera Lucida: Reflections on Photography*
Berger, John	*Ways of Seeing*
Kawabata, Yasunari	*Snow Country*
McLuhan, Marshall	*Understanding Media: The Extensions of Man*
Miller, Frank	*Batman: Year One or The Dark Knight Returns*
Molière	*The Misanthrope* (Richard Wilbur, tr.)
Spiegelman, Art	*Maus: A Survivor's Tale*

Arizona State University
Tempe, AZ 85287-0705
(602) 965-7788

Freshmen at Arizona State are required to take a composition course in which the writing is based on selections from several readers. The more reading the students have done prior to their entry into the university, the better will be their background for writing. Specific texts for Arizona's composition courses are selected from the following:

DICTIONARIES:

Webster's Ninth New Collegiate

Webster's New World Dictionary, 3rd ed., 1988

HANDBOOKS:

Guth, Hans P.	*New English Handbook*
Howell & Memering	*Brief Handbook for Writers*

RHETORICS:

Bean, John and John Rammage	*Writing Arguments: A Rhetoric with Readings*
D'Angelo, Frank	*Process and Thought in Composition*
Scholes, Robert & Nancy Comley	*The Practice of Writing*
Spatt, Brenda	*Writing from Sources*
Warnick, Barbara & Edward Inch	*Critical Thinking and Communication: The Use of Reason in Argument*

READERS:

Behrens, Laurence & L. J. Rosen	*Writing and Reading Across the Curriculum*
Booth, Wayne C. & M. W. Gregory	*The Harper & Row Reader: Liberal Education Through Reading and Writing*
Schwegler, Robert A.	*Patterns in Action*
Shrodes, Carolyn, et al.	*The Conscious Reader*

ADDITIONAL TEXTS:

Anderson, Thayle K. & Kent Forrester	*Point Counterpoint: Eight Cases for Composition*
Arnaudet, Martin L. & Mary Ellen Barrett	*Academic Reading and Writing*
Bender, David L.	*American Values: Opposing Viewpoints*
Coyle, William	*Research Papers*
Langan, John	*English Skills*
Oster, Judith	*From Reading to Writing: A Rhetoric and a Reader*
Smalley, Regina L. & Mary K. Ruetten	*Refining Composition Skills: Rhetoric & Grammar for ESL Students*

Arkansas College
PO Box 2317
Batesville, AR 72501
(501) 793-9813

Freshmen at Arkansas College take Masterpieces of the Western World, two world literature courses that are required in the core curriculum. The first course covers:

	The Song of Roland
Dante	*Inferno*
Euripides	*Medea*
Homer	*The Iliad* and *The Odyssey*

Shakespeare, William	*Hamlet*
Sophocles	*Oedipus Rex*

Studied in the second course are the following works: (The brief defining comments are those Dr. Terrell Tebbetts includes in the syllabus.)

Blake, William	Poems
Camus, Albert	"The Guest": a story on the existential self
Chekhov, Anton	*The Cherry Orchard:* realism triumphant
Coleridge, Samuel T.	"Kubla Khan"
Eliot, T. S.	"The Love Song of J. Alfred Prufrock": a poem on self-destruction
Ellison, Ralph	"King of the Bingo Game": a story on identity and power
Faulkner, William	"Barn Burning": a story on self-assertion
Flaubert, Gustave	*Madame Bovary:* the death of a romanticist
Goethe, Johann W. von	*Faust:* romantic desire
Ibsen, Henrik	*Hedda Gabler:* modern woman
Kafka, Franz	*The Metamorphosis:* a fable on imposed identity
Keats, John	Poems
Lawrence, D. H.	"Odour of Chrysanthemums"
Mann, Thomas	"Mario and the Magician": a story on the individual and society
Molière	*Tartuffe:* a satire on a religious hypocrite
Racine, Jean	*Phaedra:* a tragedy on passion
Shelley, Percy Bysshe	"Ode to the West Wind"
Stevens, Wallace	Poems: poetry on individualism
Swift, Jonathan	*Gulliver's Travels:* a satire on passions
Tolstoy, Leo	*The Death of Ivan Ilych:* the death of a realist
Voltaire	*Candide:* a fable on the limits of reason
Wordsworth, William	Poems: man and nature
Yeats, W. B.	Poems: poetry on the individual and society

Auburn University
202 Martin Hall
Auburn University, AL 36849-5145
(205) 826-4080

The Freshman English Committee at Auburn precedes its Pre-College Reading List with the following "Preliminary Word to Consumers":

"While we have had in mind the college-bound high school student in producing this list, it is more, perhaps, 'a list for all seasons,' as much for during and after college as it is for pre-college. The works in this list, we want to make clear, do not constitute an exhaustive or absolute listing of any kind. . . . They are, rather, simply our suggestions for some valuable, meaningful reading. . . .

"Two other points should be made briefly. First, because we do want the list to be a helpful guide, we have made specific recommendations for your reading. For example, W. B. Yeats is not simply named, but some Yeats poems are specifically suggested. This does not mean that these are the only or all the "good" poems by Yeats, but they are good poems and poems good for providing an introduction to Yeats' work. . . . Our specific recommendations, then, are not intended to be absolute evaluations but reasonable, helpful suggestions for valuable reading. . . .

"A glance at the list will show, too, that we have excluded writers who have only recently come into prominence. We hope that there will be some reading of contemporary works, but not enough time has elapsed at this point to test how really valuable or significant these works are. . . ."

Pre-College Reading List

(An * designates works of a high level of difficulty for pre-college readers.)

NOVELS

AMERICAN

Crane, Stephen	*The Red Badge of Courage*
Ellison, Ralph	*Invisible Man*
Faulkner, William	*The Unvanquished*
Hawthorne, Nathaniel	*The Scarlet Letter*
Hemingway, Ernest	*A Farewell to Arms*
James, Henry	*The Portrait of a Lady**
Melville, Herman	*Moby-Dick**
Steinbeck, John	*The Grapes of Wrath*

Twain, Mark   *The Adventures of Huckleberry Finn*
Wright, Richard   *Native Son*

BRITISH

Austen, Jane   *Pride and Prejudice*
Brontë, Emily   *Wuthering Heights**
Defoe, Daniel   *Robinson Crusoe*
Dickens, Charles   *David Copperfield; A Tale of Two Cities*
Eliot, George (Evans)   *Adam Bede*
Fielding, Henry   *Joseph Andrews*
Hardy, Thomas   *The Return of the Native*
Orwell, George   *1984*
Swift, Jonathan   *Gulliver's Travels*
Thackeray, William M.   *Vanity Fair*

INTERNATIONAL

Camus, Albert   *The Stranger**
Cervantes, Miguel de   *Don Quixote*
Dostoevski, Feodor   *Crime and Punishment**
Flaubert, Gustave   *Madame Bovary*
Kafka, Franz   *The Trial*
Stendhal (Beyle)   *The Red and the Black*
Tolstoy, Leo   *The Cossacks*
    *War and Peace**
Turgenev, Ivan   *Fathers and Sons*

SHORT STORIES

AMERICAN

Anderson, Sherwood   *Winesburg, Ohio*
Faulkner, William   "A Rose for Emily," "Barn Burning"
Hawthorne, Nathaniel   "The Minister's Black Veil," "Rappaccini's Daughter," "Young Goodman Brown"
Hemingway, Ernest   "The Killers," "The Snows of Kilimanjaro," "The Short Happy Life of Francis Macomber"
James, Henry   "The Beast in the Jungle," "Europe," "The Turn of the Screw"
Poe, Edgar Allan   "The Cask of Amontillado," "The Fall of the House of Usher," "The Purloined Letter"

BRITISH

Conrad, Joseph   "The Lagoon," "The Secret Sharer," "Typhoon"
Joyce, James   *Dubliners*
Stevenson, R. L.   "Dr. Jekyll and Mr. Hyde"

INTERNATIONAL

Chekhov, Anton P.	"The Kiss," "Misery"
Kafka, Franz	"The Hunter Gracchus," "Metamorphosis," "Jackals and Arabs"
Mann, Thomas	*Death in Venice,* "Disorder and Early Sorrow"
Maupassant, Guy de	"A Piece of String"

POETRY

AMERICAN

Bradstreet, Anne	"Verses upon the burning of our house"
Crane, Hart	"Proem: To Brooklyn Bridge," "The River" (both from *The Bridge*), "Repose of Rivers," "Royal Palm"
cummings, e. e.	"anyone lived in a pretty how town," "a man who had fallen among thieves," "my father moved through dooms of love," "next to of course god america i," "pity this busy monster, manunkind"
Dickinson, Emily	Numbers 49, 67, 214, 216, 303, 341, 435, 449, 465, 650, 712, 986, 1737 (from *The Complete Poems of Emily Dickinson*)
Eliot, T. S.	"The Journey of the Magi," "The Love Song of J. Alfred Prufrock," "Sweeney Among the Nightingales"
Frost, Robert	"After Apple-Picking," "Birches," "Death of the Hired Man," "Departmental," "Desert Places," "Mending Wall," "The Road Not Taken"
Hughes, Langston	"Afro-American Fragment," "As I Grew Older," "Harlem," "The Negro Sings of Rivers," "Theme for English B"
Lindsay, Vachel	"Abraham Lincoln Walks at Midnight," "The Congo"
Pound, Ezra	"The Garden," "Portrait d'une Femme," "The River Merchant's Wife: A Letter," "Salutation"
Ransom, John Crowe	"Bells for John Whiteside's Daughter," "Blue Girls," "Dead Boy," "The Equilibrists," "Janet Waking," "Prelude to an Evening," "Winter Remembered"

Robinson, Edwin A.	"Miniver Cheevy," "Richard Cory"
Stevens, Wallace	"Anecdote of the Jar," "Poems of Our Climate," "The Snow Man," "Sunday Morning"
Taylor, Edward	"Meditation Eight"
Whitman, Walt	"Out of the Cradle Endlessly Rocking," "Song of Myself," "When Lilacs Last in the Dooryard Bloom'd"

BRITISH

	The Seafarer
	The Wanderer
	Ballads: "Barbara Allan," "Edward," "Lord Randall," "Sir Patrick Spens"
Arnold, Matthew	"Dover Beach," "Thrysis"
Auden, W.H.	"In Memory of W. B. Yeats," "Lullaby," "Musée des Beaux Arts," "The Unknown Citizen"
Blake, William	"The Chimney Sweeper," "The Lamb," "London," "The Tyger"
Browning, Robert	"My Last Duchess," "Porphyria's Lover," "Soliloquy of the Spanish Cloister"
Byron, George Gordon	Canto III from *Childe Harold's Pilgrimage*, Cantos I and II from *Don Juan*, "Prisoner of Chillon," "She Walks in Beauty"
Chaucer, Geoffrey	The General Prologue and two or three tales (e.g., "The Nun's Priest's Tale") from the *Canterbury Tales*
Coleridge, Samuel Taylor	"Christabel," "Kubla Khan," *The Rime of the Ancient Mariner*
Donne, John	"The Flea," "A Hymn to God the Father," Holy Sonnets: 7, 10, 14; "The Relic," "Song," "A Valediction: Forbidding Mourning"
Hopkins, Gerard Manley	"God's Grandeur," "Spring and Fall," "Thou Art Indeed Just, Lord"
Keats, John	"Bright Star," "The Eve of St. Agnes," "La Belle Dame Sans Merci," "To Autumn," Odes: "On a Grecian Urn," "On Melancholy," "To a Nightingale"
Milton, John	Book I of *Paradise Lost*; "When I Consider How My Light Is Spent"
Pope, Alexander	"The Rape of the Lock"
Shakespeare, William	Sonnets 18, 29, 55, 71, 106, 116, 129, 130, 138, 144, 146

Shelley, Percy Bysshe	"Hymn to Intellectual Beauty," "Mutability," "Ode to the West Wind," "Ozymandias," "To a Skylark"
Spenser, Edmund	Canto I, Book I of *The Faerie Queene*
Tennyson, Alfred Lord	"The Lady of Shalott," "Ulysses"
Thomas, Dylan	"And Death Shall Have No Dominion," "Do Not Go Gentle into That Good Night," "Fern Hill"
Wordsworth, William	"Intimations of Immortality," "London, 1802"
Yeats, William Butler	"Easter, 1916," "In Memory of Major Robert Gregory," "Lapis Lazuli," "Nineteen Hundred and Nineteen," "The Second Coming," "When You Are Old," "The Wild Swans at Coole"

DRAMA

AMERICAN

Miller, Arthur	*Death of a Salesman*
O'Neill, Eugene	*Desire under the Elms**
Williams, Tennessee	*The Glass Menagerie*

BRITISH

Goldsmith, Oliver	*She Stoops to Conquer*
Shakespeare, William	*As You Like It; Hamlet; Henry IV Part 1, MacBeth; Romeo and Juliet*
Shaw, George Bernard	*Major Barbara*

INTERNATIONAL

Aeschylus	*Oresteia**
Brecht, Bertolt	*The Caucasian Chalk Circle**
Euripides	*Medea*
Molière	*Tartuffe*
Sophocles	*Antigone, Oedipus Rex*

MISCELLANEOUS

	Beowulf
	Bible
	Sir Gawain and the Green Knight
Boswell, James	*Life of Samuel Johnson* (1737–1760 and 1763)
Cellini, Benvenuto	*Autobiography*
Dante Alighieri	*The Inferno*
De Quincey, Thomas	*Confessions of an English Opium Eater*
Emerson, Ralph Waldo	Essays: "The American Scholar," "Self-Reliance"

Frank, Anne	*The Diary of a Young Girl*
Franklin, Benjamin	*Autobiography* (especially boyhood and youth portions)
Hamilton, Edith	*Mythology*
Homer	*The Iliad, The Odyssey*
Lamb, Charles	*The Essays of Elia*
Montaigne, Michel E. de	"Of Friendship," "Of Idleness," "Of Solitariness"
Plato	*Apology*
Plutarch	"Antony," "Cicero," "Pompey," from *Lives of the Noble Greeks & Romans*
Russell, Bertrand	*Unpopular Essays*
Thoreau, Henry David	*Walden*
Vergil	*The Aeneid*

Ball State University
2000 University Avenue
Muncie, IN 47306
(317) 285-8300

The Ball State English Department prefaces its suggested reading list for pre-college students with this comment: "Though most teachers of literature at the college level feel that the quality of reading is more important than the specific works read by college-bound high school students, the works listed below represent the literary tradition in our culture that well-prepared students should be acquainted with when they enter college. While many entering students will, of course, only have read a few of the works listed below, we hope that they will bring an understanding of and respect for the heritage that they represent."

Suggested Reading List in Literature for College-Bound Students

CLASSICAL LITERATURE

THE EPIC

| Homer | *The Iliad* or *The Odyssey* |
| Vergil | *The Aeneid* |

TRAGEDY

Aeschylus	*Agamemnon* or *Prometheus Unbound*
Euripides	*Medea* or *The Trojan Woman*
Sophocles	*Antigone* or *Oedipus Rex*

PHILOSOPHY

Aristotle	Discussion of tragedy in *The Poetics*
Plato	One of the Socratic Dialogues

POETRY

Sappho	Selections

BIBLICAL LITERATURE

Readings in both the Old and the New Testaments, including Genesis, Psalms, Job, and at least one of the gospels

MEDIEVAL LITERATURE

	Beowulf or *The Song of Roland*
	Everyman
	Selected medieval ballads
Dante	Readings in *The Divine Comedy*
Chaucer, Geoffrey	Selections from the *Canterbury Tales*
Julian of Norwich	Selections
Marjorie á Kempis	Selections

RENAISSANCE LITERATURE

DRAMA

Marlowe, Christopher	*Doctor Faustus*
Shakespeare, William	Two tragedies, one comedy, one history play

POETRY

Shakespeare, William	Selections from the sonnets

NOVEL

Cervantes, Miguel de	*Don Quixote* (Part 1)

PHILOSOPHY

Erasmus	*In Praise of Folly*
Machiavelli, Niccolo	*The Prince*
More, Thomas	*Utopia*

SEVENTEENTH-CENTURY

DRAMA

Milton, John	"Comus"
Molière	Two comedies

POETRY

Donne, John	Selections
Dryden, John	Selections

PROSE

Phillips, Catherine	Selections

EIGHTEENTH-CENTURY

DRAMA

Goethe, Johann W. von	*Faust* (Part 1)
Goldsmith, Oliver	*She Stoops to Conquer* (or another representative comedy)
Voltaire	*Candide*

POETRY

Selections from the poetry of **William Blake, Robert Burns, Oliver Goldsmith, Alexander Pope, Edward Taylor**

NOVELS

Burney, Fanny	*Evelina*
Defoe, Daniel	*Robinson Crusoe*
Fielding, Henry	*Joseph Andrews*
Swift, Jonathan	*Gulliver's Travels*

PROSE

Franklin, Benjamin	*Autobiography*
Wollstonecraft, Mary	"Essay on the Vindication of the Rights of Women"

NINETEENTH-CENTURY

DRAMA

Ibsen, Henrik	*A Doll's House*
Shaw, George Bernard	*Major Barbara*
Wilde, Oscar	*The Importance of Being Earnest*

POETRY

Selections from the works of the following poets: **Matthew Arnold, Emily Brontë, E. B. Browning, Robert Browning, George Gordon, Lord Byron, Samuel Taylor Coleridge:** "Christabel," *Lyrical Ballads* (esp. "The Rime of the Ancient Mariner,"); **Emily Dickinson, John Keats, Christina Rossetti, Percy Bysshe Shelley, Alfred, Lord Tennyson, Walt Whitman, William Wordsworth** (including "Ode: Intimations of Immortality" and *Lyrical Ballads*)

NOVELS

(At least one by the following writers)

Austen, Jane	*Pride and Prejudice*
Brontë, Emily	*Wuthering Heights*
Dickens, Charles	*Great Expectations*
Dostoevski, Feodor	*Crime and Punishment*
Douglass, Fredrick	*Narrative of the Life of Fredrick Douglass*
Eliot, George	*The Mill on the Floss*
Flaubert, Gustave	*Madame Bovary*
Hardy, Thomas	*Tess of the D'Urbervilles*
Hawthorne, Nathaniel	*The Scarlet Letter*
James, Henry	*The Turn of the Screw*
Melville, Herman	*Billy Budd*
Rowson, Susanna	*Charlotte Temple*
Shelley, Mary	*Frankenstein*
Stowe, Harriet Beecher	*Uncle Tom's Cabin*
Tolstoy, Leo	*Anna Karenina*
Twain, Mark	*The Adventures of Huckleberry Finn*

SHORT STORIES

Representative selections from **Kate Chopin, Mary Wilkins Freeman, Nathaniel Hawthorne, Sarah Orne Jewett,** "The Country of the Pointed Firs"; **Edgar Allan Poe, Mark Twain**

PROSE

Carlyle, Thomas	"Characteristics"
Emerson, Ralph Waldo	"Self-Reliance"
Mill, J. S.	Essay: "The Subjection of Women"
Thoreau, Henry	"Civil Disobedience" or *Walden*
Wordsworth, Dorothy	*Journals*

TWENTIETH-CENTURY

DRAMA

Beckett, Samuel	*Waiting for Godot*
Brecht, Bertholt	*Mother Courage and Her Children*
Eliot, T. S.	*Murder in the Cathedral*

Hellman, Lillian	*The Children's Hour* or *Toys in the Attic*
MacLeish, Archibald	*J.B.*
Miller, Arthur	*Death of a Salesman*
O'Neill, Eugene	*The Emperor Jones* or *The Hairy Ape*
Stoppard, Tom	*Rosencrantz and Guildenstern Are Dead*
Williams, Tennessee	*The Glass Menagerie*

AMERICAN POETRY

Selections from the works of the following poets: **e. e. cummings, Paul Laurence Dunbar, T. S. Eliot:** "The Love Song of J. Alfred Prufrock," "Old Possum's Book of Practical Cats"; **Robert Frost:** "Birches," "Death of the Hired Man," "Mending Wall"; **Langston Hughes, Amy Lowell, Claude McKay, Sylvia Plath, Adrienne Rich, W. C. Williams**

BRITISH POETRY

Selections from the following poets: **W. H. Auden, A. E. Housman, Stevie Smith, William Butler Yeats**

AMERICAN FICTION

Baldwin, James	*Another Country*
Bellow, Saul	*Seize the Day*
Cather, Willa	*O Pioneers!*
Cleaver, Eldridge	*Soul on Ice*
Faulkner, William	"The Bear," "That Evening Sun," *Light in August*
Fitzgerald, F. Scott	*The Great Gatsby*
Hemingway, Ernest	*A Farewell to Arms*
Hurston, Zora Neale	*Their Eyes Were Watching God*
Momaday, Scott	*The Way to Rainy Mountain*
Oates, Joyce Carol	A novel
Plath, Sylvia	*The Bell Jar*
Roth, Henry	*Call It Sleep*
Steinbeck, John	*Of Mice and Men*, "The Red Pony"
Wharton, Edith	*The Age of Innocence* or *Summer*
Wright, Richard	*Native Son*

BRITISH FICTION

Burgess, Anthony	*A Clockwork Orange*
Donleavy, J. P.	*The Gingerman*
Greene, Graham	A novel
Huxley, Aldous	*Brave New World*
Joyce, James	*Dubliners*
Lawrence, D. H.	"Odour of Chrysanthemums," *Sons and Lovers*
Orwell, George	*Animal Farm*
Waugh, Evelyn	A novel

| Woolf, Virginia | "The Mark on the Wall," "A Room of One's Own" |

OTHER FICTION

Achebe, Chinua	*Things Fall Apart*
Beauvoir, Simone de	*The Second Sex*
Camus, Albert	*The Stranger*
Colette	A novel
Hesse, Herman	*Siddhartha*
Kafka, Franz	"The Metamorphosis"
Paton, Alan	*Cry, The Beloved Country*

NON-FICTION

Camus, Albert	"The Myth of Sisyphus"
Eisley, Loren	*The Immense Journey*
Frank, Anne	*Diary of a Young Girl*
Gould, Stephen Jay	A selection
Russell, Bertrand	A selection
Sagan, Carl	A selection
Strachey, Lytton	*Queen Victoria*
Tuchman, Barbara	*A Distant Mirror*
Wiesel, Elie	*Night*

Barnard College
Columbia University
3009 Broadway
New York, NY 10027-6598
(212) 280-2014

The following are texts from the syllabus of a year-long introductory survey course taught at Barnard. Professor Cary H. Plotkin has appended comments to this list and to a list of classical literature he feels students would profit from reading.

INTRODUCTORY SURVEY COURSE

	Piers Plowman (excerpts)
	The Second Shepherd's Play
	Sir Gawain and the Green Knight
	Selections from sixteenth-century lyrics
Arnold, Matthew	"Dover Beach"
Austen, Jane	*Northanger Abbey*
Brontë, Emily	*Wuthering Heights*

Browning, Robert	"Andrea del Sarto," "Childe Roland to the Dark Tower Came," "Fra Lippo Lippi," "My Last Duchess," "Rabbi Ben Ezra," "Soliloquy of the Spanish Cloister"
Coleridge, Samuel Taylor	"The Eolian Harp," "Frost at Midnight," "Kubla Khan," *The Rime of the Ancient Mariner*
Collins, William	"Ode to Evening"
Congreve, William	*Love for Love*
Chaucer, Geoffrey	*Canterbury Tales* ("the whole thing, if you can." Otherwise the General Prologue, Miller's Tale, and Wife of Bath's Tale are suggested.)
Donne, John	Satires
Dryden, John	*Absalom and Achitophel*
Eliot, T. S.	*The Waste Land,* and other selections
Hopkins, Gerard Manley	"As kingfishers catch fire," "Carrion Comfort," "God's Grandeur," "The Leaden Echo and the Golden Echo," "No worst, there is none," "Pied Beauty," "That Nature Is a Heraclitean Fire and of the Comfort of the Resurrection," "Spelt from Sibyl's Leaves," "Thou art indeed just," "The Windhover"
Jonson, Ben	*Volpone*
Keats, John	"The Eve of St. Agnes," "Ode on a Grecian Urn," "Ode to a Nightingale," "To Autumn"
Marlowe, Christopher	*Dr. Faustus,* "The Passionate Shepherd to His Love," *Tamburlaine the Great* (Part 1)
Marvell, Andrew	"Bermudas," "An Horatian Ode," and his mower eclogues
Milton, John	"Lycidas," *Samson Agonistes, Paradise Lost*
Pope, Alexander	"A Discourse on Pastoral Poetry," "An Essay on Man," "The Rape of the Lock," "Windsor Forest"
Raleigh, Sir Walter	"The Nymph's Reply to the Shepherd"
Shakespeare, William	*As You Like It; A Comedy of Errors; Hamlet; Henry V; King Lear; A Midsummer Night's Dream; Timon of Athens*
Shelley, Percy Bysshe	"Hymn to Intellectual Beauty," "Mont Blanc," "Ode to the West Wind," "To a Skylark"
Sidney, Sir Philip	"Ye Goatherd Gods"

Spenser, Edmund	*The Faerie Queene,* "A Letter of the Authors," and "October" from *The Shepheardes Calendar*
Sterne, Laurence	*Tristram Shandy*
Swift, Jonathan	*Gulliver's Travels;* "A Modest Proposal"
Tennyson, Alfred Lord	From *Idylls of the King:* "The Coming of Arthur," "Lancelot and Elaine," "The Last Tournament," "The Passing of Arthur"; *In Memoriam A. H. H.*
Wordsworth, William	"Lines Written in Early Spring," *The Prelude,* "Tintern Abbey"
Yeats, William Butler	"The Second Coming," and other poems

CLASSICAL LIST

	BIBLE (King James Version): Old Testament: Genesis; Exodus (through the 10 Commandments); Deuteronomy (the death of Moses); Joshua (through the fall of Jericho); Judges (Deborah, the story of Joel, Samson); I & II Samuel; I Kings (through Ahab); Job; Psalms 1, 8, 19, 22, 23, 24, 91, 100, 104, 123, 137, 139; Proverbs 1-7, 22, 24-29, 31; Ecclesiastes; Song of Solomon; Jeremiah; Isaiah; Ezekiel; Daniel; Jonah; New Testament: The Four Gospels; Romans; Ephesians; Hebrews; Revelation
Aeschylus	*The Oresteia*
Aristophanes	*The Birds; Lysistrata*
Aristotle	*Poetics* (a minimum)
Boccaccio	*The Decameron*
Catullus	*Carmina* iii, v, lxii, lxx, lxxxv, cl
Dante	*The Divine Comedy* (There are many serviceable translations. Sinclair's has the advantage of clarity and helpful notes; it makes no pretenses to beauty. Others include John Ciardi's and a recent one by Alan Mandelbaum.)
Euripides	*Electra; Medea*
Homer	*Iliad; Odyssey* (Fitzgerald, tr.)
Homeric Hymns	"Hymn to Demeter"
Horace	*The Art of Poetry* and a couple of odes and satires
Ovid	*Metamorphoses* (Humphries, tr.)

Plato	*Ion; Meno; Phaedrus; Republic:* Books 2, 3, 6, 7, 10; *Symposium; Timaeus*
St. Augustine	*Confessions*
Sappho	Selected lyrics
Sophocles	*Antigone; Oedipus Rex*
Vergil	*The Aeneid* (Alan Mandelbaum, tr.)

Baylor University
PO CSB 361
Waco, TX 76798
(817) 755-1813

In its brochure, "An Invitation: Voyage of Discovery," the Baylor College of Arts and Sciences Committee for Suggested Reading presents the following list. They preface it with "any list of recommended books, including this one, is incomplete and, to some extent, arbitrary. The books suggested here many have read with profit and pleasure. Therefore, we offer this list, which represents a variety of topics and points of view, not as an end, but as a beginning of a voyage of discovery."

ARTS AND LETTERS

Cather, Willa	*The Professor's House*
Cervantes, Miguel de	*Don Quixote*
Dostoevski, Feodor	*The Brothers Karamazov*
Melville, Herman	*Moby-Dick*
Tolstoy, Leo	*Anna Karenina*
Woolf, Virginia	*A Room of One's Own*
Wright, Richard	*Native Son*

THE SCIENCES

Darwin, Charles	*The Voyage of the Beagle*
Eiseley, Loren	*The Immense Journey*
Freud, Sigmund	*Character and Culture*
Kuhn, Thomas S.	*The Copernican Revolution*
Skinner, B. F.	*Beyond Freedom and Dignity*
Thomas, Lewis	*The Medusa and the Snail*

PHILOSOPHY

Gandhi, M. K.	*Autobiography*
Hughes, Robert	*The Shock of the New*
James, William	*The Varieties of Religious Experience*
Marx, K. and F. Engels	*The Communist Manifesto*

Mill, J. S.	*On Liberty*
Niebuhr, H. Richard	*Christ and Culture*

HISTORY

Boorstin, Daniel	*The Discoverers*
Burckhardt, Jacob	*The Civilization of the Renaissance in Italy*
Catton, Bruce	*Civil War Trilogy: The Coming Fury; Terrible Swift Sword; Never Call Retreat*
Hofstadter, Richard	*Anti-Intellectualism in American Life*
Spence, Jonathan	*The Gate of Heavenly Peace*
Tuchman, Barbara	*The Proud Tower*

In a Baylor literature course open to freshmen and sophomores the following novels are recommended:

Agee, James	*A Death in the Family*
Austen, Jane	*Emma; Mansfield Park; Pride and Prejudice*
Bellow, Saul	*Dangling Man; Henderson the Rain King; Seize the Day*
Bowden, Elizabeth	*The Death of the Heart*
Bradford, Richard	*Red Sky at Morning*
Brontë, Charlotte	*Jane Eyre*
Brontë, Emily	*Wuthering Heights*
Butler, Samuel	*The Way of All Flesh*
Cather, Willa	*Death Comes for the Archbishop; My Antonia*
Conrad, Joseph	*Lord Jim; Nostromo*
Dickens, Charles	*Dombey and Son; Great Expectations; Hard Times*
Eliot, George	*The Mill on the Floss*
Faulkner, William	*As I Lay Dying; The Reivers*
Fitzgerald, F. Scott	*The Great Gatsby*
Golding, William	*Lord of the Flies*
Hardy, Thomas	*Mayor of Casterbridge; Return of the Native; Tess of the D'Urbervilles*
Hemingway, Ernest	*A Farewell to Arms; For Whom the Bell Tolls*
Huxley, Aldous	*Brave New World*
James, Henry	*The American; Washington Square*
Kesey, Ken	*One Flew over the Cuckoo's Nest*
Knowles, John	*A Separate Peace*
Lawrence, D. H.	*Sons and Lovers*
Lewis, Sinclair	*Babbitt; Main Street*
Miller, Walter	*A Canticle for Leibowitz*
Norris, Frank	*The Octopus*
Orwell, George	*Burmese Days; 1984*
Porter, Katherine Anne	*Ship of Fools*

Scott, Walter	*Waverley*
Sinclair, Upton	*The Jungle*
Steinbeck, John	*Grapes of Wrath*
Styron, William	*Lie Down in Darkness*
Trollope, Anthony	*Barchester Towers*
Wolfe, Thomas	*Look Homeward, Angel*
Wright, Richard	*Native Son*

Bloomsburg University of Pennsylvania
Room 10, Ben Franklin Building
Bloomsburg, PA 17815
(717) 389-4316

Louis F. Thompson, Chairman of the Bloomsburg Department of English, suggests the following as a "useful list from which college-bound students may select works for summer reading." He says that "all of these works are indisputably part of our literary heritage; they both reflect and propound ideas fundamental to Western civilization." The Bloomsburg English Department brochure in its section on high school preparation points out that works such as these "have achieved immortality because each is unique and excellent as a literary production, has had a powerful influence on later writers, and is a source of ideas and perceptions of life that remain important even to this day."

	Bible
Arnold, Matthew	Essays (esp. "Function of Criticism at the Present Time"); poems ("Buried Life," "To Marguerite," "Dover Beach")
Baldwin, James	Selection
Bulfinch, Thomas	*Mythology*
Bunyan, John	*Pilgrim's Progress*
Carlyle, Thomas	*Sartor Resartus* (Chapters on "Everlasting Nay," "Center of Indifference," "Everlasting Yea")
Cervantes, Miguel de	*Don Quixote* (Putnam, tr., in Viking Portable Cervantes)
Chaucer, Geoffrey	*Canterbury Tales*
Chopin, Kate	*The Awakening*
Conrad, Joseph	*Heart of Darkness*
Dickens, Charles	*Great Expectations*
Dickinson, Emily	Poetry selections
Dostoevski, Feodor	*Crime and Punishment*
Emerson, Ralph Waldo	Essays (esp. "Self-Reliance," "The American Scholar")
Faulkner, William	"The Bear"
Fielding, Henry	*Joseph Andrews; Tom Jones*

Fitzgerald, F. Scott	Selections
Hansberry, Lorraine	*A Raisin in the Sun*
Hardy, Thomas	*The Mayor of Casterbridge*
Hawthorne, Nathaniel	*The Scarlet Letter;* short stories
Hemingway, Ernest	*A Farewell to Arms; For Whom the Bell Tolls*
Homer	*The Iliad* and *The Odyssey* (Rouse, tr.)
Ibsen, Henrik	*Ghosts*
Kafka, Franz	Stories
Koestler, Arthur	*Darkness at Noon*
Matthew, Saint	*Matthew:* Christ's Sermon on the Mount
Melville, Herman	*Moby-Dick*
Meredith, George	*The Ordeal of Richard Feverel*
Morrison, Toni	A novel
Orwell, George	*1984*
Shakespeare, William	*Henry IV, Part 1; King Lear; Midsummer Night's Dream; Twelfth Night*
Shaw, George Bernard	*Man and Superman*
Sophocles	*Antigone; Oedipus at Colonus; Oedipus Rex*
Swift, Jonathan	*Gulliver's Travels*
Thoreau, Henry	*Walden*
Thurber, James	Selections
Toomer, Jean	Selections
Twain, Mark	Selections
Vergil	*The Aeneid* (Rolfe Humphries, tr.)
Walker, Alice	Selections

Boston College
Lyons Hall 120
Chestnut Hill, MA 02167-3835
(617) 552-3100

Fr. William B. Neenan, S.J., Academic Vice President and Dean of Faculties at Boston, has composed a reading list that is given to incoming freshmen at the college. A letter prefaces the list: "Welcome to Boston College!

"During your college years, you will enjoy opportunities for leisure such as most likely you will never have again. Hence, I encourage you to develop the habit of reading good books. The attached list may assist you. It represents responses I might make to the question, 'Have you read a good book recently?'

"These titles are not necessarily my candidates for the 'Great Books' category. They are simply books I have read over the course of many years and for various reasons remain memorable. Absent from the list are the Classics, Dante, and Shakespeare—no need to state the obvious—as well as books of poetry. But don't spurn the poets. Other books are absent either because I have not read them, they didn't impress me or because they have slipped my mind.

"And your list? What will it look like in four years? In twenty years?"

The Dean's List

Agee, James	*A Death in the Family*
Amis, Kingsley	*Lucky Jim*
Bellah, Robert N., et al.	*Habits of the Heart*
Bernanos, George	*Diary of a Country Priest*
Bolt, Robert	*A Man for All Seasons*
Burns, Olive Ann	*Cold Sassy Tree*
Camus, Albert	*The Fall*
Dillard, Annie	*An American Childhood*
Donovan, Charles F., S.J.	*History of Boston College*
Ellison, Ralph	*The Invisible Man*
Endo, Shusaku	*Silence*
Fitzgerald, F. Scott	*The Great Gatsby*
Greene, Graham	*The Power and the Glory*
Hillesum, Etty	*An Interrupted Life*
Joyce, James	*Portrait of the Artist as a Young Man*
Keegan, John	*Face of Battle*
Kingsolver, Barbara	*The Bean Trees*
Kundera, Milan	*The Joke*
Lampedusa, Giuseppe	*The Leopard*
Landon, H. C. Robbins	*1791 Mozart's Last Year*
O'Neill, Thomas P., Jr.	*Man of the House*
Pelikan, Jaroslav	*Jesus through the Centuries*
Silone, Ignazio	*Bread and Wine*
Stegner, Wallace	*Collected Short Stories*
Undset, Sigrid	*Kristin Lavransdatter*
Warren, Robert Penn	*All the King's Men*
Woolf, Virginia	*Mrs. Dalloway*

Brandeis University
415 South Street
Waltham, MA 02254
(617) 736-3500

According to Professor Mitsue Miyata Frey, "*all* entering Brandeis freshmen must take" a two-step program of University Studies in the Humanities. Step-1 courses "include an Homeric text, a selection from the *Old Testament* and the *New Testament*" in addition to other texts which the individual faculty members choose. For Step-2 instructors select works from two of the following authors: Dante, William Shakespeare, Denis Diderot, Jane Austen, Emily Dickinson, Sigmund Freud, Franz Fanon as well as other readings.

In Step-1, authors and their works have recently included:

	Bhagavad Gita
	Bible: Genesis, Exodus, I & II Samuel, Job, Proverbs, Jonah, Matthew, Luke, John; I Corinthians, other Pauline letters
	Enuma Elish
	The Gilgamesh Epic
	Upanishads
Aeschylus	*The Oresteia*
Apuleius	*The Golden Ass*
Aristophanes	*The Birds; The Clouds*
Aristotle	*Nicomachean Ethics*
Cicero	*De Officiis*
Euripides	*The Bacchae; Iphigenia in Aulis; Medea; Electra; Hippolytus; Ion*
Hesiod	*Theogony; Works and Days*
Homer	*The Odyssey; The Iliad*
Morrison, Toni	*Beloved*
O'Brien, Tim	"How to Tell a War Story"
Petronius, Gaius	*Satyricon*
Plato	*Dialogues: Apology, Crito, Euthyphro to Phaedo*
Plutarch	*Lives*
Pritchard, James B., ed.	*The Ancient Near East I*
Procopius	*Secret History*
Sappho	*Sappho: A New Translation* (Mary Barnard, tr.)
Sophocles	*Trachineae; The Oedipus Cycle: Oedipus Rex; Oedipus at Colonus; Antigone*
Theognis of Megara	Poetry
Vergil	*The Aeneid*

In the second semester, authors and their works have recently included:

	Beowulf
	The Cid
	The Elder Edda
	The Nibelungenlied
	One Thousand and One Nights
	Song of Roland
Achebe, Chinua	*Things Fall Apart*
Anouilh, Jean	*Antigone*
Ayer, Sir Alfred Jules	*Language, Truth, and Logic*
Augustine, Saint	*Confessions*
Austen, Jane	*Emma; Pride and Prejudice*
Baldwin, James	"Sonny's Blues"
Baudelaire, Charles	*The Flowers of Evil*
Bellah, Robert N., et al.	*Habits of the Heart*
Brontë, Charlotte	*Jane Eyre*
Calderón de la Barca, Pedro	*Life Is a Dream*
Camus, Albert	*The Stranger; The Plague*
Cesaire, Aimé	*A Tempest*
Conrad, Joseph	*Heart of Darkness*
Dante	*Inferno; Vita Nuova*
Descartes, René	*Meditations*
Dickens, Charles	*Hard Times*
Diderot, Denis	*Rameau's Nephew; The Supplement to Bougainville's Voyage*
Dostoevski, Feodor	*Crime and Punishment;* "White Nights"; "The Dream of a Ridiculous Man"
Ellison, Ralph	*Invisible Man*
Erasmus, Desiderius	*The Praise of Folly*
Fanon, Frantz	*The Wretched of the Earth*
Ferdowsi, Aboe-Quasem	*Shahname*
Fitzgerald, F. Scott	*The Great Gatsby*
Flaubert, Gustave	*Madame Bovary*
Forster, E. M.	*A Passage to India*
Frankl, Victor	*Man's Search for Meaning*
Freud, Sigmund	*Civilization and Its Discontents; Dora; Wit and Its Relation to the Unconscious*
Gaskell, Elizabeth Cleghorn	*Mary Barton*
Gilman, Charlotte P.	"The Yellow Wallpaper"
Gottfried, V. Strassburg	*Tristan*
Hardy, Thomas	*The Mayor of Casterbridge*
Hardy, G. H.	*A Mathematician's Apology*
Hegel, George Frederick W.	*Phenomenology of Spirit*
Heine, Heinrich	*Germany: A Winter's Tale*
Hoffman, E. T. A.	*The Golden Pot*
Hsi-Yu Chi	*Monkey (selections)*

Hume, David	*An Inquiry Concerning the Principles of Morals*
Hurston, Zora Neale	*Their Eyes Were Watching God*
Huysmans, Joris K.	*Against Nature*
Jacobs, Harriet	*Incidents in the Life of a Slave Girl, Written by Herself*
James, William	"The Will to Believe," "The Moral Philosopher and the Moral Life," essays on Pragmatism
Kafka, Franz	"A Hunger Artist," *Metamorphosis*
Kant, Immanuel	*Metaphysics of Virtue*
Kauffman, Walter	*Existentialism From Dostoevsky to Sartre*
Kerouac, Jack	*The Dharma Bums*
Kipling, Rudyard	*Kim*
Kraus, Karl	*The Last Days of Mankind*
Machiavelli, Niccolò	*The Prince*
Malcolm X	*The Autobiography of Malcolm X*
Mann, Thomas	*Death in Venice*
Marx, Karl and Friedrich Engels	*The Communist Manifesto*
Mill, John Stuart	*Utilitarianism; On Liberty*
Miller, Arthur	*Death of a Salesman*
Mishima, Yukio	*The Sailor Who Fell From Grace With the Sea*
Molière	*Tartuffe*
Montaigne, Michel de	*Essays*
Moore, George Edward	*Principia Ethica*
Morrison, Toni	*Sula; The Bluest Eye; Beloved*
Murdoch, Iris	*The Sovereignty of Good*
Nabokov, Vladimir	*Lolita*
Nietzsche, F. W.	*The Genealogy of Morals*
Pascal, Blaise	*Pensées*
Paton, Alan	*Cry the Beloved Country*
Petronius, Gaius	*Satyricon*
Poe, Edgar Allan	Selected short stories
Rabelais, François	*Gargantua and Pantagruel*
Rojas, Fernando de	*The Spanish Bawd; Celestina*
Rousseau, Jean Jacques	*Discourse on Inequality*
Sartre, Jean-Paul	*Existentialism and Humanism*
Shakespeare, William	*King Lear; The Tempest; Hamlet*
Shelley, Mary	*Frankenstein*
Steinbeck, John	*The Grapes of Wrath*
Swift, Jonathan	*Gulliver's Travels*
Tanizaki, Junichiro	*Some Prefer Nettles*
Tolstoy, Leo	*Death of Ivan Illych; Master and Man*
Twain, Mark	*The Adventures of Huckleberry Finn*
Voltaire	*Candide*
Wright, Richard	*Almost a Man; Native Son*

Brigham Young University
Abraham Smoot Building
Provo, UT 84602
(801) 378-2507

Brigham Young has a "minimum reading list" that includes the authors whom the university considers basic for students working for a B.S. in English. The standards governing the list are that it 'include representative works of the major periods, movements, types, and writers in our cultural heritage; include works which are available and understandable to the undergraduate student; and be within fair limits for the student. . . .

"Some writers are represented with relatively short and easy works rather than with their longer, more complex and difficult 'masterpieces.'" The list is helpful to the pre-college student because it contains these 'simpler' works and because the titles "are usually the best-known and often the most frequently reprinted."

Suggested Minimum Reading List

(Dates indicate year work was first published)

PLAYS

	Abraham and Isaac (*c* 1450)
	Everyman (*c* 1500)
	The Second Shepherd's Play (*c* 1450)
Aeschylus	*Agamemnon* (*c* 475 BC)
Aristophanes	*The Frogs* (412 BC)
Beckett, Samuel	*Waiting for Godot* (1952)
Congreve, William	*The Way of the World* (1700)
Euripides	*Medea* (*c* 435 BC)
Ibsen, Henrik	*Hedda Gabler* (1890)
Jonson, Ben	*Volpone* (*c* 1616)
Marlowe, Christopher	*Doctor Faustus* (*c* 1590)
Miller, Arthur	*Death of a Salesman* (1949)
Molière	*Tartuffe* (1664)

O'Neill, Eugene	*Long Day's Journey Into Night* (1955)
Shakespeare, William	*Hamlet; Henry IV Part 1; King Lear; Macbeth; Measure for Measure; Othello; Troilus and Cressida* (1598–1611)
Shaw, George Bernard	*Man and Superman* (1903)
Sheridan, Richard B.	*The School for Scandal* (1777)
Sophocles	*Oedipus Rex* (*c* 534 BC)
Synge, J. M.	*The Playboy of the Western World* (1907)
Wilde, Oscar	*The Importance of Being Earnest* (1895)
Williams, Tennessee	*A Streetcar Named Desire* (1947)

PROSE FICTION: NOVELS

"Major novels are listed below, but an equally relevant list with different titles could be assembled."

Austen, Jane	*Pride and Prejudice* (1813)
Brontë, Emily	*Wuthering Heights* (1847)
Cervantes, Miguel de	*Don Quixote* (1605–16)
Conrad, Joseph	*Lord Jim* (1900)
Dickens, Charles	*Great Expectations* (1860)
Dostoevski, Feodor	*Brothers Karamazov* (1880) or *Crime and Punishment* (1866)
Dreiser, Theodore	*Sister Carrie* (1907)
Eliot, George	*Middlemarch* (1859)
Ellison, Ralph	*Invisible Man* (1947)
Faulkner, William	*Absalom, Absalom!* (1936)
Fielding, Henry	*Tom Jones* (1726–27)
Fitzgerald, F. Scott	*The Great Gatsby* (1925)
Flaubert, Gustave	*Madame Bovary* (1857)
Greene, Graham	*The Power and the Glory* (1940)
Hardy, Thomas	*Tess of the D'Urbervilles* (1891)
Hawthorne, Nathaniel	*The Scarlet Letter* (1850)
Hemingway, Ernest	*A Farewell to Arms* (1929)
James, Henry	*The Portrait of a Lady* (1881)
Joyce, James	*A Portrait of the Artist as a Young Man* (1916)
Lawrence, D. H.	*Sons and Lovers* (1913)
Melville, Herman	*Moby-Dick* (1851)
Steinbeck, John	*The Grapes of Wrath* (1939)
Swift, Jonathan	*Gulliver's Travels* (1726–27)
Thackeray, W. M.	*Vanity Fair* (1848)
Tolstoy, Leo	*Anna Karenina* (1875–1877) or *War and Peace* (1865–1869)
Twain, Mark	*The Adventures of Huckleberry Finn* (1884)

PROSE FICTION: SHORT STORIES

Authors here include Maxwell Anderson, Willa Cather, Stephen Crane, E. M. Forster, William Faulkner, Ernest Hemingway, Henry James, Franz Kafka, Rudyard Kipling, D. H. Lawrence, Bernard Malamud, Thomas Mann, Katherine Mansfield, Guy de Maupassant, Flannery O'Connor, Frank O'Connor, Edgar Allan Poe, Katherine Anne Porter, James Thurber, Edith Wharton, Eudora Welty, Virginia Woolf

POETRY: EPIC AND MOCK-EPIC

	Beowulf
Byron, G. G., Lord	*Don Juan,* Cantos I–IV (1819–21)
Dante	*The Divine Comedy (c* 1307)
Homer	*The Iliad (c* 9th century BC)
Milton, John	*Paradise Lost* (1667)
Pope, Alexander	"The Rape of the Lock" (1714)
Spenser, Edmund	*The Faerie Queene,* Book I (1500)
Vergil	*The Aeneid,* Books I–VI (*c* 25 BC)

POETRY: NARRATIVE, DRAMATIC, PHILOSOPHIC, DIDACTIC

English Ballads, *Sir Gawain and the Green Knight,* and poets William Cullen Bryant, Robert Browning, Geoffrey Chaucer, Samuel Taylor Coleridge, John Dryden, T. S. Eliot, Edward Fitzgerald, Robert Frost, John Keats, A. E. Housman, Robinson Jeffers, Samuel Johnson, John Keats, George Meredith, John Milton, E. A. Robinson, Christina Rossetti, D. G. Rossetti, James Thomson, Francis Thompson, Alfred, Lord Tennyson, William Wordsworth

POETRY: LYRIC AND ELEGIAC

Poets here include Browning, Coleridge, Eliot, Emerson, Frost, Housman, Jonson, Keats, Marlowe, Poe, Robinson, Rossetti (D. G.), Sidney, Spenser, Shakespeare (Sonnets), Tennyson, Wordsworth, Matthew Arnold, W. H. Auden, William Blake, Robert Burns, Thomas Campion, Hart Crane, e. e. cummings, Emily Dickinson, John Donne, Michael Drayton, Thomas Gray, George Herbert, Robert Herrick, Gerard Manley Hopkins, H. W. Longfellow, Richard Lovelace, Archibald MacLeish, Andrew Marvell, Marianne Moore, Wilfred Owen, Ezra Pound, Theodore Roethke, Carl Sandburg, Percy Bysshe Shelley, Stephen Spender, Wallace Stevens, Sir John Suckling, Algernon Swinburne, Dylan Thomas, J. G. Whittier, Walt Whitman, William Carlos Williams, Thomas Wyatt, William Butler Yeats

BIOGRAPHY, AUTOBIOGRAPHY, AND OTHER NON-FICTION PROSE

Adams, Henry	*The Education of Henry Adams* (1907)
Addison and Steele	*Spectator* Papers 2 and 70 (1711)
Bacon, Francis	"Of Marriage and Single Life," "Of Studies," (1579–1612)
Boswell, James	*Life of Johnson* (1791)
Carlyle, Thomas	Selections from *Sartor Resartus* (1833–34)
Donne, John	"Meditation 17" (1624)
Ellman, Richard	*James Joyce*
Edel, Leon	*Henry James*
Emerson, Ralph Waldo	"The American Scholar," "Nature," "The Divinity School Address"
Franklin, Benjamin	*Autobiography*, "The Sale of the Hessians" (1771)
Jefferson, Thomas	"Declaration of Independence," Letters (1776)
Johnson, Samuel	*Life of Milton*
Lamb, Charles	"A Chapter on Ears," "Old China," "Poor Relations"
Lincoln, Abraham	"Second Inaugural Address" (1865)
Mill, John Stuart	from *On Liberty:* "Applications" (1859)
Milton, John	*Areopagitica* to 9 (1644)
Newman, J. H. Cardinal	from *The Idea of a University:* "Knowledge Its Own End" (1852)
Sheaffer, Louis	Biographies of O'Neill
Strachey, Lytton	*Queen Victoria* (1921)
Thoreau, Henry	*Civil Disobedience, Walden* (1846–48)

FOLKLORE

Buchan, David	*The Ballad of the Folk* (1972)
Thompson, Stith	*The Folktale* (1946)

Bucknell University
Lewisburg, PA 17837-9988
(717) 524-1101

Entering students have a number of freshman courses they can choose from at Bucknell. Some of the courses and the books they require follow:

I. MYTH, REASON, FAITH

In this course, works by major writers from Homer to Dante are studied "to illustrate the development of Western culture from its origins in the Greek, Roman, Judaic, and Christian traditions." The Bible and the writings of such authors as **Aristotle, Dante, Homer, Plato, Sophocles, and Vergil** are considered.

II. MAJOR FIGURES AND COMPOSITION

Representative works in this course are examined "in relationship to the histories that shaped them" and the writing styles and techniques used by the writers. Texts include:

	Beowulf
	Sir Gawain and the Green Knight
Brontë, Emily	*Wuthering Heights*
Camus, Albert	*The Stranger*
Conrad, Joseph	*Heart of Darkness*
Homer	*The Odyssey*
Twain, Mark	*The Adventures of Huckleberry Finn*
Updike, John	*Rabbit, Run*

In the spring semester, this course focuses on British literature from the eighteenth century to the mid-twentieth. It begins with the poetry of **Alexander Pope** and the letters of **Lady Mary Wortley Montagu**. Romanticism in poetry and fiction is illustrated by the works of **Jane Austen, William Blake,** and **Emily Brontë**. The "high Romantic" is considered through "two related pairs of writers: **Mary** and **Percy Bysshe Shelley, Dorothy** and **William Wordsworth**." The Victorian period is investigated through the poetry of **Elizabeth Barrett Browning** and **Robert Browning**, and modernism through the novels of **James Joyce** and **Virginia Woolf**. The *Norton Anthology of English Literature* (Major Authors Edition) is one of the main texts in addition to the paperback novels.

III. DRAMA AND COMPOSITION

The two sections of this course are intended to allow the student "to read, to interpret, and to judge representative great plays in the Western tradition." Some of the dramatists considered are **Samuel Beckett, Steven Berkoff, Anton Chekov, Henrik Ibsen, Luigi Pirandello, August Strindberg**. Specific texts include:

	The Second Shepherd's Play
Albee, Edward	*The Zoo Story*
Baraka, Imamu Amiri	
(LeRoi Jones)	*Dutchman*
Esslin, Martin	*The Field of Drama*
Miller, Arthur	*Death of a Salesman*
Shakespeare, William	*Othello*
Sophocles	*Antigone*
Williams, Tennessee	*A Streetcar Named Desire*

IV. FICTION AND COMPOSITION

In the two sections of this course students are encouraged "to read, feel, think, and write—and to become more aware of the interdependence of these processes" as they interact with short stories. Some of the authors studied are **John Barth, James Baldwin, Ambrose Bierce, John Cheever, Stephen Crane, Ralph Ellison, William Faulkner, F. Scott Fitzgerald, Ernest Hemingway, Richard Hughes, James Joyce, D. H. Lawrence, Ursula LeGuin, Doris Lessing, Jean Rhys, John Updike, Kurt Vonnegut.** Depending on the section, specific texts are:

McHahan, Elizabeth, Susan Day, et al.	*The Elements of Writing About Literature*
Scholes, Robert	*Elements of Fiction: An Anthology*
Strunk and White	*The Elements of Style*
Trimmer & Jennings, eds.	*Fictions* (2nd Ed)

V. FICTION AND COMPOSITION: WOMEN'S FICTION

This course considers "the broad outlines of female literary history and the major themes of women writers." Texts include an anthology of short stories and:

Austen, Jane	*Sense and Sensibility*
Brooks, Gwendolyn	*Maude Martha*
Larsen, Nella	*Quicksand*
Williams, Sherley Anne	*Dessa Rose*
Woolf, Virginia	*Mrs. Dalloway*

VI. POETRY AND COMPOSITION

In this course, three poetic genres: the sonnet, the dramatic monologue, and the song will be studied as well as poems "which lie outside these formal boundaries." The reading list includes **Elizabeth Bishop, Robert Browning, Emily Dickinson, John Donne, Robert Frost, George Herbert, Gerard Manley Hopkins, Langston Hughes, Andrew Marvell, William Shakespeare, William Wordsworth, William Butler Yeats,** and others. The texts are:

Allison, A. W., et al., eds.	*Norton Shorter Anthology of Poetry*
Hollander, John	*Rhyme's Reason*

VII. SPECIAL TOPICS AND COMPOSITION: FARCE

"The first half of the course is concerned with the past—the farces of **Aristophanes, Plautus,** the medieval writers, **Shakespeare, Jonson, Molière.** The second half focuses on the modern world"—the farces of **Noel Coward, Georges Feydeau, Gilbert and Sullivan, George Bernard Shaw, Neil Simon, Oscar Wilde,** and others.

VIII. Special Topics And Composition: The Young Woman In American Literature

The purpose of this course is to introduce "beginning students to literature of the 'bildungsroman' or novel of development, in which a young woman experiences the rites of passage from adolescence to adulthood, and to enable students to recognize archetypal patterns in narratives focused on women's experience." Among the novelists considered are **Louisa May Alcott, Maya Angelou, Rita Mae Brown, Willa Cather, Kate Chopin, Toni Morrison, Jean Stafford, Alice Walker**, and **Edith Wharton**. Also studied are four books of criticism:

Abel, Hirsch, Langland	*The Voyage In*
Christ, Carol	*Diving Deep and Surfacing*
Pratt, Annis	*Archetypal Patterns in Women's Fiction*
White, Barbara	*Growing Up Female*

IX. Special Topics And Composition: The Art Of The American Short Story And Short Novel

The course considers "how American short fiction embodies characteristics of American life and how it can contribute to a better understanding of our national character and of ourselves." The selection of short stories in the anthology *Major American Short Stories* edited by A. Walton Litz includes those by **John Barth, F. Scott Fitzgerald, Nathaniel Hawthorne, Ernest Hemingway, Edgar Allan Poe, John Updike,** and others. Students also read short novels by **Phillip Roth** and:

James, Henry	*Great Short Works of Henry James*
Salinger, J. D.	*The Catcher in the Rye*

X. Special Topics And Composition: The Psychological Roots Of Literature

The course explores "the theories of Freud and Jung; dreams, fairy tales, poems, short stories, epics, plays. The aphorism which governs [this] approach to literature, borrowed from Erich Fromm's *The Forgotten Language*, goes: 'The language of dreams is the language of literature.'" The works considered, in addition to two texts that review the theories of **Sigmund Freud** and **Carl Jung**, include fairy tales, poems by **William Blake** and **William Butler Yeats**, short stories by **Nathaniel Hawthorne, Ernest Hemingway, Rudyard Kipling,** and:

	Beowulf
	Bible: Genesis
Conrad, Joseph	*Heart of Darkness*
Shakespeare, William	*Othello* and *Twelfth Night*

XI. SPECIAL TOPICS AND COMPOSITION: THE NOVEL OF YOUTH

The course explores "the nature of adolescence (particularly initiation rites) from several perspectives." Students read:

Litz, A. Walton, ed.	*Major American Short Stories*
Ballantyne, Sheila	*Imaginary Crimes*
Brown, Rita Mae	*Rubyfruit Jungle*
Hemingway, Ernest	*In Our Time*
Knowles, John	*A Separate Peace*
Zinsser, William	*On Writing Well*

XII. SPECIAL TOPICS AND COMPOSITION: THE AUTOBIOGRAPHY

In this course students read "a series of autobiographies, ranging from antiquity to the present day." Included are:

Augustine, St.	*Confessions* (selections)
Douglass, Frederick	*Narrative of the Life of Frederick Douglass*
Franklin, Benjamin	*Autobiography*
Johnson, James Weldon	*Autobiography of an Ex-Coloured Man*
Kingston, Maxine Hong	*The Woman Warrior*
Mingus, Charles	*Beneath the Underdog*
Rousseau, Jean Jacques	*Confessions* (selections)
Watson, James	*The Double Helix*

XIII. ART, NATURE, KNOWLEDGE

"This course introduces the student to some of the major artists, writers, and texts in the humanities.... Among the twenty-five or so authors, artists, and composers" considered are **Johann Sebastian Bach, Ludwig Van Beethoven, Gustave Courbet, Charles Darwin, Rene Descartes, Feodor Dostoevski, Galileo, Karl Marx, John Milton, Rembrandt Van Rijn, William Shakespeare, Voltaire.**

XIV. SPECIAL TOPICS AND COMPOSITION: LITERATURE AND REBELLION

The general purpose of the course is "to study literature with respect to the following ideas: that, while literature always expresses a culture, it also always expresses an individual. The artist always tends toward subversion, because writing is an individual act leading to independent thinking. Rulers, historically, have distrusted the poet and the writer knowing they will not fit into predestined slots." The readings include:

Baraka, Imamu Amiri (LeRoi Jones)	*Dutchman*
Blake, William	"London," "Preface to *Milton*"

Camus, Albert	"Rebellion and Art"
King, Martin Luther	"I Have a Dream"
Malraux, Andre	*Man's Fate*
Melville, Herman	*Billy Budd;* "The Paradise of Bachelors & the Tartarus of Maids"
Miller, Arthur	*Death of a Salesman*
Orwell, George	"Politics and the English Language"
Plato	Selections from *The Republic*
Thoreau, Henry	"Civil Disobedience"

XV. SPECIAL TOPICS AND COMPOSITION: RENDEZVOUS WITH THE THIRD WORLD

Novels studied in this course are from a number of Third World countries, including Ghana, Nigeria, some Caribbean states, Latin America, and India. The works are by such writers as **Chinua Achebe, Ayi K. Armah, Alejo Carpentier, Jamaica Kincaid, George Lamming, Paule Marshall, V. A. Naipaul, R. K. Narayan, Salman Rushdie, Wole Soyinka.**

XVI. SPECIAL TOPICS AND COMPOSITION: FILM AND LITERATURE

The emphasis in this course is on the relationship between fiction and film. It examines "what literature can do that film can't, and vice versa." Treated are the following and their film adaptations:

Short stories by **William Faulkner, Stephen King,** and (paired with Hitchcock's *Psycho*) **Edgar Allan Poe**

Brontë, Emily	*Wuthering Heights*
Conrad, Joseph	*Heart of Darkness* (paired with *Apocalypse Now*)
James, Henry	*The Turn of the Screw* (paired with *The Innocents*)
Oates, Joyce Carol	"Where Are You Going, Where Have You Been?" (paired with Frank Capra's *Smooth Talk*)
Shelley, Mary	*Frankenstein*
Steinbeck, John	*East of Eden*
Vonnegut, Kurt	*Slaughterhouse Five*
Walker, Alice	*The Color Purple*
Wright, Richard	*Native Son*

Butler University
4600 Sunset Avenue
Indianapolis, IN 46208
(317) 283-9255

During the first semester of Butler's two-term freshman English course, students are normally working with readings from texts such as *The Harper & Row Reader* (Booth and Gregory), *Theme and Variations: The Impact of Great Ideas* (Behrens and Rosen), or *Audiences and Intentions: A Book of Arguments* (Bradbury and Quinn). For the second semester, instructors choose the works they wish to use for their individual sections. A list of typical selections would include these ancients and moderns:

Barth, John	"Lost in the Funhouse"
Blake, William	Selected poems
Brontë, Charlotte	*Jane Eyre*
Brontë, Emily	*Wuthering Heights*
Brooks, Gwendolyn	Selected poems
Chaucer, Geoffrey	*Canterbury Tales*
Conrad, Joseph	*Heart of Darkness; Lord Jim*
Dickens, Charles	*Bleak House*
Dickinson, Emily	Selected poems
Dostoevski, Feodor	*Crime and Punishment*
Euripides	*Medea*
Faulkner, William	"The Bear"
Fitzgerald, F. Scott	*The Great Gatsby*
Hawthorne, Nathaniel	Short stories
Hardy, Thomas	*Tess of the d'Ubervilles*
Heaney, Seamus	Selected poems
Hemingway, Ernest	*For Whom the Bell Tolls*
Homer	*The Odyssey*
Joyce, James	*A Portrait of the Artist as a Young Man*
Lawrence, D. H.	*Sons and Lovers*
Levertov, Denise	Selected poems
Orwell, George	*1984*
Poe, Edgar Allan	Tales
Pope, Alexander	*The Rape of the Lock*
Shakespeare, William	*Othello; King Lear; Hamlet*
Shaw, George Bernard	*Candida; Major Barbara*
Sophocles	*Antigone; Oedipus the King*
Swift, Jonathan	*Gulliver's Travels*
Twain, Mark	Selections
Vonnegut, Kurt Jr.	*Slaughterhouse Five*
Wolfe, Thomas	*Look Homeward, Angel*
Wright, Richard	*Native Son*
Yeats, William Butler	Selected poems

California Institute of Technology
1201 East California Boulevard
Pasadena, CA 91125
(818) 356-6341

Freshmen entering Caltech are required to take two terms of freshman humanities. Depending on the particular course, European, American, and Asian literature are studied. The content of the prescribed reading material is up to the individual instructor; however, some of the humanities courses typically teach certain works.

Homer and **Aristotle**, for example, are among the "Greeks" taught in Humanities 1, Greek Civilization. In Humanities 3, Early European Literature, the selections are usually English literature, but **Dante, Molière**, and **Rabelais** are also frequently taught.

Humanities 11, Literature and Psychology, introduces the student to "literature and psychology considered as parallel investigations of such essential human issues as development of a sense of self, the nature of dreams, levels (conscious and unconscious) of communication." Works studied include, among others, those by **Samuel Taylor Coleridge, Feodor Dostoevski, Thomas Mann, Robert Louis Stevenson**.

Clarkson University
Holcroft House
Potsdam, NY 13676
(315) 268-6479

Great Ideas in Western Culture is the title of the core program at Clarkson. Required reading for its courses include four of the following books each semester of the academic year, plus one additional work of the faculty member's choice.

	Bible, Oxford Study Edition (New English translation, annotated)
Austen, Jane	*Pride and Prejudice*
Camus, Albert	*The Stranger*
Dante	*Inferno*
Darwin, Charles	*Darwin* (Appleman, ed.)
Freud, Sigmund	*Civilization and Its Discontents*
Homer	*The Odyssey*
Locke, John	*Second Treatise on Government*
Machiavelli, Niccolo	*The Prince*
Marx, Karl	*The Marx-Engels Reader* (Tucker, ed.)
Plato	*The Last Days of Socrates*

Shakespeare, William	Any play
Sophocles	*The Oedipus Cycle*
Voltaire	*Candide and Other Writings*

Colby College
Waterville, ME 04901
(207) 872-3168

There are a variety of works used to provide inspiration for writing in Colby's freshman English course. Some of the sections read, discuss, and write about works by **Henry David Thoreau, Mark Twain, Annie Dillard, Norman MacClean, Robert M. Pirsig, Helen Keller, Roland Barthes,** and **Salman Rushdie.** Describing his section, Professor John R. Sweney says, "As Samuel Johnson reminds us, 'What is written without effort is in general read without pleasure.' But what is it that pleases readers, and how and where do we focus our efforts as writers?" The following are some of the works considered in the various sections of English 115 at Colby College:

Brecht, Bertolt	Plays
Cassill, R. V.	*Norton Anthology of Contemporary Fiction*
Colombo, Gary, et al., eds.	*Rereading America: Cultural Contexts for Critical Thinking and Writing*
Dorsen, Norman, ed.	*The Rights of Americans*
Eagleton, Terry	*Literary Theory*
Fante, John	*Wait Until Spring; Bandini*
Freud, Sigmund	*Three Case Histories*
Henley, Beth	*The Wake of Jamey Foster*
Kazin, Alfred	*A Walker in the City*
Kingston, Maxine Hong	*Woman Warrior*
Lurie, Nancy O., ed.	*Mountain Wolf Woman, Sister of Crashing Thunder: The Autobiography of a Winnebago Indian*
Marius, Richard	*Writing on History, A Writer's Companion*
Mathabane, Mark	*Kaffir Boy in America*
Scholes, Robert	*Textual Power: Literary Theory and the Teaching of English*
Scholes, Robert and Nancy Comley	*The Practice of Writing*
Sontag, Susan	*AIDS and its Metaphors*
Woolf, Virginia	*A Room of One's Own*
Wycherley, William	*The Country Wife*
Ziff, Linda	*The Responsible Reader*

Colorado College
Colorado Springs, CO 80903
(719) 473-2233

According to Professor George Butte, Chairman of the Department of English at Colorado, the college has no set list of recommended titles nor a common freshman reading list, but the following are the works required in several of the entering-level courses:

ENGLISH 201: INTRODUCTION TO LITERATURE

Bain, C. E., et al., eds.	*The Norton Introduction to Literature,* 3rd ed.
Chekhov, Anton	*The Three Sisters*
Dickens, Charles	*A Tale of Two Cities*
Durrenmatt, Friedrich	*The Visit*
Aristophanes	*The Birds*
Malamud, Bernhard	*The Natural*
Pinter, Harold	*The Dumb Waiter*
Shakespeare, William	*Twelfth Night*
Soyinka, Wole	*Death and the King's Horseman*

Recommended:

Holman, C. Hugh	*Handbook to Literature*

And students must choose one of the following:

Fugard, Athol	*Master Harold and the Boys* or *Siswe Banzi is Dead*
Morrison, Toni	*Sula*
Orwell, George	*Animal Farm* or *Road to Wigan Pier*

Short fiction read in the course includes:

Anderson, Sherwood	"The Egg"
Baldwin, James	"Sonny's Blues"
Bambara, Toni Cade	"My Man Bovanne"
Chekhov, Anton	"The Lady with the Dog"
Doyle, Sir Arthur Conan	"The Adventure of the Speckled Band"
Garcia Marquez, Gabriel	"A Very Old Man with Enormous Wings"
Hawthorne, Nathaniel	"Young Goodman Brown"
Hemingway, Ernest	"The Short Happy Life of Francis Macomber"
Kafka, Franz	"The Hunger Artist"
Lawrence, D. H.	"Odour of Chrysanthemums"
Le Guin, Ursula	"The Ones Who Walk Away from Omelas"

Lessing, Doris	"Our Friend Judith"
O'Connor, Flannery	"The Artificial Nigger"
Olson, Tillie	"O Yes"
Richler, Mordecai	"The Summer My Grandmother Was Supposed to Die"
Twain, Mark	"The Celebrated Jumping Frog of Calaveras County"

Poetry selections include:

	Ballads: "Lord Randall," "Sir Patrick Spens"
Blake, William	"The Sick Rose"
Brooke, Rupert	"The Soldier"
Browning, Robert	"Soliloquy of the Spanish Cloister"
Chasin, Helen	"Joy Sonnet"
Donne, John	"A Valediction: Forbidding Mourning," "Batter My Heart"
Eliot, T. S.	"The Love Song of J. Alfred Prufrock"
Giovanni, Nikki	"Poetry"
Harper, F. E.	"Dear John, Dear Coltrane"
Knight, Etheridge	"The Idea of Ancestry"
Marvell, Andrew	"To His Coy Mistress"
Owen, Wilfred	"Dulce Et Decorum Est"
Plath, Sylvia	"Lady Lazarus"
Pound, Ezra	"In a Station of the Metro"
Rich, Adrienne	"Diving Into the Wreck"
Shakespeare, William	"Th' Expense of Spirit"
Tennyson, Alfred Lord	"Break, Break, Break"
Thomas, Dylan	"Do Not Go Gentle Into That Good Night," "Fern Hill"
Wordsworth, William	"London, 1802"
Yeats, William Butler	Selections

COMPOSITION-LITERATURE 100: THEORY AND PRACTICE OF LITERATURE

Harari, Josue V.	*Textual Strategies*
Hulme, Keri	*The Bone People*
Mann, Thomas	*Mario the Magician*
Molière	*Tartuffe*
Morrison, Toni	*Sula*
Plato	*Phaedrus*
Puig, Manuel	*Pubis Angelical*
Tutuola, Amos	"Homecoming," "Tra-la-la"

COMPARATIVE LITERATURE 100

Aristophanes	*The Birds*
Conrad, Joseph	*Lord Jim*

Freud, Sigmund	*Dora*
Hesiod	*Theogony; Works and Days*
Shakespeare, William	*Twelfth Night*
Shelley, Mary	*Frankenstein*

ENGLISH 203: CONVENTION AND CHANGE: THE NATURE OF COMEDY

Aristophanes	*The Clouds* (Arnott, tr.)
Amado, Jorge	*The Two Deaths of Quincas Watervell*
Austen, Jane	*Pride and Prejudice*
Beckett, Samuel	*Waiting for Godot*
Böll, Heinrich	*The Clown*
Faulkner, William	*As I Lay Dying*
Freud, Sigmund	*Jokes and Their Relation to the Unconscious*
Heller, Joseph	*Catch-22*
Homer	*The Odyssey* (Fitzgerald, tr.)
Shakespeare, William	*Twelfth Night*
Shaw, George Bernard	*Pygmalion*
Stoppard, Tom	"Jumpers," "The Real Inspector Hound," "The Real Thing"

Columbia College, Columbia University
 212 Hamilton Hall
 New York, NY 10027
 (212) 280-2521

Since 1919, Columbia College has had a required core curriculum made up of Literature Humanities, Contemporary Civilization, Music Humanities, and Art Humanities courses. Required and recommended works for the Literature Humanities and Contemporary Civilization sections are listed below.

LITERATURE HUMANITIES

(Fall Semester Assignments)

Aeschylus	*Aeschylus I: Oresteia* (Lattimore, tr.)
Aristophanes	*Aristophanes: Four Comedies* (Arrowsmith, tr.)
Aristotle	*Nichomachean Ethics* (Ross, tr.); *Poetics* (Janko, tr.)
Euripides	*Euripides I* (Warner, tr.) *Medea; Euripides V* (Arrowsmith, tr.); *Bacchae*

Homer	*The Iliad* (Lattimore, tr.); *The Odyssey* (Lattimore, tr.);
Homeric Hymns	*Homeric Hymns* (Athanassakis, tr.), "Homeric Hymn to Demeter"
Plato	*Apology* (Grube, tr.) "Trial and Death of Socrates"; *Republic* (Grube, tr.); *Symposium* (Hamilton, tr.)
Sappho	Selections
Sophocles	*Sophocles I: Oedipus the King* (Grene, tr.); *Antigone* (Wyckoff, tr.); *Oedipus at Colonus* (Fitzgerald, tr.)
Thucydides	*Peloponnesian War* (Warner, tr.)
Vergil	*Aeneid* (Fitzgerald, tr.)

LITERATURE HUMANITIES

(Spring Semester Assignments)

	Bible: Old and New Testaments, Revised Standard or King James Version
Augustine, Saint	*Confessions* (Pine-Coffin, tr.)
Austen, Jane	*Pride and Prejudice*
Boccaccio, Giovanni	*Decameron* (McWilliam, tr.)
Dante	*Inferno* (Mandelbaum, tr.)
Descartes, René	*Discourse on Method* and *Meditations on the First Philosophy* (Cress, tr.)
Goethe, Johann W. von	*Faust, Part I* (Salm, tr.)
Lafayette, Mde. de	*Princesse de Cleves* (Mitford/Tancock, tr.)
Montaigne, Michel de	*Essays* (Cohen, tr.)
Shakespeare, William	*King Lear*

CONTEMPORARY CIVILIZATION

(Fall Semester)

SECTION I: THE GREEK AND ROMAN WORLD

Required:	
Plato	*Republic* (Lee, tr.)
Recommended:	
Plato	*Last Days of Socrates*
Required:	
Aristotle	*The Politics* (Barker, ed.)
Recommended:	
Aristotle	*Nichomachean Ethics*

Required:

> *CHW [Columbia History of the World,* Garrety, Gay, eds.], Chs. 18–21

Recommended:

Cicero	*On the Good Life* (Grant, tr.)
Epictetus	*The Handbook of Epictetus*
Livy	*History of Rome* (Selincourt, tr.)

SECTION II: THE SOURCES OF THE JUDEO-CHRISTIAN TRADITION

Required:

> Hebrew Bible, minimally Genesis, Exodus, Isaiah; New Testament, minimally Matthew, Acts (selections), and Galatians or Romans

SECTION III: THE MIDDLE AGES

Required:

> *CHW* Chs. 32–33, 35

Aquinas, St. Thomas	*Aquinas on Ethics and Politics* (Sigmund, ed.)
Augustine, Saint	*City of God*

Recommended:

> *Medieval Political Philosophy* (Lerner, ed.): "Alfarabi," "Maimonides"

SECTION IV: RENAISSANCE AND REFORMATION

Required:

> *CHW* Chs. 39–44

Braudel, Fernand	"European Expansion and Capitalism, 1450–1650" in *Chapters in Western Civilization* 3rd ed., Vol. 1
Calvin, John	*Institutes* Bk. IV, Ch. 20
Hillerbrand, H. J., ed.	*Protestant Reformation*
Machiavelli, Niccolo	*Prince* and *Discourses*
More, Thomas	*Utopia*

SECTION V: THE NEW SCIENCE

Required:

Bacon, Francis	*The New Organon*
Galileo	*Discoveries and Opinions*
Descartes, René	*Discourse on Method* or *Meditations*

Recommended:

CHW Ch. 59

SECTION VI: NEW PHILOSOPHY AND THE POLITY

Required:

	CHW Ch. 48
Hobbes, Thomas	*Leviathan*
Locke, John	*Two Treatises on Government*

CONTEMPORARY CIVILIZATION

(Spring Semester)

SECTION I: THE ENLIGHTENMENT AND THE FRENCH REVOLUTION

Required:

Rousseau, Jean Jacques   *Discourse on the Origin of Inequality* and *Social Contract*

Recommended:

Rousseau, Jean Jacques   *Émile* (entire text recommended)

Wollstonecraft, Mary   *Vindication of the Rights of Women*

Required:

Hume, David   Selection from *Inquiry Concerning the Principles of Morals* in *ICCW [Introduction to Contemporary Civilization in the West]*, Vol. I

Recommended:

Hume, David   *Inquiry Concerning Human Understanding; Inquiry Concerning the Principles of Morals; Treatise on Human Nature; Essays: Moral, Political and Literary*

Required:

     CHW, Chs. 64, 65, 66 (on American and French Revolutions); Documents on the French Revolution; *Federalist Papers* #10, #51

Kant, Immanuel   *Grounding for the Metaphysics of Morals* and "What is Enlightenment"

Recommended:

Burke, Edmund   *Reflections on the Revolution in France*

SECTION II: ECONOMY, SOCIETY, AND THE STATE

Required:

	CHW Chs. 72, 73, 74
Hegel, Georg	"Ethics" from *The Philosophy of Right* in C. J. Friedrich ed., *The Philosophy of Hegel* 3rd part, or *Reason in History*
Marx, Karl	Selections from *Marx-Engels Reader* (R. Tucker, ed.)
Mill, J. Stuart	"On Liberty," "The Subjection of Women," selections from "On Representative Government," in *Three Essays*

Recommended:

Bentham, Jeremy	"Principles of Legislation" in *ICCW*, Vol. II

SECTION III: DARWIN, FREUD, NIETZSCHE

Required:

Darwin, Charles	*Descent of Man* or *Origin of Species* in *Darwin* (Appleman, ed.)

Recommended:

	"Illustrations of Universal Progress" in *ICCW*, Vol 2.; "Social Darwinism, Gender, and Race" in the *Appleman Reader*, Part V

Required:

Freud, Sigmund	*Civilization and its Discontents; Three Essays on the Theory of Sexuality* or Selections from *Introductory Lectures*
Nietzsche, Friedrich	*Genealogy of Morals*

SECTION IV: MODERNITY AND ITS DISCONTENTS (TENTATIVE)

A. Science and Revolutions in the 20th Century

Arendt, Hannah	*On Violence*
	The Origins of Totalitarianism
Gramsci, Antonio	*The Modern Prince*
Habermas, Jurgen	*Toward a Rational Society*
Lenin, V. I.	*Imperialism* or *State and Revolution*
Merleu-Ponty, Maurice	*Humanism and Terror*
Weber, Max	"Science as a Vocation" and "Politics as a Vocation" in *Essays in Sociology*

B. The Ambiguities of Integration: Class, Race, and
Gender

Beauvoir, Simone de	*The Second Sex*
Fanon, Frantz	*The Wretched of the Earth*
Harrington, Michael	*The Other America*
Mahowald, Mary B., ed.	*Philosophy of Women*
Malcolm X	*Autobiography*
Rawls, John	*A Theory of Justice*
Snitow, Ann, ed.	*Powers of Desire*

Supreme Court cases, such as *Brown* vs. *Board of Education* (1954); *Serrano* vs. *Priest* (1971); *San Antonio School District* vs. *Rodriguez* (1973); *De Funis* vs. *Odegaard* (1974); *University of California Regents* vs. *Bakke* (1978).

Cornell University
410 Thurston Avenue
Ithaca, NY 14850
(607) 255-5241

Most freshmen at Cornell must take two freshman writing seminars. The John S. Knight Writing Program gives them a choice of more than 125 different courses to fulfill this requirement. Each seminar is limited to 17 students. The reading assignments of 100 pages or less a week may be in humanities, social sciences, expressive arts, or sciences depending upon the particular course. Examples of readings in a few of the seminars follow:

PLAIN TALES FROM THE RAJ: LANGUAGE, LITERATURE, AND EXPERIENCE IN BRITISH INDIA

This course focuses "on Anglo-Indian literature as a product of a particular historical situation and as exemplary of the problems that arise from contact between two alien cultures." The course examines the theme that the British images that authors put forth "are imaginative inventions, reflections derived from British views of their own civilization and from the declining fortunes of British rule on the Indian subcontinent." Writers studied include, among others, **Rudyard Kipling, E. M. Forster.**

KAFKA, HESSE, BRECHT, AND MANN

The course is "based on complete works (in English translation) by four representative German authors of the first half of the century." Among the works studied are:

Brecht, Bertolt	*Mother Courage and Her Children; Galileo*
Hesse, Herman	*Demian; Siddhartha*
Kafka, Franz	*The Metamorphosis*
Mann, Thomas	*Death in Venice*

INTENSIVE WORKSHOP IN GERMANIC STUDIES FOR FRESHMEN I AND II

These courses, taught in German, may be used to satisfy the freshman writing requirement. The first semester provides "an intensive introduction to the study of German literature through the discussion of exemplary prose works, dramas, and poems from the eighteenth century to the present." In the second semester the emphasis is on German literature since 1900. Some of the authors studied are G. Benn, Bertolt Brecht, Paul Celan, Friedrich Durrenmatt, Herman Hesse, Franz Kafka, Thomas Mann, Ulrich Plenzdorf, Rainer Maria Rilke, Peter Weiss.

CLASSICS OF RUSSIAN THOUGHT AND LITERATURE

The course, taught in English, looks "in particular at the conflict between the Slavophiles, those who thought Russia had its own unique destiny, and the Westernizers, those who thought Russia should look to the West for a model in its development." Authors studied (in English translation) include Feodor Dostoevski, Aleksander Herzen, Aleksandr Solzhenitsyn, Ivan Turgenev.

NINETEENTH-CENTURY RUSSIAN LITERARY MASTERPIECES

This and several other seminars in the Russian Department examine the writings of such authors as Isaac Babel, Anton Chekov, Nikolai Gogol, Mikhail Lermontov, Vladimir Nabokov, Olesha, Boris Pasternak, Alexander Pushkin, Leo Tolstoy, Fyodor Tiutchev, Mikhail Zoshchenko.

WRITERS ON WRITING

This course looks at how "writers of nineteenth- and twentieth-century Russian literature from Gogol to Olesha portray reading or writing processes in their works." It also examines selections from Georges Poulet, Friedrich Von Schiller, Jean Paul Sartre, and others to see how and why we read and write.

PARADISE LOST: BICULTURALISM IN AMERICA

This course "dissect[s] the myth of the American Dream through a study of literature written by American ethnic minority authors."

Barrio, Raymond	*The Plum Plum Pickers*
Galarza, Ernesto	*Barrio Boy*
Kingston, Maxine Hong	*China Men*
Momaday, Scott	*House Made of Dawn*
Thomas, Piri	*Down These Mean Streets*

SEARCHING FOR SELF IN HISPANIC FICTION

Through selected works of Hispanic fiction, this course explores "the problem of self-definition." Texts include:

Arias, Ron	*Road to Tamazunchale*
Fuentes, Carlos	*The Good Conscience*
Mohr, Nicholasa	*Rituals of Survival*
Paz, Octavia	Essay
Puig, Manuel	*Betrayed by Rita Hayworth*

MYTH AND LEGEND IN THE ANCIENT NEAR EAST

This course considers "classic myths and legends from various ancient Near Eastern civilizations (*c* 3000–1000 BCE)" including Sumer, Egypt, Assyria, Babylonia, Anatolia, Canaan, and Israel. Among the texts read are:

From Egypt

> The God and His Unknown Name of Power
> The Story of Two Brothers
> The Theology of Memphis

Atum — The Creation

From Sumer

> The Deluge
> A Paradise Myth
> Inanna's Descent to the Nether World

From Assyria and Babylonia

> Atrahasis
> The Creation Epic
> The Epic of Gilgamesh
> A Vision of the Nether World

From Ugarit

> The Legend of King Keret
> Poems of Baal and Anat

From Israel

The Creation Stories
Noah's Flood

THE LITERATURE OF CHIVALRY

This course explores the development of chivalric culture in such works as French and German stories of Tristan and Perceval and:

	Sir Gawain and the Green Knight
Chrétien de Troyes	Romances
Marie de France	*Lais*
Malory, Sir Thomas	*Morte d'Arthur*

LEGEND, FANTASY, AND VISION

The course surveys examples of medieval writers from various medieval cultures and considers "the continuity of these writings with selected works of modern fiction." Medieval texts include such works as Icelandic sagas, French and German romances of King Arthur and his knights, and:

	Beowulf (Anglo-Saxon epic)
	Voyage of St. Brendan (Irish)
Dante	*The Divine Comedy*

WRITING IN THE HUMANITIES

This seminar is open to some freshmen and to all sophomores. Student essays are based on viewings of paintings by such artists as **Leonardo da Vinci** and **Velasquez** and books such as:

Conrad, Joseph	*Heart of Darkness*
Euripides	*The Bacchae*
Nabokov, Vladimir	*Pale Fire*
Nietzsche, Friedrich	*Birth of Tragedy*
Plato	*Gorgias*
Weiss, Peter	*Marat/Sade*

Creighton University
2500 California Street
Omaha, NE 68178
(402) 280-2703

The following list was developed within Creighton's Department of English and Speech, which is chaired by Professor Gordon Bergquist.

List of Books Suggested for Pre-College Reading

Arthurian Tales
Robin Hood Tales
Song of Roland
Bible

Adams, Henry	The Education of Henry Adams
Adler, Mortimer	How to Read a Book
Allen, Frederick L.	Only Yesterday
Austen, Jane	Emma; Pride and Prejudice
Barnett, Lincoln K.	The Universe and Dr. Einstein
Bellamy, Edward	Looking Backward
Boswell, James	Life of Johnson
Brontë, Charlotte	Jane Eyre
Brontë, Emily	Wuthering Heights
Buck, Pearl	The Good Earth
Bulfinch, Thomas	Mythology
Bunyan, John	Pilgrim's Progress
Butler, Samuel	The Way of All Flesh
Carroll, Lewis	Alice's Adventures in Wonderland
Carson, Rachel	The Sea Around Us
Cather, Willa	Death Comes for the Archbishop; My Antonia
Cervantes, Miguel de	Don Quixote
Chaucer, Geoffrey	Canterbury Tales
Clark, Walter V. T.	The Ox-Bow Incident
Conrad, Joseph	Lord Jim; Heart of Darkness
Crane, Stephen	The Red Badge of Courage
Defoe, Daniel	Robinson Crusoe
Dickens, Charles	A Tale of Two Cities; David Copperfield; Great Expectations; Oliver Twist
Dostoevski, Feodor	Crime and Punishment; The Brothers Karamazov
Doyle, Sir Arthur Conan	Sherlock Holmes
Dumas, Alexandre	The Three Musketeers
Eliot, George	Adam Bede; The Mill on the Floss
Faulkner, William	Intruder in the Dust
Fielding, Henry	Tom Jones
Fitzgerald, F. Scott	The Great Gatsby
Flaubert, Gustave	Madame Bovary
Forster, E. M.	A Passage to India
Franklin, Benjamin	Autobiography
Galsworthy, John	The Forsyte Saga
Golding, William	Lord of the Flies
Goldsmith, Oliver	She Stoops to Conquer
Greene, Graham	The Power and the Glory
Hamilton, Edith	The Greek Way
Hamilton, A., et al.	The Federalist Papers

Hardy, Thomas	*Tess of the D'Urbervilles; The Return of the Native*
Hawthorne, Nathaniel	*The House of The Seven Gables; The Scarlet Letter*
Hemingway, Ernest	*For Whom the Bell Tolls; A Farewell To Arms; The Old Man and the Sea*
Hersey, John	*Hiroshima*
Homer	*The Iliad; The Odyssey*
Hudson, W. H.	*Green Mansions*
Hugo, Victor	*Les Misérables*
Huxley, Aldous	*Brave New World*
James, Henry	*The Turn of the Screw*
Joyce, James	*A Portrait of the Artist as a Young Man*
Lewis, Sinclair	*Arrowsmith; Babbitt; Main Street*
London, Jack	*The Call of the Wild*
Maugham, Somerset	*Of Human Bondage*
Melville, Herman	*Moby-Dick*
Miller, Arthur	*Death of a Salesman*
Nordhoff & Hall	*Mutiny on the Bounty*
O'Neill, Eugene	*The Emperor Jones*
Orwell, George	*Animal Farm; 1984*
Parkman, Francis	*The Oregon Trail*
Paton, Alan	*Cry, The Beloved Country*
Plutarch	*Lives*
Remarque, Erich Maria	*All Quiet on the Western Front*
Roberts, Kenneth	*Northwest Passage*
Rolväag, O. E.	*Giants in the Earth*
Rostand, Edmond	*Cyrano de Bergerac*
Saint Exupery, A. de	*Wind, Sand, and Stars*
Salinger, J. D.	*The Catcher in the Rye*
Scott, Sir Walter	*Ivanhoe*
Shakespeare, William	*Hamlet; Henry IV; MacBeth; Romeo and Juliet*
Shaw, George Bernard	*Pygmalion; Saint Joan*
Sophocles	*Oedipus Rex*
Steinbeck, John	*The Grapes of Wrath*
Stevenson, Robert L.	*Treasure Island*
Swift, Jonathan	*Gulliver's Travels*
Thackeray, William M.	*Vanity Fair*
Thoreau, Henry	*Walden*
Tolstoy, Leo	*War and Peace*
Turgenev, Ivan	*Fathers and Sons*
Twain, Mark	*The Adventures of Huckleberry Finn; Life on the Mississippi; The Adventures of Tom Sawyer*
Vergil	*The Aeneid*
Warren, Robert Penn	*All the King's Men*
Wharton, Edith	*Ethan Frome*
Wilder, Thornton	*Our Town; The Bridge of San Luis Rey*
Wolfe, Thomas	*Look Homeward, Angel*

Davidson College
PO Box 1737
Davidson, NC 28036
(704) 892-2000

The following books are required for Davidson's first-year Humanities program:

For Both Semesters:

Fowler, H. Ramsey	*The Little, Brown Handbook* 3rd ed.

Fall Semester:

Aeschylus	*The Oresteia* (Fagles, tr.)
Apuleius	*The Golden Ass* (Lindsay, tr.)
Aristotle	*Nicomachean Ethics* (Ross, tr.)
Chamber, Mortimer	*Ancient Greece*
Euripides	*Medea & Other Plays* (Vellacott, tr.)
Gruen, Erich	*The Roman Republic*
Homer	*The Iliad of Homer* (Lattimore, tr.)
Plato	*Protagoras and Meno* (Guthrie, tr.)
Plato and Aristophanes	*Four Texts on Socrates* (West and West, tr.)
Pollitt, J. J.	*Art and Experience in Classical Greece*
Sophocles	*The Three Theban Plays* (Fagles, tr.)
Tacitus	*The Annals of Imperial Rome* (Grant, tr.)
Thucydides	*History of the Peloponnesian War* (Warner, tr.)
Vergil	*The Aeneid of Vergil* (Humphries, tr.)

Spring Semester:

	Beowulf (Raffel, tr.)
	The Epic of Gilgamesh (Sanders, tr.)
	The Lais of Marie De France (Hanning and Ferrante, tr.)
	The New Oxford Annotated Bible with the Apocrypha, Revised Standard Version
	The Quest of the Holy Grail (Matarasso, tr.)
	The Song of Roland (Harrison, tr.)
Augustine, Saint	*The Confessions of St. Augustine* (Warner, tr.)
Benedict, Saint	*The Rule of St. Benedict in English* (Fry and Baker, eds.)
Chaucer, Geoffrey	*Canterbury Tales* (Wright, tr.)
Dante Alighieri	*The Divine Comedy: The Inferno, The Purgatorio, The Paradiso* (Ciardi, tr.)

Eibhard and Notker the Stammerer	*Two Lives of Charlemagne* (Thorpe, tr.)
Hollister, C. Warren	*Medieval Europe: A Short History,* 5th ed.
Kelber, Werner H.	*Mark's Story of Jesus*
O'Brien & Major	*In the Beginning: Creation Myths from Ancient Mesopotamia, Greece, and Israel*
Aquinas, Thomas	*The Pocket Aquinas* (Vernon J. Bourke, ed.)

Optional texts are:

Anderson, Bernhard W.	*Understanding the Old Testament,* 4th ed.
Spivey & Smith	*Anatomy of the New Testament,* 4th ed.

Denison University
PO Box H
Granville, OH 43023
(614) 587-6276

According to Denison's Department of English, this reading list is a carefully selected compilation of "works important to literature in English." Although the list was composed primarily for college students, it is certainly a relevant one for the pre-college student to scan.

DRAMA

	The Second Shepherd's Play
	Everyman
Beckett, Samuel	*Waiting for Godot*
Chekhov, Anton	*The Cherry Orchard*
Congreve, William	*The Way of the World*
Fuller, Charles	*A Soldier's Play*
Goldsmith, Oliver	*She Stoops to Conquer*
Ibsen, Henrik	*Hedda Gabler*
Miller, Arthur	*Death of a Salesman*
Norman, Marsha	*'Night, Mother*
O'Neill, Eugene	*Long Day's Journey into Night*
Pinter, Harold	"The Dumb Waiter"
Pirandello, Luigi	*Six Characters in Search of an Author*
Shakespeare, William	*Hamlet; Henry IV, Part I; The Tempest; Twelfth Night*
Shaw, George Bernard	*Major Barbara*
Sheridan, Richard B.	*The School for Scandal* or *The Rivals*
Sherman, Martin	*Bent*

Sophocles	*Oedipus Rex*
Webster, John	*The Duchess of Malfi*

POETRY

	Beowulf
	Sir Gawain and the Green Knight
Arnold, Matthew	"Dover Beach"
Auden, W. H.	"Musée de Beaux Arts," "In Memory of W. B. Yeats," "In Praise of Limestone"
Bishop, Elizabeth	"Man-Moth," "The Fish," "The Armadillo," "In the Waiting Room"
Blake, William	*Songs of Innocence:* "The Lamb," "The Chimney Sweeper," *Songs of Experience:* "The Tyger," "The Chimney Sweeper," "London"
Bradstreet, Anne	"The Author to Her Book," "In Reference to her Children," "Upon the Burning of Our House"
Brooks, Gwendolyn	"We Real Cool," "Sadie and Maud," "Boy Breaking Glass," "The Lovers of the Poor," "A Bronzeville Mother Loiters in Mississippi . . ."
Browning, Robert	"My Last Duchess," "Andrea del Sarto," "Fra Lippo Lippi"
Browning, E. B.	Sonnets 21, 22, 32, 43
Chaucer, Geoffrey	*Canterbury Tales:* "General Prologue," "The Nun's Priest's Tale," "The Wife of Bath's Prologue and Tale," "The Pardoner's Introduction, Prologue, and Tale"
Coleridge, S. T.	"The Rime of the Ancient Mariner," "Frost at Midnight," "The Eolian Harp"
Dickinson, Emily	"Because I could not stop for Death—," "There's a certain Slant of light," "I heard a Fly buzz—when I died," "A narrow Fellow in the Grass," "Safe in their Alabaster Chambers—," "I started Early—Took my Dog—," "I taste a liquor never brewed—," "I felt a Funeral, in my Brain," "After great pain, a formal feeling comes—," "I died for Beauty—but was scarce," "My Life had stood—a Loaded Gun," "I'm Nobody! Who are you?"

Donne, John	"The Canonization," "The Sun Rising," "A Valediction: Forbidding Mourning," "A Nocturnal Upon St. Lucy's Day," Holy Sonnet 14, Elegy 19
Dryden, John	"MacFlecknoe"
Eliot, T. S.	"The Love Song of J. Alfred Prufrock," "The Waste Land," "Gerontion"
Frost, Robert	"Home Burial," "After Apple-Picking," "The Death of the Hired Man," "Design"
Ginsberg, Allen	"Howl"
Hayden, Robert	"Those Winter Sundays," "Middle Passage," "Night, Death, Mississippi"
Hopkins, Gerard Manley	"Spring and Fall," "The Windhover," "God's Grandeur," "Pied Beauty"
Keats, John	"Ode to a Nightingale," "Ode on a Grecian Urn"
Lowell, Robert	"Skunk Hour," "For the Union Dead"
Marvell, Andrew	"To His Coy Mistress," "The Garden"
Milton, John	*Paradise Lost,* Books I, II, IX; "Lycidas," "When I Consider How My Light Is Spent," "On My Late Espoused Saint," "How Soon Hath Time"
Moore, Marianne	"Poetry," "The Fish," "England," "A Grave," "In Distrust of Merits"
Plath, Sylvia	"Daddy," "Tulips," "Lady Lazarus," "Ariel"
Poe, Edgar Allan	"The City in the Sea"
Pope, Alexander	"The Rape of the Lock"
Rich, Adrienne	"Diving into the Wreck," "Transcendental Etude," "Snapshots of a Daughter-in-Law"
Roethke, Theodore	"My Papa's Waltz," "Four for Sir John Davies," "The Waking," "In a Dark Time"
Shakespeare, William	Sonnets 15, 18, 55, 64, 73, 116, 129, 130
Shelley, P. B.	"Ode to the West Wind," "To a Skylark," "Ozymandias,"
Spenser, Edmund	*The Faerie Queene,* Book I, "Epithalamion"
Stevens, Wallace	"The Emperor of Ice Cream," "Thirteen Ways of Looking at a Blackbird," "Sunday Morning," "The Idea of Order at Key West"

Tennyson, Alfred Lord	"Ulysses," "Tithonus," "Song of the Lotos-Eaters"
Whitman, Walt	"Song of Myself," "Crossing Brooklyn Ferry," "When Lilacs Last in the Dooryard Bloom'd"
Williams, W. C.	"Tract," "The Red Wheelbarrow," "The Yachts," "Spring and All," "The Dance"
Wordsworth, William	"Tintern Abbey," "Ode: Intimations of Immortality"
Wright, James	"A Blessing," "Lying in a Hammock at William Duffy's Farm in Pine Island, Minnesota," "This Journey," "The Jewel," "At the Executed Murderer's Grave," "Autumn Begins in Martin's Ferry, Ohio"
Yeats, W. B.	"The Second Coming," "Among School Children," "Sailing to Byzantium," "Easter 1916"

FICTION

Atwood, Margaret	*Surfacing*
Austen, Jane	*Emma* or *Pride and Prejudice*
Baldwin, James	*Go Tell It on the Mountain*
Bellow, Saul	*Seize the Day*
Black Elk	*Black Elk Speaks*
Brontë, Charlotte	*Jane Eyre*
Brontë, Emily	*Wuthering Heights*
Chopin, Kate	*The Awakening*
Douglass, Frederick	*Narrative of the Life of Frederick Douglass*
Ellison, Ralph	*Invisible Man*
Faulkner, William	*The Sound and the Fury* or *Light in August* or *As I Lay Dying* or *Absalom, Absalom!*
Fielding, Henry	*Joseph Andrews* or *Tom Jones*
Fitzgerald, F. Scott	*The Great Gatsby*
Gordimer, Nadine	*Burger's Daughter* or *A Guest of Honour*
Hardy, Thomas	*Jude the Obscure* or *The Mayor of Casterbridge* or *The Return of the Native* or *Tess of the D'Urbervilles*
Hawthorne, Nathaniel	*The Scarlet Letter,* "Young Goodman Brown," "My Kinsman, Major Molineux," "Rappaccini's Daughter"
Hemingway, Ernest	*The Sun Also Rises* or *In Our Time* or *A Farewell to Arms*
Hurston, Zora Neale	*Their Eyes Were Watching God*
James, Henry	*Daisy Miller; The Turn of the Screw*

Joyce, James	*Dubliners* or *A Portrait of the Artist as a Young Man*
Lawrence, D. H.	*Women in Love* or *The Rainbow* or *Sons and Lovers*
Melville, Herman	*Moby-Dick*
Morrison, Toni	*Sula* or *Song of Solomon*
O'Connor, Flannery	"A Good Man is Hard to Find," "Everything That Rises Must Converge," "The Artificial Nigger"
Porter, Katherine Anne	"Flowering Judas," "The Jilting of Granny Weatherall," "Rope"
Swift, Jonathan	*Gulliver's Travels*
Twain, Mark	*The Adventures of Huckleberry Finn*
Walker, Alice	*The Color Purple*
Welty, Eudora	"Why I Live at the P.O.," "A Worn Path," "The Petrified Man"
Wharton, Edith	*The House of Mirth* or *The Age of Innocence*
Woolf, Virginia	*Mrs. Dalloway* or *To the Lighthouse*
Wright, Richard	*Native Son*

ESSAYS AND CRITICISM

Aristotle	*Poetics*
Bentley, Eric	"Plot" from *The Life of the Drama*
Coleridge, S. T.	*Biographia Literaria*, Chapter 13
Dryden, John	"An Essay of Dramatic Poesy"
Eagleton, Terry	*Literary Theory*
Edwards, Jonathan	"Sinners in the Hands of an Angry God," "Personal Narrative"
Emerson, Ralph Waldo	*Nature;* "The American Scholar"
Keats, John	*Letters:* to Benjamin Bailey, 22/11/1817; George & Thomas Keats 21, 27/12/1817; Richard Woodhouse, 27/10/1818
Lawson, John Howard	"Theory and Technique of Playwrighting"
Miller, Arthur	"Tragedy and the Common Man"
Paine, Thomas	"Thoughts on the Present State of American Affairs" from *Common Sense*
Plato	*The Republic*, Book X
Poe, Edgar Allan	"The Poetic Principle" and "The Philosophy of Composition"
Rich, Adrienne	"When We Dead Awaken: Writing as Re-Vision"
Sidney, Sir Philip	"The Defence of Poesy"
Thoreau, Henry David	*Walden*
Warren, Robert Penn	"Pure and Impure Poetry"

Whitman, Walt	Preface to 1855 edition of *Leaves of Grass*
Wordsworth, William	Preface to *Lyrical Ballads*

DePaul University
25 East Jackson Boulevard
Chicago, IL 60604
(312) 341-8300

Professor Helen Marlborough explains that DePaul freshman are required to take English 120: Understanding Literature. There are a number of sections of this course. In one section, the text is Northrop Frye et al., *The Practical Imagination: Stories, Poems, Plays.* In addition to numerous shorter works, students in this section read: **William Shakespeare**, *Hamlet*; *The Tempest* and **Sophocles**, *Oedipus Rex*.

The instructor for another section, Professor Caryn Chaden, states that English 120 "introduces you to the process of reading literature. It invites you to examine a variety of short stories, poems, and plays spanning five centuries and two continents. The course will help you develop a critical vocabulary for discussing these works, both in class and in essays. By giving you the opportunity to read literature and write about it, the course will help you perceive and articulate some of the choices a writer makes when he or she turns blank paper into art." The text for this section is Scholes, Robert, Carl H. Klaus, and Nancy R. Comley, *Elements of Literature 3: Fiction, Poetry, Drama.* Some of the required readings are:

	Everyman
Anderson, Sherwood	"I'm a Fool"
Aristophanes	*Lysistrata*
Auden, W. H.	"As I walked out one evening," "Lullaby," "Musée des Beaux Arts," "The Unknown Citizen"
Baldwin, James	"Sonny's Blues"
Baraka, Imamu Amiri (LeRoi Jones)	Poems
Beckett, Samuel	*Krapp's Last Tape*
Borges, Jorge	"Lottery in Babylon"
Boyle, Kay	"Winter Night"
Brooks, Gwendolyn	Poems
Browning, Robert	"My Last Duchess"
Browning, E. B.	Sonnets
Carter, Angela	"The Snow Child"
Cheever, John	"The Swimmer"
Chekhov, Anton	"Heartache"
Chopin, Kate	"The Story of an Hour"
Coover, Robert	"The Hat Act"

Cortazar, Julio	"Blowup"
Dickinson, Emily	Poems
Donne, John	Poems
Ellison, Ralph	"Battle Royal"
Frost, Robert	Poems
Hughes, Ted	"On the Road"; *Mother and Child*
Lessing, Doris	"Sunrise on the Veld"
Maupassant, Guy de	"The Diamond Necklace"
Molière	*The Misanthrope*
O'Conner, Frank	"Guests of the Nation"
O'Connor, Flannery	"Everything that Rises Must Converge"
Olsen, Tillie	"I Stand Here Ironing"
Parker, Dorothy	"You Were Perfectly Fine"
Porter, Katherine Anne	"Rope"
Rich, Adrienne	"Night Pieces: For a Child," "Rape"
Roethke, Theodore	Poems
Stevens, Wallace	"Anecdote of the Jar," "Thirteen Ways of Looking at a Blackbird," "The Snow Man," "A High-Toned Old Christian Woman"
Tennyson, Alfred Lord	"Ulysses," "Tears, Idle Tears"
Wells, H. G.	"The Country of the Blind"
Welty, Eudora	"Why I Live at the P. O."
Whitman, Walt	Poems
Williams, Tennessee	*Cat on a Hot Tin Roof*
Williams, W. C.	Poems

DePauw University
South Locust Street
Greencastle, IN 46135
(317) 658-4006

While DePauw has no specific official list for pre-college reading, Dr. Martha Rainbolt, Chair, Department of English, says "clearly in this area, more is better. The more a student has read the better will be that individual's reading and writing skills. . . . I would recommend that students read everything they possibly can, and I would include in my list magazines and newspapers as well as books."

Dr. Rainbolt has two unofficial lists that she gives to students at DePauw who ask what they should read. She recommends their "beginning with the nineteenth-century British fiction. These works will impress a magnificent syntax and vocabulary on the minds of their readers, so the 'right' way to write sentences will be in the ears of the readers of those books."

On the unofficial list are:

NINETEENTH-CENTURY BRITISH NOVELS

Austen, Jane	*Emma; Pride and Prejudice*
Brontë, Charlotte	*Jane Eyre*
Brontë, Emily	*Wuthering Heights*
Butler, Samuel	*The Way of All Flesh*
Dickens, Charles	*Bleak House; Great Expectations*
Eliot, George	*Middlemarch; The Mill on the Floss*
Hardy, Thomas	*Jude The Obscure; Tess of the D'Urbervilles*
Meredith, George	*The Egoist*
Scott, Sir Walter	*The Heart of Midlothian*
Thackeray, William	*Vanity Fair*
Trollope, Anthony	*Barchester Towers*

BRITISH NOVELS OTHER THAN 19TH-CENTURY

Beerbohm, Max	*Zuleika Dobson*
Bennett, Arnold	*The Old Wives' Tale*
Conrad, Joseph	*Lord Jim; Nostromo*
Defoe, Daniel	*Moll Flanders*
Durrell, Lawrence	*The Alexandria Quartet*
Fielding, Henry	*Joseph Andrews; Tom Jones*
Ford, Ford Madox	*The Good Soldier*
Forster, E. M.	*A Passage to India*
Galsworthy, John	*The Forsyte Saga*
Huxley, Aldous	*Point Counter Point*
Joyce, James	*A Portrait of the Artist as a Young Man; Ulysses*
Lawrence, D. H.	*Sons and Lovers; The Rainbow*
Orwell, George	*1984*
Powell, Anthony	*A Dance to the Music of Time*
Richardson, Samuel	*Clarissa*
Smollett, Tobias	*Humphrey Clinker*
Sterne, Laurence	*Tristram Shandy*
Waugh, Evelyn	*A Handful of Dust*
Wells, H. G.	*Tono-Bungay*
Woolf, Virginia	*Mrs. Dalloway; To the Lighthouse*

AMERICAN NOVELS

Cather, Willa	*My Antonia*
Crane, Stephen	*The Red Badge of Courage*
Dos Passos, John	*U.S.A.*
Dreiser, Theodore	*An American Tragedy; Sister Carrie*
Faulkner, William	*Light in August; The Sound and the Fury*
Fitzgerald, F. Scott	*Tender is the Night; The Great Gatsby*
Hawthorne, Nathaniel	*The Scarlet Letter*

Heller, Joseph	*Catch-22*
Hemingway, Ernest	*A Farewell to Arms; The Sun Also Rises*
Howells, William Dean	*The Rise of Silas Lapham*
James, Henry	*The Ambassadors; The Portrait of a Lady*
Kesey, Ken	*One Flew over the Cuckoo's Nest*
Lewis, Sinclair	*Babbitt*
Melville, Herman	*Moby-Dick*
Steinbeck, John	*The Grapes of Wrath*
Twain, Mark	*The Adventures of Huckleberry Finn*
Wharton, Edith	*The Age of Innocence*
Wolfe, Thomas	*Look Homeward, Angel*

OTHER NOVELS

Balzac, Honoré de	*Lost Illusions; Père Goriot*
Camus, Albert	*The Plague*
Cervantes, Miguel de	*Don Quixote*
Dostoevski, Feodor	*Crime and Punishment; The Brothers Karamazov*
Flaubert, Gustave	*Madame Bovary; A Sentimental Education*
Gide, André	*The Counterfeiters*
Goethe, Johann von	*The Sorrows of Young Werther*
Gogol, Nikolai	*Dead Souls*
Goncharov, Ivan	*Oblomov*
Grass, Gunter	*The Tin Drum*
Hugo, Victor	*Les Misérables*
Kafka, Franz	*The Trial*
Laclos, Choderlos de	*Les Liaisons Dangereuses*
Lermontov, Mikhail	*A Hero of Our Time*
Malraux, Andre	*Man's Fate*
Mann, Thomas	*Buddenbrooks; The Magic Mountain*
Manzoni, Alessandro	*The Betrothed*
Montherlant, Henry de	*The Bachelors*
Murasaki, Lady	*The Tale of Genji*
Musil, Robert	*The Man Without Qualities*
Pasternak, Boris	*Doctor Zhivago*
Proust, Marcel	*Remembrance of Things Past*
Rolväag, O. E.	*Giants in the Earth*
Silone, Ignazio	*Bread and Wine*
Solzhenitsyn, Alexander	*The First Circle*
Stendhal	*The Charterhouse of Parma; The Red and the Black*
Svevo, Italo	*The Confessions of Zeno*
Tanizaki, Junichiro	*The Makioka Sisters*
Tolstoy, Leo	*Anna Karenina; War and Peace*
Turgenev, Ivan	*Fathers and Sons*
Undsett, Sigrid	*Kristin Lavransdatter*
Voltaire	*Candide*
Zola, Émile	*Germinal*

GREAT SATIRES

Austen, Jane	*Northanger Abbey*
Carroll, Lewis	*Alice's Adventures in Wonderland*
Cervantes, Miguel de	*Don Quixote*
Fielding, Henry	*Tom Jones*
Heller, Joseph	*Catch-22*
Kesey, Ken	*One Flew over the Cuckoo's Nest*
Orwell, George	*Animal Farm or 1984*
Swift, Jonathan	*Gulliver's Travels*
Updike, John	*Rabbit, Run*
Vonnegut, Kurt	*Player Piano*

Duquesne University
600 Forbes Avenue
Pittsburgh, PA 15282
(412) 434-6220

Two introductory classes at Duquesne help freshman learn to think about, write about, and discuss literature. Anthologies are used in these classes rather than single author texts. The required texts are Blanche Ellsworth's *English Simplified* and Kelly Griffith Jr.'s *Writing Essays About Literature: A Guide and Style Sheet*. In addition they use two of the following anthologies:

Bain, C. E., Jerome Beaty, J. P. Hunter	*The Norton Introduction to Literature* (4th ed.)
Behrens, Laurence & Leonard Rosen	*Theme and Variations: The Impact of Great Ideas*
Diyanni, Robert	*Literature: Reading Fiction, Poetry, Drama, and the Essay*
Guerin, Wilfred, et al.	*Lit: Literature and Interpretive Techniques*
Jacobus, Lee A.	*A World of Ideas: Essential Reading for College Writers*
Perrine, Laurence & Thomas Arp	*Literature: Structure, Sound, and Sense*

Elizabethtown College
Leffler House, 1 Alpha Drive
Elizabethtown, PA 17022
(717) 367-1151

According to Dr. John A. Campbell, Jr., Chairman of the Department of English at Elizabethtown, all freshmen are required to take the Introduction to Literature course, which is "designed to enhance the students' ability to analyze, evaluate, and appreciate literature through the study of several classic and traditional masterworks." The students are introduced to "basic concepts, themes, and world views and trained in the application of literary terms and concepts to enhance reading and writing skills . . . and sharpen their ability in critical thinking." Required texts for the course include:

Hardy, Thomas	*Tess of the D'Urbervilles*
Homer	*The Iliad* (William Rouse, tr.)
Perrine, Laurence, ed.	*Sound and Sense*
Shakespeare, William	*Hamlet* (Cyrus Hoye, ed.)
Sophocles	*The Oedipus Cycle* (Fitts and Fitzgerald, tr.)

Florida Institute of Technology
150 West University Boulevard
Melbourne, FL 32901-6988
(305) 768-8000

Beginning students at Florida Institute of Technology take a humanities course called The Human Imperative. Texts vary according to the theme of the particular class, and in some classes film and texts are combined to stimulate discussion and writing. The following include the books and films recently used in some of the sections:

I. TEXTS:

Clark, Brian	*Whose Life Is It Anyway?*
Hellman, Lillian	*The Little Foxes*
Ibsen, Henrik	*An Enemy of the People* (Miller adaptation)
Miller, Arthur	*All My Sons*
Rabe, David	*Sticks and Bones*
Shaffer, Peter	*Amadeus; Equus*

Simon, Neil   *Plaza Suite*
Williams, Tennessee   *The Glass Menagerie*

FILMS:

*All My Sons; Amadeus; Cocoon; Equus;
The Glass Menagerie; Hearts and
Minds; The Little Foxes; Plaza Suite*

II. TEXTS:

Barrett, William   *The Illusion of Technique*
Eliade, Mircea   *The Sacred and the Profane*
Percy, Walker   *The Thanatos Syndrome*

FILMS:

*The Elephant on the Hill; The Gods
Must Be Crazy*

III. TEXTS:

Eliot, T. S.   *T. S. Eliot: Selected Poems*
Hesse, Herman   *Magister Ludi: The Glass Bead Game*
West, Nathanael   *Miss Lonelyhearts* and *The Day of the
Locust*

IV. TEXTS:

Auel, Jean   *The Clan of the Cave Bear*
Capra, Fritjof   *The Turning Point: Science, Society, and
the Rising Culture*
Herr, Michael   *Dispatches*

*The Florida State University
216B WJB
Tallahassee, FL 32306-1036
(904) 644-6200*

Florida State has compiled a Suggested Reading List for High School
Students which includes selected poetry from **Robert Browning,
George Gordon, Lord Byron, e. e. cummings, Emily Dickinson, John
Donne, T. S. Eliot, Robert Frost, John Milton, Alfred, Lord Tennyson,
Walt Whitman, William Wordsworth,** and **William Butler Yeats.** In ad-
dition the following works are listed:

Austen, Jane   *Pride and Prejudice* or *Sense and Sensi-
bility*

Carroll, Lewis	*Alice's Adventures in Wonderland*
Chaucer, Geoffrey	*Canterbury Tales*
Dickens, Charles	*Great Expectations* or *Oliver Twist*
Faulkner, William	*The Hamlet* or *Light in August*
Fitzgerald, F. Scott	*The Great Gatsby*
Hardy, Thomas	*Jude the Obscure* or *Tess of the D'Urbervilles*
Hawthorne, Nathaniel	*The Scarlet Letter*
Hemingway, Ernest	*The Old Man and the Sea* or *The Sun Also Rises*
Lee, Harper	*To Kill A Mockingbird*
Lessing, Doris	*Martha Quest*
Olds, Sharon	*The Gold Cell*
Shakespeare, William	*MacBeth; Romeo and Juliet*
Thoreau, Henry	*Walden* ("Economy" or whole book)
Twain, Mark	*The Adventures of Huckleberry Finn*
Vonnegut, Kurt	*Breakfast of Champions*
Walker, Alice	*The Color Purple*
Wright, Richard	*Black Boy*

Fordham University
East Fordham Road
Bronx, NY 10458-5158
(212) 579-2133

Fordham's freshman core literature course is a survey of English literature from the early 18th century to the 20th century. Professor Philip Sicker, Chairman of the Department of English, lists the following works as being among those frequently taught in the course:

Blake, William	*Songs of Innocence and Experience*
Browning, Robert	Dramatic monologues
Coleridge, Samuel Taylor	"The Rime of the Ancient Mariner"
Conrad, Joseph	*Heart of Darkness*
Eliot, T. S.	"The Love Song of J. Alfred Prufrock"
Swift, Jonathan	*Gulliver's Travels*
Wordsworth, William	Early lyrics

Gallaudet University
800 Florida Ave. NE
Washington, DC 20002-3625
(202) 651-5114

The following reading list is for pre-college students at Gallaudet, the only liberal arts institution of higher learning for the deaf and hearing-impaired in the United States. The Chair of the Department of English, Professor Nancy E. Kensicki, D. A., writes that "since most of our students are not native speakers of English (American sign language is their first language), we adapt English as a Second Language techniques to teach them.... Students [in the English Language Program] must pass our developmental English courses before they are allowed to register for Freshman English."

Ackert, Patricia	*Cause & Effect; Concepts & Comments; Facts & Figures; Insights & Ideas*
Adams, W. Royce	*Reading Beyond Words*
Alexander, Felicia M. & Jack Gannon	*Deaf Heritage: A Narrative; Take a Stand*
Cake, Cathleen & H. D. Rogerson	*Gaining Ground*
Christ, Henry	*World Biographies*
Clements, Zacharie J. & Leon F. Burrell	*Profiles: A Collection of Short Biographies*
D'Aulaire, Ingri	*Book of Greek Myths*
DeVillez, Randy	*Step by Step*
Dixon, Robert J.	*Easy Reading Selections in English; Essential Idioms in English; Graded Exercises in English*
Ghirasawa & Markstein	*Developing Reading Skills*
Gruber, Edward	*Stories That Are Not Boring*
Holcomb, Roy	*Silence is Golden*
Jupp, T. C. & John Milne	*Guided Course in English Composition*
Kieszak, Kenneth	*Turning Point*
Langan, John	*English Skills*
Milan, Deanne	*Forms of the Essay*
Ronstadt/McGony	*Reading Strategies for University Students*
Schinke-Llano, Linda	*Time: We, the People*
Smalley, Regina L. & Mary K. Ruetten	*Refining Composition Skills*
Van Nostrond, A. D., et al.	*The Process of Writing: Discovery and Control*

Georgetown University
37th and O Streets, Northwest
Washington, DC 20057
(202) 687-3600

In Georgetown's Literature and Writing Workshop, a course for freshmen only, students read "different kinds of texts (both literary and non-literary) organized around a particular intellectual and cultural problem. These readings introduce students to various writing strategies and to the different uses to which writing is put—in different eras, perhaps, or in different cultures, or in different generic forms." The course can count as one of the university's two General Education Requirements in literature. The following are among the works considered in the various sections of the course:

	The Epic of Gilgamesh
Albee, Edward	*Who's Afraid of Virginia Woolf?*
Angelou, Maya	*I Know Why the Caged Bird Sings*
Aristophanes	A play
Atwood, Margaret	*The Handmaid's Tale*
Beckett, Samuel	*Waiting for Godot*
Bellow, Saul	Selections
Berman, Marshall	*All That is Solid Melts into Air*
Brecht, Bertolt	*The Threepenny Opera*
Brontë, Charlotte	*Jane Eyre*
Burgess, Anthony	*A Clockwork Orange*
Butler, Samuel	*Erewhon*
Cassill, R. V.	*The Norton Anthology of Short Fiction*
Cheever, John	Selected stories
Chekhov, Anton	*The Three Sisters*
Conrad, Joseph	*Heart of Darkness*
Dick, Philip K.	*Do Androids Dream of Electric Sheep?*
Dickens, Charles	Short Story
Doyle, Sir Arthur Conan	Short story
Eliot, George	*The Mill on the Floss*
Faulkner, William	*Go Down, Moses; Light in August*
Fitzgerald, F. Scott	*The Great Gatsby*
Forster, E. M.	*The Aspect of the Novel*
Fox and Lears	*The Culture of Consumption*
Fugard, Athol	*Sizwe Bansi Is Dead*
Gardner, John	*Grendel*
Gaskell, Elizabeth	Short story
Gay, John	*The Beggar's Opera*
Gilman, Charlotte P.	*The Yellow Wallpaper*
Hardy, Thomas	*The Mayor of Casterbridge*
Hawthorne, Nathaniel	*The Scarlet Letter*
Heilbroner, Robert	*The Nature and Logic of Capitalism*

Hemingway, Ernest	*The Old Man and the Sea*
Hongo, Garrett	*Yellow Light*
Hwang, David Henry	*M. Butterfly*
Ibsen, Henrik	*A Doll's House*
Janowitz, Tama	*Slaves of New York*
Johnson, Owen	*Lawrenceville Stories*
Kafka, Franz	Selection
Kennedy, X. J.	*An Introduction to Poetry*
Kingston, Maxine Hong	*The Woman Warrior*
Kipling, Rudyard	Short story
Kundera, Milan	*The Unbearable Lightness of Being*
Lawrence, D. H.	*Sons and Lovers*
McInerney, Jay	*Bright Lights, Big City*
Malamud, Bernard	Selection
Melville, Herman	*Billy Budd*
Miller, Arthur	*Death of a Salesman*
More, Sir Thomas	*Utopia*
Morrison, Toni	*Beloved; The Bluest Eye*
O'Connor, Flannery	"A Good Man is Hard to Find"
Paton, Alan	*Cry, The Beloved Country*
Pinter, Harold	*The Homecoming*
Scholes, Robert	*The Nature of Narrative*
Shakespeare, William	*Hamlet; Macbeth; Othello; The Taming of the Shrew; Twelfth Night*
Shange, Ntosake	*for colored girls who have considered suicide when the rainbow is enuf*
Shaw, George Bernard	*Pygmalion*
Shelley, Mary	*Frankenstein*
Sophocles	*Antigone; Oedipus Rex*
Stoppard, Tom	*Rosencrantz and Guildenstern Are Dead*
Tolstoy, Leo	*What is Art?*
Updike, John	*Rabbit, Run; Rabbit Redux; Rabbit is Rich*
Vergil	*The Aeneid*
Vonnegut, Kurt	*God Bless You, Mr. Rosewater*
Warren, Robert Penn	*All the King's Men*
Weiss, Samuel	*Drama in the Modern World*
Wells, H. G.	*The Time Machine*
Welty, Eudora	*Collected Stories*
White, E. B.	*The Once and Future King*
Wicomb, Zoe	*You Can't Get Lost in Capetown*
Wiesel, Elie	*Night*
Wilde, Oscar	Short story
Williams, Tennessee	*Cat on a Hot Tin Roof*
Wister, Owen	*The Virginian*
Wright, Richard	*Native Son*

George Washington University
2121 I Street Northwest
Washington, DC 20052
(202) 994-6040

Professor Miriam Dow, Director of the Writing Program at George Washington, says that most instructors for the writing classes "design their own courses and choose their own texts, frequently anthologies." One syllabus consistently used, however, is for a Humanities/ Composition course for freshmen. The course "does two related things: it is an exploration of texts that have been recognized as formative of our civilization; it is also a composition course, training students in the techniques of expository and argumentative writing." Texts for the course include **Altshuler** et al., *Western Civilization: An Owner's Manual* and the *Random House Handbook*. Although there are "minor variations among the various instructor teams," the following texts are from a syllabus that is "quite representative."

	Bible (Revised Standard Version): Old Testament: Genesis 1–11; II Samuel 9–20; I Kings 1–2; Deuteronomy; Job; New Testament: Mark; John; Romans
Aeschylus	*Prometheus Bound* (Grene & Lattimore, ed.)
Aristophanes	*The Clouds*
Aristotle	*Nicomachean Ethics; Poetics* in *Introduction to Aristotle*
Augustine, Saint	*The Confessions*, Bks. I–X
Cicero	"The Dream of Scipio," *On the Good Life*
Euripides	*Hippolytus* (Grene & Lattimore, ed.)
Mishna and **Philo**	*The Origins of Christianity: Sources and Documents* (Kee, ed.)
Plato	*The Republic*
Sophocles	*Oedipus the King* (Grene & Lattimore, ed.)
Thucydides	*History of the Peloponnesian War*
Vergil	*The Aeneid*, Bks. I–X

Hamilton College
Clinton, NY 13323
(315) 859-4421

For its first-year English 200, a writing-intensive course, the Hamilton College English Department requires the following literature texts:

Austen, Jane	*Pride and Prejudice*
Chaucer, Geoffrey	*Canterbury Tales* (The General Prologue and any one of the tales)
Donne, John	Some lyrics and some Holy Sonnets
Gottesman, Ronald	*Norton Anthology of English Literature,* Vol. 1
Milton, John	*Paradise Lost,* Books I and IX
Pope, Alexander	One of the following: "An Essay on Criticism," "An Essay on Man," "The Rape of the Lock"
Shakespeare, William	Many sonnets and one play
Swift, Jonathan	*Gulliver's Travels,* Book I or II or IV; or "A Modest Proposal"

In the freshman Writing 100 course, the literature texts vary according to the sections. Among the works studied are:

	Bible (King James ed.): Matthew
	The Harper & Row Reader
Abrams, M. H.	*A Glossary of Literary Terms*
Bielenberg, Christabel	*Right Out of the Dark*
Bulgakov, Mikhail	*The White Guard*
Cassill, R. V.	*Norton Anthology of Short Fiction*
Cather, Willa	*O Pioneers!*
Comley, Nancy M., et al.	*Fields of Writing: Readings Across the Disciplines*
Dickens, Charles	*Great Expectations*
Didion, Joan	*Slouching Towards Bethlehem*
Doig, Ivan	*This House of Sky*
Dreiser, Theodore	*Sister Carrie*
Emerson, Ralph Waldo	"The American Scholar"
Forster, E. M.	*A Passage to India*
Franklin, Benjamin	*Autobiography*
Kingston, Maxine Hong	*The Woman Warrior*
Kureishi, Hanif	*My Beautiful Laundrette*
Plato	*Apology, The Last Days of Socrates*
Rivera, Edward	*Family Installments*
Rushdie, Salman	*Midnight's Children*
Simon, Kate	*Bronx Primitive*
Thomas, Lewis	*The Lives of a Cell*
Thoreau, Henry	*Walden*
Woolf, Virginia	*A Room of One's Own*

Harvard University
Byerly Hall, 8 Garden Street
Cambridge, MA 02138
(617) 495-1551

Principal Reading sections of Harvard's Bibliography for English Undergraduate Concentrators indicate those literary works regarded as most significant by members of the Tutorial Board and of the Department of English and American Literature and Language. Since 1938, the Harvard English Department has provided a bibliography for Harvard undergraduates. The booklet, most recently revised in 1983, was compiled by a committee consisting of Professors Larry Benson (Chairman), W. J. Bate, Marjorie Garber, Alan Heimert, Walter Kaiser, Elizabeth McKinsey, and David Perkins.

The following are portions of the Principal Reading sections from the various literary periods. Except for the medieval period and the section on the Theory and Criticism of Literature, all authors have been included, but not all specific works. The entire booklet may be purchased from the Harvard University Department of English.

I. THE BIBLE AND CLASSICAL BACKGROUNDS

Bible:
Old Testament: Genesis; Exodus; Judges, chs. 13–16 (Samson); Ruth; I Samuel; Job; Psalms; Proverbs, chs. 1–9; Ecclesiastes; Song of Songs; Isaiah; Lamentations; Daniel
New Testament: The Four Gospels; Acts of the Apostles; Romans; I Corinthians; Hebrews; James; Revelation

CLASSICAL EPIC

Aristotle	*Poetics*
Homer	*The Iliad; The Odyssey*
Vergil	*The Aeneid*

CLASSICAL TRAGEDY

Aeschylus	*Agamemnon; Choephoroi; Eumenides; Prometheus Bound*
Aristotle	*Poetics*
Euripides	*Alcestis; Hippolytus; Ion; Medea; The Trojan Women*

| Seneca | *Hercules furens; Medea* |
| Sophocles | *Ajax; Antigone; Oedipus at Colonus; Oedipus Tyrannos; Philoctetes* |

CLASSICAL COMEDY

Aristophanes	*The Acharneans; The Birds; The Clouds; The Frogs; Lysistrata*
Aristotle	*Poetics*
Menander	*Dyskolos*
Plautus	*Amphitruo; Menaechmi; Miles Gloriosus; Mostellaria; Rudens*
Terence	*Andria; Heauton Timorumenos; Phormio*

CLASSICAL MYTHOLOGY

A.

Aeschylus	*Promethus Bound* (Grene and Lattimore, tr.)
Catullus	*Poems 63* and *64* (Quinn, tr.)
Euripides	*Medea* (Grene and Lattimore, tr.)
Hesiod	*Works and Days*, 11.1–201
Homer	*The Iliad* I–III, XVI–XXIV (Lattimore, tr.)
Ovid	*Metamorphoses* I–VIII, X, XII–XIII (Golding or A. E. Watts, tr.)
Sophocles	*Oedipus Rex* (Grene and Lattimore, tr.)
Vergil	*The Aeneid* I–VI (Fitzgerald, tr.)

B.

Bulfinch, Thomas	*Mythology* (1947), pp. 1–317
Bush, Douglas	*Mythology and the Renaissance Tradition in English Poetry* (2nd. ed., 1963); *Mythology and the Romantic Tradition in English Poetry*
Harvey, Sir Paul	*The Oxford Companion to Classical Literature* (1937)
Lemprière, J. A.	*Classical Dictionary of Proper Names Mentioned in Ancient Authors*, rev. F. A. Wright (1951)
Seznec, Jean	*The Survival of the Pagan Gods: The Mythological Tradition and Its Place in Renaissance Humanism and Art* (B. F. Sessions, tr.)

II. ENGLISH LITERATURE FROM THE BEGINNING TO 1500: MAJOR MEDIEVAL ENGLISH WRITERS

	Beowulf
	Narrative poems; "The Battle of Brunnanburg," "The Battle of Maldon," "The Dream of the Rood," "The Seafarer," "The Wanderer"
Chaucer, Geoffrey	*Canterbury Tales; Troilus and Criseyde*
The "Gawain" Poet	*Pearl; Sir Gawain and the Green Knight*
Langland, William	*Piers Plowman*, Passus I–VI, XVII–XIX
Malory, Sir Thomas	"Lancelot and Guenevere," "Le Morte D'Arthur," "The Tale of the Sankgreal," "The Tale of Sir Lancelot"

III. ENGLISH LITERATURE FROM 1500 TO 1660

DRAMA (EXCLUSIVE OF SHAKESPEARE)

Baskerville, C. R., et al.	*Elizabethan and Stuart Plays* (1934)
Fraser, R. A. & N. Rabkin, eds.	*Drama of the English Renaissance* (2 vols., 1976)

Listed as Principal Reading in the above texts are two plays by anonymous authors: *Everyman* and *Gammer Gurton's Needle* and plays by **Francis Beaumont, Francis Beaumont and John Fletcher, George Chapman, Thomas Dekker, John Ford, Robert Greene, John Heywood, Ben Jonson, Philip Marlowe, John Marston, Philip Massinger, Thomas Middleton, Thomas Sackville and Thomas Norton, Cyril Tourneur, Nicholas Udall, and John Webster.**

DRAMA: SHAKESPEARE, WILLIAM

Evans, G. B., et al., eds.	*The Riverside Shakespeare* (Most of the Shakespeare plays are considered principal reading.)

PROSE

Authors listed in this section are **Roger Ascham, Sir Francis Bacon, Robert Burton, Castiglione, Thomas Deloney, John Donne, Sir Thomas Browne, Sir Thomas Elyot, Thomas Hobbes, Richard Hooker, John Lyly, John Milton, Montaigne, Sir Thomas More, Sir Philip Sidney, Jeremy Taylor, Izaak Walton.**

POETRY (EXCLUSIVE OF SPENSER AND MILTON)

Broadside Ballads and A Mirror for Magistrates are the anonymous works listed in this section. The authors are Thomas Campion, Thomas Carew, George Chapman, Abraham Cowley, Richard Crashaw, Samuel Daniel, Sir John Davies, John Donne, Michael Drayton, George Gascoigne, Robert Greene, Fulke Greville, George Herbert, Robert Herrich, Ben Jonson, Thomas Lodge, Richard Lovelace, Christopher Marlowe, Andrew Marvell, John Milton ("On the Death of a Fair Infant Dying of a Cough"), Sir Walter Raleigh, William Shakespeare (sonnets and other lyric poetry are in the text mentioned above), Sir Philip Sidney, John Skelton, Robert Southwell, Edmund Spenser, Sir John Suckling, Earl of Surrey, Thomas Traherne, Henry Vaughan, Sir Thomas Wyatt.

SPENSER AND MILTON

Selincourt, Ernest de & J. D. Smith, eds.	The Poetical Works of Edmund Spenser (1926)
Hughes, Merritt Y., ed.	John Milton: Complete Poems and Major Prose (1957)
Carey, John & Alistair Fowler, eds.	The Poems of John Milton (1968)

IV. ENGLISH LITERATURE FROM 1660 TO 1790

RESTORATION AND EIGHTEENTH CENTURY DRAMA

Authors listed are Sir Joseph Addison, William Congreve, Sir William Davenant, John Dryden, Sir George Etherege, Henry Fielding, George Farquhar, John Gay, Oliver Goldsmith, Thomas Otway, Richard Brinsley Sheridan, Sir Richard Steele, Sir John Vanbrugh, Sir George Villiers, William Wycherley.

RESTORATION AND AUGUSTAN LITERATURE

In this section, the authors are Joseph Addison, Daniel Defoe, John Dryden, Bernard Mandeville, Alexander Pope, Earl of Shaftsbury, Jonathan Swift.

THE AGE OF JOHNSON

Authors include William Blake, James Boswell, Edmund Burke, Robert Burns, William Collins, William Cowper, Edward Gibbon, Oliver Goldsmith, Thomas Gray, Samuel Johnson, Joshua Reynolds.

ENGLISH FICTION BEFORE 1800

In this section the writers are **William Beckford, Aphra Behn, John Bunyan, Fanny Burney, Daniel Defoe, Thomas Deloney, Henry Fielding, William Godwin, Oliver Goldsmith, Samuel Johnson, M. G. Lewis, Thomas Lodge, Henry Mackenzie, Thomas Nashe, Ann Radcliffe, Samuel Richardson, Tobias Smollett, Laurence Sterne, Horace Walpole.**

V. ENGLISH LITERATURE FROM 1790 TO 1890

ROMANTIC POETRY

The poets listed are **William Blake, George Gordon, Lord Byron, Samuel Taylor Coleridge, John Keats, Percy Bysshe Shelley, William Wordsworth.**

VICTORIAN POETRY

Poets are **Matthew Arnold, Elizabeth Barrett Browning, Robert Browning, Arthur Hugh Clough, Edward Fitzgerald, Thomas Hardy, Gerard Manley Hopkins, George Meredith, Christina Rossetti, Dante Gabriel Rossetti, Algernon Charles Swinburne, and Alfred, Lord Tennyson.**

FICTION

The Principal Reading includes two Dickens novels and one novel by each of seven other authors.

Austen, Jane	*Emma; Pride and Prejudice*
Brontë, Charlotte	*Jane Eyre; Villette*
Brontë, Emily	*Wuthering Heights*
Dickens, Charles	*Bleak House; David Copperfield; Great Expectations; Our Mutual Friend*
Eliot, George	*Middlemarch; The Mill on the Floss*
Hardy, Thomas	*Jude the Obscure; The Mayor of Casterbridge; Tess of the D'Urbervilles*
Meredith, George	*The Egoist; The Ordeal of Richard Feverel*
Scott, Sir Walter	*The Heart of Midlothian*
Thackeray, W. M.	*Vanity Fair*
Trollope, Anthony	*Barchester Towers*

PROSE

Listed are **Matthew Arnold, Thomas Carlyle, S. T. Coleridge, Thomas DeQuincey, William Hazlitt, T. H. Huxley, Charles Lamb, J. S. Mill, J. H. Newman, Walter Pater, John Ruskin.**

VI. AMERICAN LITERATURE TO 1890

Principal Reading includes selections from Bradford, Bradstreet, John Cotton, Hooker, Cotton Mather, Shepard, Sewall, Taylor, Wigglesworth, Winthrop, and Wise in Alan Heimert and Andrew Delbanco, *The Puritans in America: A Narrative Anthology* (1985) and J. F. Cooper, Emily Dickinson, Jonathan Edwards, R. W. Emerson, Benjamin Franklin, Nathaniel Hawthorne, William Dean Howells, Henry James, Washington Irving, Herman Melville, E. A. Poe, H. D. Thoreau, Mark Twain, Walt Whitman.

VII. ENGLISH AND AMERICAN
LITERATURE FROM 1890 TO THE PRESENT

POETRY

Ellman, Richard & Robert O'Clair	*The Norton Anthology of Modern Poetry* (1973)

Principal Reading includes the poets John Ashbery, W. H. Auden, Hart Crane, e. e. cummings, Walter de la Mare, T. S. Eliot, Robert Frost, Allen Ginsberg, Thom Gunn, Thomas Hardy, Seamus Heaney, Langston Hughes, Ted Hughes, Philip Larkin, D. H. Lawrence, Robert Lowell, Archibald MacLeish, Marianne Moore, Wilfred Owen, Sylvia Plath, Ezra Pound, John Crowe Ransom, E. A. Robinson, Wallace Stevens, Dylan Thomas, W. C. Williams, W. B. Yeats.

ENGLISH FICTION

Conrad, Joseph	*Heart of Darkness; Lord Jim; Nostromo*
Ford, Ford Madox	*The Good Soldier*
Forster, E. M.	*Howard's End; Passage to India*
Hardy, Thomas	*The Mayor of Casterbridge; Tess of the D'Urbervilles*
Joyce, James	*Dubliners; A Portrait of the Artist as a Young Man*
Lawrence, D. H.	*The Rainbow; Sons and Lovers; Women in Love*
Woolf, Virginia	*Mrs. Dalloway; To the Lighthouse;* Selected Essays from *The Common Reader, First* and *Second Series*

DRAMA

Baraka, Imamu Amiri (LeRoi Jones)	*Dutchman*
Beckett, Samuel	*Endgame; Waiting for Godot*
Eliot, T. S.	*The Cocktail Party; The Family Reunion; Murder in the Cathedral*
Miller, Arthur	*Death of a Salesman*

O'Casey, Sean	*Juno and the Paycock; The Plough and the Stars*
O'Neill, Eugene	*Desire Under the Elms; The Hairy Ape; Long Day's Journey Into Night*
Pinter, Harold	*The Birthday Party; The Caretaker*
Shaw, George Bernard	*Caesar and Cleopatra; Heartbreak House; Man and Superman; Saint Joan*
Shepard, Sam	*Angel City*
Stoppard, Tom	*Rosencrantz and Guildenstern Are Dead*
Synge, J. M.	*In the Shadow of the Glen; The Playboy of the Western World; Riders to the Sea*
Thomas, Dylan	*Under Milkwood*
Wilde, Oscar	*The Importance of Being Earnest*
Wilder, Thornton	*Our Town*
Williams, Tennessee	*A Streetcar Named Desire*
Yeats, W. B.	*On Baile's Strand; The Death of Cuchulain; At the Hawk's Well; The Only Jealousy of Emer*

AMERICAN PROSE

Adams, Henry	*The Education of Henry Adams*
Anderson, Sherwood	*Winesburg, Ohio*
Bellow, Saul	*Seize the Day*
Cather, Willa	*My Antonia* or *O Pioneers!*
Chopin, Kate	*The Awakening*
Crane, Stephen	*Maggie; The Red Badge of Courage;* short stories
Dreiser, Theodore	*An American Tragedy* or *Sister Carrie*
Ellison, Ralph	*Invisible Man*
Faulkner, William	*Absalom, Absalom!; The Sound and the Fury*
Fitzgerald, F. Scott	*The Great Gatsby*
Hemingway, Ernest	*A Farewell to Arms* or *The Sun Also Rises;* short stories
James, Henry	*Hawthorne; The Portrait of a Lady*
Mailer, Norman	*The Armies of the Night* or *The Naked and the Dead*
Nabokov, Vladimir	*Lolita* or *Pale Fire*
Norris, Frank	*McTeague* or *The Octopus*
O'Connor, Flannery	*Everything that Rises Must Converge* or *Wise Blood*
Stein, Gertrude	*Composition as Explanation; Three Lives*
Toomer, Jean	*Cane*
Wharton, Edith	*The Age of Innocence* or *The House of Mirth*
Welty, Eudora	*The Golden Apples;* short stories
West, Nathanael	*Miss Lonelyhearts*
Wright, Richard	*Native Son*

Hawaii Pacific College
1164 Bishop Street
Honolulu, HI 96813
(808) 544-0249

Introduction to Humanities is a required course for all freshmen at Hawaii Pacific. Not all sections have the same specific readings. Some teach the Sermon on the Mount while another section reads **Peter Weiss**, *Marat/Sade*. The selections for Dr. Deborah Ross' classes, which follow, are indicative of other works that are studied.

	Bible: Creation and Fall; Job
Confucius	Analects
Dostoevski, Feodor	*The Grand Inquisitor on the Nature of Man*
Henderson, Harold	*Introduction to Haiku: An Anthology of Poems and Poets from Basho to Shiki*
Murasaki, Shikibu	*The Tale of Genji*
Orwell, George	*Animal Farm*
Plato	*The Last Days of Socrates*
Shakespeare, William	*Romeo and Juliet*
Sophocles	*Antigone; Oedipus Rex*
Yohannan, John D., ed.	*A Treasury of Asian Literature*

Hillsdale College
Hillsdale, MI 49242
(517) 437-7341

Dr. James King, Chairman of the Department of English at Hillsdale, would urge all pre-college students to become familiar with the classics. He recommends their reading classical mythology and the Bible for literary references and also:

	Bible: selections, usually from Job
Aristotle	*Poetics:* the part pertaining to tragedy
Shakespeare, William	Any play

ONE OR MORE GREEK TRAGEDIES:

Aeschylus
Sophocles
Euripides

A GREEK COMEDY:

Aristophanes

THE EPICS:

Dante   *Inferno*
Homer   *The Iliad* or *The Odyssey*

Hofstra University
Hempstead, NY 11550
(516) 560-6700

To graduate from Hofstra, students must pass a Proficiency Test, which is designed to ensure that they "achieve at least minimum competence in writing skills, particularly logic, organization, development, sentence structure, and matters of grammar and usage." According to Dr. Robert B. Sargent, former English Department Chairman, two composition/literature courses help freshmen prepare for the test. Although skill in writing "clear expository prose and . . . a compelling argument" is a goal of the first course, it "should not obscure other important concerns, such as the writer's proper interest in the truth, in aesthetic and moral determinations, and in the identification and refinement of personal values and beliefs."

Readings for the first course are "a mix of classic and contemporary selections" chosen by the individual instructors. In the second course short critical papers and a research paper are required. Some works that have been taught recently in the second course are:

Austen, Jane	*Pride and Prejudice; Northanger Abbey*
Bellow, Saul	*Seize the Day*
Chaucer, Geoffrey	*Canterbury Tales* (Selections)
Dostoevski, Feodor	*Notes from Underground*
Ellison, Ralph	*Invisible Man*
Grubb, Davis	*Night of the Hunter*
Hawthorne, Nathaniel	*The Scarlet Letter*
Ibsen, Henrik	*An Enemy of the People*
James, Henry	*Washington Square*
Lawrence, D. H.	*Sons and Lovers*
Melville, Herman	*Redburn*
Miller, Arthur	*The Crucible*
Poe, Edgar Allan	Tales
Shakespeare, William	*Hamlet; King Lear; Henry IV, Part I*
Swift, Jonathan	*Gulliver's Travels*
Walpole, Horace	*The Castle of Otranto*

Hollins College
PO Box 9707
Roanoke, VA 24020
(703) 362-6401

Textbooks containing a wide selection of poetry and fiction are used in the freshman writing classes at Hollins according to Dr. Eric Trethewey, Chairman of the Department of English. Two texts commonly used in these classes are Barbara Drake's *Writing Poetry* and Janet Burroway's *Writing Fiction*.

In the literature courses open to freshmen the following are among the titles regularly read:

Angelou, Maya	*I Know Why the Caged Bird Sings*
Austen, Jane	*Pride and Prejudice*
Beagle, Peter	*The Last Unicorn*
Brontë, Charlotte	*Jane Eyre*
Brontë, Emily	*Wuthering Heights*
Homer	*The Odyssey*
Shakespeare, William	*Henry IV Part 1; The Taming of the Shrew*
Welty, Eudora	*The Optimist's Daughter; The Robber Bridegroom*

Holy Names College
3500 Mountain Boulevard
Oakland, CA 94619-9989
(415) 436-1322

Required courses for freshmen at Holy Names include a Humanities Core and Freshman Composition. According to Sister Francesca Cabrini, Ph.D., Professor of English, some recent selections for those courses have been:

HUMANITIES

	Epic of Gilgamesh
Goethe, Johann W. von	*Faust*
Greer, Thomas H., ed.	*Classics of Western Thought*
Plato	*The Republic*
Sophocles	*Theban Plays*
Van Over, Raymond, ed.	*Sun Songs: Creation Myths from Around the World*

FRESHMAN COMPOSITION

Generally an essay collection is chosen and other selections have been:

Anaya, Rudolfo A.	*Bless Me, Ultima*
Angelou, Maya	*I Know Why the Caged Bird Sings*
Kingston, Maxine Hong	*Woman Warrior*
Moffett, James & K. R. McElheny, eds.	*Points of View, Anthology of Short Stories*
Morgan, Edmund S.	*Meaning of Independence: John Adams, George Washington, Thomas Jefferson*
Rodriguez, Richard	*Hunger of Memory: The Education of Richard Rodriguez, an Autobiography*

Illinois Wesleyan University
Bloomington, IL 61702-9965
(309) 556-3031

Illinois Wesleyan has made up a reading list called *IWU's Select 100* to encourage undergraduates to read widely. Incoming freshmen might profitably read the following texts from that list:

Angelou, Maya	*I Know Why the Caged Bird Sings*
Austen, Jane	*Pride & Prejudice*
Brontë, Charlotte	*Jane Eyre*
Brown, Dee	*Bury My Heart at Wounded Knee*
Camus, Albert	*The Plague*
Chopin, Kate	*The Awakening*
Dickens, Charles	*Great Expectations*
Dostoievsky, Feodor	*Brothers Karamazov*
Ellison, Ralph	*Invisible Man*
Freud, Sigmund	*An Outline of Psychoanalysis*
Gilligan, Carol	*In a Different Voice*
Hawking, Stephen	*A Brief History of Time*
Hugo, Victor	*Les Miserables*
Hurston, Zora Neale	*Their Eyes Were Watching God*
Malcolm X	*The Autobiography of Malcolm X*
García Márquez, Gabriel	*One Hundred Years of Solitude*
Mill, John Stuart	*On Liberty*
Paton, Alan	*Cry, the Beloved Country*
Sinclair, Upton	*The Jungle*
Steinbeck, John	*Grapes of Wrath*
Stowe, Harriet Beecher	*Uncle Tom's Cabin*
Vonnegut, Kurt	*Slaughterhouse Five*
Walker, Alice	*The Color Purple*
Wiesel, Elie	*Night*
Woods, Donald	*Biko Cry Freedom*
Woolf, Virginia	*A Room of One's Own*
Wright, Richard	*Native Son*

Indiana University
814 East Third Street
Bloomington, IN 47405
(812) 335-0661

Prefacing Indiana's list for the pre-college student, the compilers have written: "Because college itself in some ways *is* the world of books, this list of 114 BOOKS FOR PRE-COLLEGE READING is offered with the hope it will help you get a head start. It is a list selected by a group of Indiana University faculty members and recommended to the high school student who wishes to prepare himself to do well in college.

"The books on the list are extremely varied. Some are fanciful (*Alice's Adventures in Wonderland*); some are informative (*Gods, Graves, and Scholars*); some are great early novels (*Gulliver's Travels*); and some are more recent (*The Sun Also Rises*). We do not intend to imply that these are the only books worth reading or that all are equally valuable. We mean, rather, to suggest that these books, taken together, represent a solid intellectual foundation for a college education. Like any reading list, these books can only point the way."

114 Books for Pre-College Reading

Adams, Henry	*The Education of Henry Adams*
Adler, Irving	*How Life Began*
The American Assembly	*The Population Dilemma*
Anderson, A. R.	*Minds and Machines*
Asimov, Isaac	*The Genetic Code*
Augustine, St.	*Confessions*
Austen, Jane	*Pride and Prejudice*
Ballou, Robert O., ed.	*The Portable World Bible*
Bellamy, Edward	*Looking Backward*
Benedict, Ruth	*Patterns of Culture*
Benet, Stephen Vincent	*John Brown's Body*
Bowen, Catherine D.	*Yankee from Olympus*
Brinton, Crane	*Ideas and Men: The Story of Western Thought*
Brogan, D. W.	*The American Character*
Brown, Harrison	*The Challenge of Man's Future*
Brown, Robert McAfee	*Observer in Rome*
Buckingham, Walter	*Automation: Its Impact on Business and People*
Bulfinch, Thomas	*Mythology*
Bunyan, John	*The Pilgrim's Progress*
Camus, Albert	*The Stranger*

Carroll, Lewis	*Alice's Adventures in Wonderland*
Carson, Rachel	*The Sea Around Us*
Cather, Willa	*Death Comes for the Archbishop*
Catton, Bruce	*A Stillness at Appomattox*
Ceram, C. W.	*Gods, Graves, and Scholars*
Chase, Stuart	*The Tyranny of Words*
Churchill, Winston	*A History of the English-Speaking Peoples*
Clark, Walter Van T.	*The Ox-Bow Incident*
Commager and Nevins	*Freedom, Loyalty, and Dissent*
Conant, James B.	*Modern Science and Modern Man*
Conrad, Joseph	*Lord Jim*
Courant & Robbins	*What is Mathematics?*
Crane, Stephen	*The Red Badge of Courage*
Curie, Eve	*Madame Curie*
Darwin, Charles	*Autobiography*
Davis, Elmer	*But We Were Born Free*
Dickens, Charles	*David Copperfield*
Dostoevski, Feodor	*Crime and Punishment*
Dreiser, Theodore	*An American Tragedy*
Durant, Will	*The Story of Philosophy*
Edmonds, Walter D.	*Drums Along the Mohawk*
Faulkner, William	*Three Famous Short Novels*
Franklin, Benjamin	*Autobiography*
Frost, Robert	*Poems*
Galbraith, John K.	*The Affluent Society*
Gardner, Martin, ed.	*Great Essays in Science*
Gilson, Etienne	*God and Philosophy*
Golding, William	*Lord of the Flies*
Goldwater and Treves	*Artists on Art*
Gombrich, Ernst H.	*The Story of Art*
Hamilton, Madison, Jay	*On the Constitution* (selections from *The Federalist Papers*)
Hardy, Thomas	*The Return of the Native*
Hawthorne, Nathaniel	*The Scarlet Letter*
Heilbronner, Robert	*The Worldly Philosophers*
Hemingway, Ernest	*The Sun Also Rises*
Hersey, John	*Hiroshima*
Highet, Gilbert	*The Art of Teaching*
Hofstadter, Richard	*The American Political Tradition*
Housman, A. E.	*A Shropshire Lad*
Hoyle, Fred	*The Nature of the Universe*
Hugo, Victor	*Les Misérables*
Huxley, Julian	*Man in the Modern World*
James, William	*The Varieties of Religious Experience*
Joyce, James	*A Portrait of the Artist as a Young Man*
Kasuer and Newman	*Mathematics and the Imagination*
Kitto, H. D. F.	*The Greeks*
Koestler, Arthur	*Darkness at Noon*
Ley, Willy	*The Conquest of Space*
Lomax, Louis E.	*The Negro Revolt*

Lucretius	*On the Nature of Things*
Lynd and Lynd	*Middletown, U.S.A.*
McNeill, William	*The Rise of the West*
Maeterlinck, Maurice	*The Life of the Bee*
Mann, Thomas	*The Magic Mountain; Buddenbrooks*
Maugham, Somerset	*Of Human Bondage*
Mead, Margaret	*New Lives for Old*
Melville, Herman	*Moby-Dick*
Mill, John Stuart	*On Liberty*
Muller, Herbert J.	*The Uses of the Past*
Orwell, George	*Animal Farm*
Parkman, Francis	*The Oregon Trail*
Paton, Alan	*Cry, The Beloved Country*
Pepys, Samuel	*Diary*
Pevsner, Nikolaus	*An Outline of European Architecture*
Poe, Edgar Allan	*Poems and Selected Tales*
Proust, Marcel	*Swann's Way*
Rawlings, Marjorie K.	*The Yearling*
Reade, Charles	*The Cloister and the Hearth*
Russell and Pirani	*ABC of Relativity*
St. Exupery, Antoine de	*Wind, Sand, and Stars*
Sandburg, Carl	*Harvest Poems*
Schweitzer, Albert	*Out of My Life and Thought*
Scientific American, eds.	*New Chemistry; The Planet Earth; The Physics and Chemistry of Life: The Universe*
Shakespeare, William	*Hamlet; Henry IV, Part I; Julius Caesar; MacBeth; Othello; Romeo and Juliet;* Selections from Sonnets
Shaw, Bernard	*Arms and the Man; Caesar and Cleopatra; Candida; Major Barbara; Man and Superman; Pygmalion; St. Joan*
Snow, C. P.	*The New Men*
Steffens, Lincoln	*Autobiography of Lincoln Steffens*
Steinbeck, John	*The Grapes of Wrath*
Swift, Jonathan	*Gulliver's Travels*
Thackeray, William	*Vanity Fair*
Thoreau, Henry	*Civil Disobedience; Walden*
Tocqueville, Alexis de	*Democracy in America*
Turgenev, Ivan	*Fathers and Sons*
Twain, Mark	*The Adventures of Huckleberry Finn*
Veblen, Thorstein	*The Theory of the Leisure Class*
Ward, Barbara	*The Rich Nations and the Poor Nations*
Wedgwood, C. V.	*Truth and Opinion*
Whitehead, Alfred North	*Science and the Modern World*
Whitman, Walt	*Leaves of Grass*
Wilder, Thornton	*Three Plays*
Williams, Oscar, ed.	*A Pocket Book of Modern Verse*
Wolfe, Thomas	*Look Homeward, Angel*
Yutang, Lin	*The Wisdom of China and India*
Zinsser, Hans	*Rats, Lice, and History*

James Madison University
Harrisonburg, VA 22807
(703) 568-6147

In a Summer Reading List leaflet sent to all incoming freshmen, the faculty of James Madison University list six books that they regard as central to a student's education. According to the leaflet, these works are studied in the Freshman Seminar, "the foundation of the Liberal Studies program, a course which is designed to promote the ethic of life-long learning; to develop the skills of analysis, problem solving, critical thinking, informed discussion and writing; and to establish a common ground of understanding and values through knowledge of our cultural heritage." The books and accompanying annotations are:

Bible: Genesis, Job, Matthew: The Bible presents the most prominent and pervasive Western way of understanding the world. It has also been a source of allusions in literature and justifications for actions and ideas throughout its history. Although most of us have a general familiarity with the themes and ideas in the Bible, in order to be culturally fluent, one must know the sources of these themes and ideas in some detail.

Achebe, Chinua, *Things Fall Apart:* At the turn of the last century, the Ibo of what is now Biafra (Nigeria) were caught between two cultures. Their traditions were increasingly challenged by white Christian culture as whites settled West Africa in greater numbers. This novel explores the breakup of tribal traditions under the pressures of modern life and the consequences for the individual lives of the Ibo.

Adams, Henry, *Mont-Saint-Michel and Chartres:* In this study of cathedrals, Henry Adams finds that these buildings reflect the values and aspirations of man. They can also serve to show how much we have changed since the time these edifices were built. This work helps us see how human works are expressions of the human character.

Bronowski, Jacob, *Science and Human Values:* In this work, Jacob Bronowski explores science as an activity that expresses and embodies human values. Instead of presenting science as an arena of dry facts and obscure theories, Bronowski shows us its relationship to other forms of human endeavor and encourages us to value the creative quality of scientific inquiry.

Carson, Rachel, *Silent Spring:* In this ground-breaking work on our effect on the environment, Rachel Carson presents a terrifying but prophetic view of our threat to the ecosystem of which we are a part. In her exploration of the effect of pesticide contamination on the ecology, she sends a warning to all of us. This book is frequently cited as influential in the founding of the world-wide ecology movement.

Paton, Alan, *Cry, the Beloved Country:* South Africa is the setting of this novel which explores the ways in which people live under apartheid. The characters in this book search for a way of living that is just under a system that denies them justice. Although this is a work of fiction, it shows how the creative imagination in literature can help us experience and understand contemporary events.

Kalamazoo College
1200 Academy St.
Kalamazoo, MI 49007
(616) 383-8408

Kalamazoo, according to Professor Gail B. Griffin, Chairperson of the Department of English, "has a freshman General Education Program, 'Discovering the Liberal Arts,' which includes self-selected students and offers four courses in different divisions of the college." The literature component, entitled 'Literary Questing in the Western World,' has used the following works:

	Sir Gawain and the Green Knight
Chrètien de Troyes	*Iwain the Knight of the Lion*
Conrad, Joseph	*Heart of Darkness*
Homer	*The Odyssey*
Mann, Thomas	*Death in Venice*
Shakespeare, William	*King Lear; MacBeth*
Shelley, Mary	*Frankenstein*
Welty, Eudora	*The Golden Apples*

Kansas State University
Anderson Hall, Room 118
Manhattan, KS 66506
(913) 532-6250

The Department of English at Kansas State lists sixteen books students should have read before entering college.

	Bible
Brontë, Emily	*Wuthering Heights*
Chaucer, Geoffrey	*Canterbury Tales* (selections)
Crane, Stephen	*The Red Badge of Courage*
Defoe, Daniel	*Robinson Crusoe*
Dickens, Charles	*A Tale of Two Cities*

Fitzgerald, F. Scott	*The Great Gatsby*
Hamilton, Edith	*Mythology*
Hawthorne, Nathaniel	*The Scarlet Letter*
Hemingway, Ernest	*A Farewell to Arms*
Poe, Edgar Allan	*Selected Tales*
Salinger, J. D.	*The Catcher in the Rye*
Shakespeare, William	*Julius Caesar; MacBeth; Romeo and Juliet*
Steinbeck, John	*The Grapes of Wrath*
Swift, Jonathan	*Gulliver's Travels*
Twain, Mark	*The Adventures of Huckleberry Finn*

Kenyon College
Gambier, OH 43022-9623
(614) 427-2244

Students in Kenyon's Freshman English course 1–2(3) write essays throughout the year, approximately eight during the first semester. Both writing skill and critical ability are evaluated. A sample syllabus from the course includes the anthologies and critical analysis texts *Poetic Meter and Poetic Form*; **Alexander W. Allison,** ed., *The Norton Anthology of Poetry* (Shorter Ed.); **R. V. Cassill,** *The Norton Anthology of Short Fiction* (Longer Ed.). Other books studied are:

Brontë, Charlotte	*Jane Eyre*
Dickens, Charles	*Great Expectations*
Homer	*The Odyssey* (Fitzgerald, tr.)
Shakespeare, William	*Henry IV, Part I; King Lear; Much Ado About Nothing*
Swift, Jonathan	*Travels into Several Remote Nations* (Normally known as *Gulliver's Travels*)
Thoreau, Henry	*Walden*
Woolf, Virginia	*A Room of One's Own*
Wright, Richard	*Black Boy*

Knox College
Box 148
Galesburg, IL 61401-4999
(309) 343-0112

Professor William E. Brady, Chairman of the Department of English, writes that although "you need not have read any particular books before you enter Knox College, it might not be a bad idea to have consumed some of these":

Austen, Jane	*Emma*
Conrad, Joseph	*Heart of Darkness; Lord Jim;* "The Secret Sharer"
Dickens, Charles	*Great Expectations*
Fitzgerald, F. Scott	*The Great Gatsby*
Ford, Ford Madox	*The Good Soldier*
Hemingway, Ernest	"The Killers," "The Short Happy Life of Francis Macomber," "The Snows of Kilimanjaro," and other short stories
James, Henry	"The Turn of the Screw"
Joyce, James	*A Portrait of the Artist as a Young Man*
Turgenev, Ivan	*Fathers and Sons*
Woolf, Virginia	*Mrs. Dalloway*

Dr. Brady also recommends "the student get a copy of any anthology of poetry and read the poetry of some of the most famous poets. **Chaucer, Shakespeare,** and **Milton** are standard," and others are **W. H. Auden, Emily Dickinson, Samuel Taylor Coleridge, T. S. Eliot, Robert Frost, Gerard Manley Hopkins, Alfred, Lord Tennyson, Walt Whitman, William Wordsworth,** and **William Butler Yeats.**

He thinks that students should be familiar with the following dramas:

Aeschylus	*Agamemnon; Prometheus Bound*
Marlowe, Christopher	*Doctor Faustus*
Miller, Arthur	*Death of a Salesman*
Shakespeare, William	*Hamlet; Macbeth; Romeo and Juliet*
Sophocles	*Oedipus Rex*

The chairman feels the preceding titles "are basic for anyone's education; psychoanalysis, Marxism, deconstructionism, and other studies can be dealt with later in the student's college career."

Loyola College
4501 North Charles Street
Baltimore, MD 21210-2699
(301) 323-1010

Loyola's reading list is prefaced by the following admonition: "We suggest that you use the list as a guide to the wealth of literature in English that awaits your discovery, not as a checklist of approved works; stray from it freely, explore writers and works that are not listed on it-but keep reading!" While, as Professor Brennan O'Donnell notes, the list is intended primarily for English majors, it offers valuable suggestions for any reader.

BRITISH LITERATURE

OLD ENGLISH

(translations)   *Beowulf*

MIDDLE ENGLISH

(translations)   *Sir Gawain and the Green Knight*
Chaucer, Geoffrey   *The Canterbury Tales* (selections)
Langland, William   *Piers Plowman* (selections)
Malory, Sir Thomas   *Morte D'Arthur* (selections)

16TH- AND 17TH-CENTURY DRAMA

Jonson, Ben   *Volpone; The Alchemist*
Marlowe, Christopher   *Dr. Faustus*
Shakespeare, William   *Romeo and Juliet, Hamlet* or *King Lear, Twelfth Night* or *A Midsummer Night's Dream, Richard II* or *I Henry IV* and *The Winter's Tale* or *The Tempest*

RESTORATION AND 18TH CENTURY

Drama

Congreve, William   *The Way of the World*
Goldsmith, Oliver   *She Stoops to Conquer*
Sheridan, Richard Brinsley   *School for Scandal*
Wycherley, William   *The Country Wife*

Prose

Pepys, Samuel   *Diary* (selections)
Swift, Jonathan   *Gulliver's Travels*

18TH-CENTURY NOVEL

Austen, Jane	*Pride and Prejudice; Emma*
Defoe, Daniel	*Moll Flanders; Robinson Crusoe*
Fielding, Henry	*Joseph Andrews; Tom Jones*
Goldsmith, Oliver	*The Vicar of Wakefield*
Richardson, Samuel	*Pamela or Clarissa* (abridged)
Smollett, Tobias	*Humphrey Clinker*
Sterne, Laurence	*Tristram Shandy*

19TH-CENTURY NOVEL

Brontë, Charlotte	*Jane Eyre*
Brontë, Emily	*Wuthering Heights*
Dickens, Charles	*Bleak House; David Copperfield;* or *Great Expectations*
Eliot, George	*Middlemarch*
Godwin, William	*Caleb Williams*
Hardy, Thomas	*Tess of the D'Urbervilles* or *Jude the Obscure*
Scott, Sir Walter	*Waverly* or *The Heart of Midlothian*
Shelley, Mary	*Frankenstein, or the Modern Prometheus*
Thackeray, William	*Vanity Fair*
Trollope, Anthony	*The Warden; Barchester Towers*

20TH-CENTURY BRITISH LITERATURE

Burgess, Antony	*A Clockwork Orange* or *Enderby;*
Conrad, Joseph	*Heart of Darkness; The Secret Sharer;* or *Lord Jim;*
Ford, Ford Maddox	*The Good Soldier*
Forster, E. M.	*A Passage to India*
Fowles, John	*The French Lieutenant's Woman*
Greene, Graham	*The Heart of the Matter*
Joyce, James	*Dubliners; A Portrait of the Artist as a Young Man;* selections from *Ulysses*
Lawrence, D. H.	*Sons and Lovers; The Rainbow;* or *Women in Love*
Murdoch, Iris	*A Severed Head*
Orwell, George	*1984* or *Animal Farm*
Woolf, Virginia	*To the Lighthouse* or *Mrs. Dalloway*

Drama

Beckett, Samuel	*Endgame* or *Waiting for Godot*
Osborne, John	*Look Back in Anger*
Pinter, Harold	*The Homecoming* or *The Birthday Party*
Shaw, G. B.	*Arms and the Man; Man and Superman; St. Joan;* or *Major Barbara*
Stoppard, Tom	*Rosencrantz and Guildenstern are Dead* or *Jumpers*
Schaffer, Peter	*Equus* or *Amadeus*

AMERICAN LITERATURE

17TH, 18TH AND 19TH CENTURIES

Non-fiction

Edwards, Jonathan	Selected writings
Emerson, Ralph Waldo	Representative essays
Franklin, Benjamin	*Autobiography*
Fuller, Margaret	Selected writings
Irving, Washington	*A History of New York* (selections)
Poe, Edgar Allan	Representative essays
Thoreau, Henry David	*Walden;* "Civil Disobedience"

Novels

Cooper, James Fenimore	One of the Leatherstocking novels
Crane, Stephen	*A Red Badge of Courage* or *Maggie, A Girl of the Streets*
Hawthorne, Nathaniel	*The Scarlet Letter*
Howells, W. D.	*The Rise of Silas Lapham*
James, Henry	*The American; The Portrait of a Lady;* or *The Ambassadors*
Melville, Herman	*Moby-Dick*
Stowe, Harriet Beecher	*Uncle Tom's Cabin*
Twain, Mark	*The Adventures of Huckleberry Finn*

Poetry selections from **Emily Dickinson, Edgar Allan Poe, Walt Whitman**

20TH CENTURY

Fiction

Anderson, Sherwood	*Winesburg, Ohio*
Baldwin, James	*Go Tell It on the Mountain;* "Sonny's Blues"
Barth, John	*The Floating Opera;* selected short fiction
Bellow, Saul	*The Adventures of Augie March; Henderson the Rain King; Humboldt's Gift*
Cather, Willa	*O Pioneers!* or *My Antonia*
Chopin, Kate	*The Awakening*
Dos Passos, John	One of the U.S.A. novels
Dreiser, Theodore	*Sister Carrie* or *An American Tragedy*
Ellison, Ralph	*Invisible Man*
Farrell, James T.	*The Young Manhood of Studs Lonigan*
Faulkner, William	*Absalom! Absalom; The Sound and the Fury; Light in August;* selected short fiction
Fitzgerald, F. Scott	*The Great Gatsby*
Heller, Joseph	*Catch 22*
Hemingway, Ernest	*The Sun Also Rises* or *A Farewell to Arms;* selected short fiction

Hurston, Zora Neale	*Their Eyes Were Watching God* or selected short stories
Kesey, Ken	*One Flew Over the Cuckoo's Nest*
Lewis, Sinclair	*Babbit*
Malamud, Bernard	*The Natural*
Mailer, Norman	*The Naked and the Dead*
Morrison, Toni	*Song of Solomon*
Norris, Frank	*McTeague* or *The Octopus*
O'Connor, Flannery	Selected short stories
Porter, Katherine Anne	*Pale Horse, Pale Rider*
Pynchon, Thomas	*The Crying of Lot 49;* "Entropy"
Roth, Philip	*Goodbye, Columbus* and selected short stories
Salinger, J. D.	*The Catcher in the Rye*
Sinclair, Upton	*The Jungle*
Stein, Gertrude	*Three Lives*
Steinbeck, John	*The Grapes of Wrath*
Updike, John	*Rabbit, Run; The Centaur;* or *Rabbit Redux;* selected stories
Warren, Robert Penn	*All the King's Men*
Welty, Eudora	Selected short stories
West, Nathanael	*Miss Lonelyhearts*
Wharton, Edith	*The House of Mirth* or *The Age of Innocence*
Wright, Richard	*Native Son*

Drama

Albee, Edward	*Who's Afraid of Virginia Woolf?* or *Zoo Story*
Miller, Arthur	*Death of a Salesman*
O'Neill, Eugene	*Beyond the Horizon; Desire under the Elms; The Iceman Cometh;* or *Long Day's Journey into Night*
Shepard, Sam	*Buried Child; The Curse of the Starving Class* or *True West*
Williams, Tennessee	*The Glass Menagerie* or *A Streetcar Named Desire*
Wilson, Lanford	*Fifth of July*

Marietta College
5th Street
Marietta, OH 45750
(614) 374-4600

For several years Marietta has required its new students to read a particular book as part of an integrated program of lectures, discussions, and other presentations. According to Dr. Gerald L. Evans, Chairman of the Department of English, "The book is also used as a basis for at least one essay in English 101, and one oral presentation in Speech 101. A copy of the book selected is sent to each entering freshman in the summer before matriculation."

Some of the books in recent years have been:

Eiseley, Loren	*All the Strange Hours*
Frankel, Victor	*Man's Search for Meaning*
Hersey, John	*Hiroshima*
Niess, Judith	*Seven Women*
O'Neill, William L.	*Coming Apart: An Informal History of America in the 60's*

Marquette University
1217 West Wisconsin Avenue
Milwaukee, WI 53233
(414) 224-7302

Marquette's booklet "An Incomplete Reading List" is addressed to students entering or already in the university. It is a long list that makes frequently annotated recommendations across the disciplines. All the authors on the list have been included below as well as representative samples of the annotations in the various sections. Students interested in Marquette may obtain the entire pamphlet from the Department of English.

In his preface to the booklet, the Dean of the College of Arts & Sciences, the Rev. John P. Schlegel, SJ, writes that the list is "an invitation to join the ranks of educated people who passionately enjoy reading and firmly believe, along with John Milton, that books 'do contain a potency of life in them to be as active as that soul was whose progeny they are.'..."

An Incomplete Reading List

ANTHROPOLOGY

Gould, Stephen Jay   *Ontogeny and Phylogeny*

A very important critique of the social use of biology with clear implications for evaluating the use of science to support social policies.

Marriott, Alice   *The Ten Grandmothers*

A beautifully told biography showing what it is to be human in another cultural tradition. Looks at American history from the viewpoint of America's native people.

Beauvoir, Simone de   *The Second Sex*
Douglas, Mary   *Purity and Danger*
Hudson, Liam   *The Cult of the Fact*
Schneider, David   *American Kinship*

BIOLOGY

Attenborough, David   *Life on Earth, The Living Planet*

Explores the survival strategies of various species. Illustrated with photographs.

Darwin, Charles   *The Origin of Species by Means of Natural Selection or The Preservation of Favored Races in The Struggle for Life*

Presents the major evidence for evolution known in 1872.

The Voyage of the Beagle

Darwin's own chronicle of the expedition that produced the discoveries and observations that eventually led him to a theory of evolution.

Sagan, Carl   *Broca's Brain: Reflections on the Romance of Science*

Explores a wide range of topics about the universe and ourselves.

The Dragons of Eden: Speculations on the Evolution of Human Intelligence

A speculative explanation of the evolution of our central nervous system. Winner of the Pulitzer Prize.

Bronowski, Jacob — *Insight; On Being an Intellectual; Science and Human Values; The Ascent of Man; A Sense of the Future: Essays in Natural Philosophy; Magic, Science, and Civilization; The Origins of Knowledge and Imagination; The Visionary Eye; Essays in the Arts, Literature, and Science*

Burnet, F. MacFarlane — *Immunology, Aging, and Cancer*

Carson, Rachel — *The Sea Around Us; Silent Spring; The Sense of Wonder; The Edge of the Sea*

Drlica, Karl — *Understanding DNA and Gene Cloning*

Ehrlich, Paul and Anne — *Extinction*

Gould, Stephen Jay — *The Panda's Thumb*

Heyerdahl, Thor — *Kon Tiki*

Leopold, Aldo — *A Sand County Almanac*

Lewin, Roger — *Thread of Life: The Smithsonian Looks at Evolution*

Lorenz, Konrad — *King Solomon's Ring*

Miller, Jonathan — *The Body in Question; Darwin for Beginners*

Restak, Richard — *The Brain*

Romer, Alfred — *The Procession of Life*

Schaller, George — *The Serengeti Lion: A Study of Predator-Prey Relations*

Stableford, Brian — *Future Man*

Stebbins, G. Ledyard — *Darwin to DNA: Molecules to Humanity*

Storer, John H. — *The Web of Life*

Thomas, Lewis — *The Lives of a Cell: Notes of a Biology Watcher; The Medusa and the Snail: More Notes of a Biology Watcher*

Watson, James D. — *The Double Helix*

Zinsser, Hans — *Rats, Lice, and History*

CHEMISTRY

Schrodinger, Erin C. — *Science, Theory, and Man*

Essays written by a Nobel Laureate in physics on man and the changing world of science.

Glasstone, Samuel — *Sourcebook on Atomic Energy*

MacDonald, Malcolm M. and Robert E. Davis — *Chemistry and Society*

Pauling, Linus — *The Architecture of Molecules; The Nature of the Chemical Bond*

Weinberg, Alvin M. — *Reflections on Big Science*

CRIMINOLOGY AND LAW STUDIES

Abbot, Jack H.   *In the Belly of the Beast*
Cullen, Francis T.   *Reaffirming Rehabilitation*
Krisberg, Barry, and James   *The Children of Ishmael: Critical Per-*
  Austin   *spectives on Juvenile Justice*
Silberman, Charles E.   *Criminal Violence, Criminal Justice*
Walker, Samuel   *The Police in America*

ESSAYS AND LETTERS

Lewis, C. S.   *The Screwtape Letters*

An exchange of letters between two devils on how to under-
mine human hopes, efforts, and desires. Acutely understanding
of human beings and of why and how they go wrong.

White, E. B.   *Essays of E. B. White; Letters of E. B.*
                                        White

White has been described as a "civilized human being—an order of man that has always been distinguished for its rarity." His
essays and letters are urbane, witty, and graceful. Arguably the
best American prose stylist of this century, White is not to be
missed.

Brown, John Mason, ed.   *The Portable Charles Lamb*
Chesterton, G. K.   *Orthodoxy*
Davies, Robertson   *A Voice from the Attic*
Howarth, William L., ed.   *The John McPhee Reader*
O'Connor, Flannery   *The Habit of Being: Letters of Flannery*
                                        O'Connor
Percy, Walker   *The Message in the Bottle; Lost in the*
                                        Cosmos: The Last Self-Help Book
Weaver, Richard   *The Ethics of Rhetoric*

FINE ARTS

Belloli, Andrea   *A Day in the Country: Impressionism and*
                                        the French Landscape

Over 130 color plates each accompanied by a descriptive and
interpretive statement. Excellent, thought-provoking text on the
nature of impressionist painting. Monet, Pissaro, and Sisley are
featured primarily.

Arnheim, Rudolf   *Art and Visual Perception*
Berenson, Bernard   *The Italian Painters of the Renaissance*
Bodkin, Maud   *Archetypal Patterns in Poetry*
Bowness, Alan   *Forty Years of Modern Art, 1945–1985*
Brooks, Cleanth & Robert   *Understanding Poetry*
  Penn Warren, eds.
Byron, Robert   *The Appreciation of Architecture*

Clark, Kenneth	*Looking at Pictures; The Nude: A Study of Ideal Form*
Cooke, Deryck	*The Language of Music*
Copland, Aaron	*What to Listen for in Music*
Cross, Milton	*The Story of the Opera*
Frye, Northrop	*The Anatomy of Criticism*
Gordey, Beverly	*The World of Marc Chagall*
Haviland, Jenny	*A Picture History of Art*
Hitchcock, H. R.	*Architecture*
Langer, Susanne K.	*Feeling and Form; Philosophy in a New Key*
Machlis, Joseph	*The Enjoyment of Music: An Introduction to Perceptive Listening*
Maritain, Jacques	*Creative Intuition in Art and Poetry*
Panofsky, Erwin	*Meaning in the Visual Arts*
Pratt, Carroll C.	*The Meaning of Music*
Read, Sir Herbert	*The Art of Sculpture*
Sessions, Roger	*The Musical Experience of Composer, Performer, Listener*
Sullivan, J. W. N.	*Beethoven: His Spiritual Development*
Weitz, Morris	*Philosophy of the Arts*
Zevi, Bruno	*Architecture as Space*

HISTORY

Fraser, Antonia — *Queen of Scots*

The story of the romantic, adventurous, and bloody career of Mary Stuart.

Moorhead, Alan — *Gallipoli*

An account of the disastrous landing in the Dardanelles by the British and their allies during World War I. The studies the Marine Corps made of this operation formed the basis of U. S. amphibious doctrine in World War II.

Tuchman, Barbara — *The Guns of August*

Retells the events of the opening months of World War I. The best work of one of America's most widely-read historians.

Wiesel, Elie — *Night*

A spellbinding account of the author's experiences as a young boy in a Nazi death camp.

Aries, Phillippe	*Centuries of Childhood: A Social History of Family Life*
Auerbach, Jerold	*Unequal Justice: Lawyers and Social Change in Modern America*
Bartlett, Merrill L.	*Assault from the Sea*
Blake, Robert	*Disraeli*
Castillo, Bernal D. del	*The Conquest of New Spain*

Fieldhouse, David	*The Colonial Empires: A Comparative Survey from the 18th Century*
Freeman, Douglas S.	*Lee's Lieutenants: A Study of Command*
Gross, Robert A.	*The Minutemen and Their World*
Guevara, Ernesto "Che"	*Guerrilla Warfare* (Brian Loveman and Thomas Davies, eds.)
Keegan, John	*The Face of Battle: A Study of Agincourt, Waterloo, and the Somme*
Lafeber, Walter	*Inevitable Revolutions: The United States and Central America*
Laslett, Peter	*The World We Have Lost: England Before the Industrial Age*
Lukacs, John	*The Last European War: September 1939–December 1941*
Mallon, Floencia	*The Defense of Community in Peru's Highlands: Peasant Struggle and Capitalist Tradition*
Mandrou, Robert	*Introduction to Modern France: An Essay in Historical Psychology*
Mattingly, Garrett	*The Armada*
Morgan, Edmund	*American Slavery, American Freedom: The Ordeal of Colonial Virginia*
Nash, Gary B.	*Red, White, and Black: The Peoples of Early America*
Pluvier, J. M.	*South-East Asia from Colonialism to Independence*
Preston, Robert and Sydney Wise	*Men in Arms*
Ruiz, Ramon	*The Great Rebellion: Mexico, 1905–1924*
Schlesinger, Jr., Arthur	*The Imperial Presidency*
Singer, Peter	*Marx*
Smith, Tony	*The Pattern of Imperialism: The U.S., Great Britain, and the Late-Industrializing World Since 1815*
Solzhenitsyn, Alexander	*Cancer Ward*
Soustelle, Jacques	*Daily Life of the Aztecs on the Eve of the Spanish Conquest*
Toynbee, Arnold	*The Study of History*
Weber, Eugen	*Peasants and Frenchmen: The Modernization of Rural France*
Wiebe, Robert	*A Search For Order*

WORLD LITERATURE

CLASSICAL

Aeschylus	*Oresteia*
Herodotus	*History*
Homer	*The Iliad; The Odyssey*
Horace	*Carmina*

| St. Augustine | *Confessions* |
| Vergil | *The Aeneid* |

AMERICAN

Ellison, Ralph	*Invisible Man*
Faulkner, William	*The Sound and the Fury*
Fitzgerald, F. Scott	*The Great Gatsby*
Hawthorne, Nathaniel	*The Scarlet Letter*
Hemingway, Ernest	*The Sun Also Rises*
James, Henry	*The Portrait of a Lady*
Melville, Herman	*Moby-Dick*
Miller, Arthur	*Death of a Salesman*
Thoreau, Henry David	*Walden*
Twain, Mark	*The Adventures of Huckleberry Finn*

Poems of **Emily Dickinson, Robert Frost, Edgar Allan Poe, Ezra Pound, Wallace Stevens, William Carlos Williams,** and **Walt Whitman.**

ENGLISH

Austen, Jane	*Pride and Prejudice*
Chaucer, Geoffrey	*Canterbury Tales*
Conrad, Joseph	*Heart of Darkness*
Dickens, Charles	*Great Expectations*
Eliot, George	*Middlemarch*
Fielding, Henry	*Tom Jones*
Joyce, James	*Ulysses*
Milton, John	*Paradise Lost*
Shakespeare, William	*Hamlet; King Lear; The Tempest*
Shaw, George Bernard	*Major Barbara*
Swift, Jonathan	*Gulliver's Travels*

Poems of **Robert Browning, Samuel Taylor Coleridge, T. S. Eliot, John Keats, Alfred, Lord Tennyson, William Wordsworth, W. B. Yeats.**

FRENCH

Balzac, Honoré de	*Eugenie Grandet (The Human Comedy)*
Flaubert, Gustave	*Madame Bovary*
Molière	*The Misanthrope*
Montaigne, Michel de	*The Essays*
Pascal, Blaise	*Thoughts*
Proust, Marcel	*Swann's Way (Remembrance of Things Past)*
Rabelais, François	*Gargantua*
Racine, Jean	*Phèdre*
Rousseau, Jean-Jacques	*Emile (On Education)*
Voltaire	*Candide*

GERMAN

	The Song of the Nibelungs
Böll, Heinrich	*The Lost Honor of Katharina Blum*
Brecht, Bertolt	*Mother Courage and Her Children*
Eschenbach, Wolfram von	*Parzifal*
Fontane, Teodor	*Effie Briest*
Goethe, Johann W. von	*Faust*
Grass, Günter	*The Tin Drum*
Kafka, Franz	*The Trial*
Kleist, Henrich von	*Michael Kohlhaas*
Lessing, Gotthold E.	*Nathan the Wise*
Mann, Thomas	*The Magic Mountain*
Rilke, Rainer Maria	*New Poems*
Schiller, Friedrich	*Wilhelm Tell*
Wolf, Christa	*Divided Heaven*

ITALIAN

Calvino, Italo	*The Cosmicomics*
Dante Alighieri	*The Divine Comedy*
Eco, Umberto	*The Name of the Rose*
Fallaci, Oriana	*Interview with History*
Ginzberg, Natalia	*Valentine; Le Voci Della Sera*
Goldini, Carlo	*Autobiography; The Fan*
Machiavelli, Niccolò	*The Prince*
Manzoni, Alessandro	*The Betrothed*
Morante, Elsa	*History*
Pirandello, Luigi	*The Late Mattia Pascal; Henry IV*
Pomilio	*Natale 1848*
Sciascia, Leonardo	*Gli Zii D'America*
Silone, Ignazio	*Bread and Wine*
Svevo, Italo	*The Confessions of Zeno*
Verga, Giovanni	*The House by the Medlar Tree*

RUSSIAN

Aksyonov, Vasilii	*Crimea Island; A Starry Ticket*
Dostoevski, Feodor	*The Brothers Karamazov; Crime and Punishment*
Fadeyev, Alexander	*Young Guard*
Gogol, Nikolae	*Dead Souls*
Gorky, Maxim	*The Lower Depths; The Mother*
Pasternak, Boris	*Dr. Zhivago*
Pushkin, Alexander	*Captain's Daughter; Eugene Onegin*
Rasputin, Valentin	*Live and Remember*
Sholokov, Mikhail	*The Silent Don*
Shukshin, Vasilii	*Snowball Berry Red*
Solzhenitsyn, Alexander	*Cancer Ward; First Circle*
Tolstoy, Leo	*Anna Karenina; War and Peace*
Turgenev, Ivan	*Fathers and Sons*

SPANISH

Cervantes, Miguel de	*Don Quixote*
García Márquez, Gabriel	*One Hundred Years of Solitude*
Lorca, Federico Garcia	*Three Tragedies* (including *House of Bernarda Alba, Yerma, Blood Wedding*)
Paz, Octavio	*The Labryinth of Solitude*
Unamuno, Miguel de	*Abel Sanchez and Other Stories*

MATHEMATICS

Davis, Phillip & Reuben Hersh	*The Mathematical Experience*
Hardy, G. H.	*A Mathematician's Apology*
Hofstadter, Douglas	*Gödel, Escher, Bach*
Kidder, Tracy	*The Soul of a New Machine*
Klein, Felix	*Famous Problems of Elementary Geometry*
Kline, Morris	*Mathematical Thought from Ancient to Modern Times*
Newman, James R.	*The World of Mathematics*
Poincare, Henri	*Science and Hypotheses*
Polya, George	*Mathematics and Plausible Reasoning*
Reid, Constance	*Hilbert*
Weizenbaum, Joseph	*Computer Power and Human Reason*

MYSTERIES

A good mystery is ideal for whiling away a quiet evening or staving off the tedium of travel. But mysteries can also be delicate probes into the nature of justice, the conflict of good and evil, and the perplexities of human motivation. There is no shortage of writers in this genre: **Agatha Christie, Michael Innes, P. D. James, Ngaio Marsh, Dorothy Sayers** in the "classic" school; **Raymond Chandler, Dashiell Hammet,** and **Robert Parker** in the "hard-boiled" one. You will find your favorites; however, the three below are especially recommended.

Buchan, John	*The Thirty-Nine Steps*
Collins, Wilkie	*The Moonstone*
Sayers, Dorothy L.	*Gaudy Night; The Nine Tailors*

PHILOSOPHY

ANCIENT PERIOD

Plato	*Dialogues* (especially *Apology, Phaedo,* and *The Republic*)

Plato raises basic questions about the nature of man, the origin of knowledge, the immortality of the soul, and the nature of justice.

Aristotle *Nicomachean Ethics*

MEDIEVAL PERIOD

St. Augustine *City of God*
Confessions

A mixture of autobiography, philosophy, and theology containing some unusual reflections on memory and time.

Boethius *The Consolation of Philosophy*
St. Anselm *Proslogion*
St. Bonaventure *Journey of the Mind to God*
St. Thomas Aquinas *Summa Theologia, I. q.2*

CLASSICAL MODERN PERIOD

Descartes, René *Meditations on First Philosophy*

Written with verve and style, this work opened the new way of philosophizing of the classic modern period.

Berkeley, George *Three Dialogues Between Mylas and Philonous*
Hume, David *Enquiry Concerning Human Understanding*
Kant, Immanuel *Grounding for the Metaphysics of Morals*
Locke, John *An Essay Concerning Human Understanding*
Pascal, Blaise *Les Pensées*

MODERN PERIOD

Nietzsche, Friedrich *Thus Spake Zarathustra*

A manifesto of creative individualism, breaking with mass movements and culture and arguing for a transformation of the pivotal values that shape human life.

Bergson, Henri *Introduction to Metaphysics*
Hegel, Georg *The Philosophy of History*
Kierkegaard, Søren *Fear and Trembling*
Marx, Karl *The Communist Manifesto*

CONTEMPORARY PERIOD

Heidegger, Martin *Being and Time*

Issues a call to contemporary persons to rediscover the temporal and historical foundations of their lives, and, in the process, to recover their proper truth as participants in the global community. One of the most influential works of the twentieth century.

Buber, Martin   *I and Thou*
Moore, G. E.   *Principia Ethica*
Sartre, Jean-Paul   *Existentialism and Humanism*

AMERICAN PHILOSOPHY

Dewey, John   *Reconstruction in Philosophy*

  Presents the view that philosophy at once is influenced by and is the necessary critic of history and changing social conditions.

James, William   *Pragmatism*
Whitehead, Alfred North *Adventures in Ideas*

CONTEMPORARY CATHOLIC PHILOSOPHY

Marcel, Gabriel   *Man Against Mass Society*

  A critique of contemporary techniques of degradation and depersonalization.

Gilson, Etienne   "The Middle Ages and Philosophy,"
           The Spirit of Medieval Philosophy
Maritain, Jacques   "The Tragedy of Humanism," *True*
           Humanism

PHYSICS

Bohr, Niels   *Atomic Physics and Human Knowledge*

  Essays on the impact of atomic physics on human thought and culture.

Bronowski, Jacob   *Science and Human Values*
Cohen, I. Bernard   *The Birth of a New Physics*
Duhem, Pierre   *To Save the Phenomena: An Essay on*
           the Idea of Physical Theory from Plato
           to Galileo
Dyson, Freeman   *Disturbing the Universe*
Feynman, Richard   *The Character of Physical Law*
Heisenberg, Werner   *Physics and Philosophy; Across the Fron-*
           tier; Physics and Beyond
Langford, Jerome J.   *Galileo, Science, and the Church*
Weinber, Stephen   *The First Three Minutes*
Ziman, John   *Public Knowledge: The Social Dimension*
           of Science

POLITICAL SCIENCE

Aristotle   *Ethics; Politics*
Art, Robert and Robert *International Politics*
 Jervice
Bagehot, Walter   *The English Constitution*
Baradat, Leon P.   *Political Ideologies*

Barber, James David	*Presidential Character,* 2nd ed.
Ebenstein, William	*Today's "Isms"*
Hamilton, Alexander; John Jay; James Madison	*The Federalist Papers*
Lowi, Theodore	*The End of Liberalism*
Neustadt, Richard	*Presidential Power: The Politics of Leadership from Roosevelt to Carter*
O'Connor, James	*The Fiscal Crisis of the State*
Plato	*The Republic*
Reich, Robert	*The Next American Frontier*
Simon, Yves	*Philosophy of Democratic Government*
Sola Pool, Ithiel de	*Technologies of Freedom*
Tocqueville, Alexis de	*Democracy in America*
Waltz, Kenneth	*Man, the State, and War*
Wolfer, Arnold	*Discord and Collaboration*
White, Theodore	*The Making of the President 1960*

PSYCHOLOGY

Allport, Gordon	*Becoming*
Arieti, Silvano	*Creativity: The Magic Synthesis*
Coleman, J. C.; J. N. Butcher; R. C. Carson	*Abnormal Psychology & Modern Life*
Cronbach, Lee J.	*Essentials of Psychological Testing*
Erikson, Erik	*Childhood & Society*
Flavell, John H.	*The Developmental Psychology of Jean Piaget*
Freud, Sigmund	*The Interpretation of Dreams*
Hall, C. and G. Lindzey	*Theories of Personality,* 3rd ed.
James, William	*Principles of Psychology*
Loehlin, J. C. and J. N. Spuhler	*Race Differences in Intelligence*
MacCoby, Eleanor E.	*Social Development: Psychological Growth and the Parent-Child Relationship*
Maslow, Abraham	*Toward a Psychology of Being*
May, Rollo	*Existence*
Neisser, Ulric	*Memory Observed*
Penfield, Wilder	*The Mystery of the Mind*
Skinner, B. F.	*Beyond Freedom and Dignity*

SCIENCE AND LIBERAL EDUCATION

Conant, James Bryant	*On Understanding Science*

Emphasizes the importance of an understanding of science for all citizens and the advantage of a historical approach to teaching science. Lectures by a chemist and former president of Harvard.

Dubos, René	*Reason Awake: Science for Man*
Harrington, J. W.	*Discovering Science*
Whitehead, Alfred North	*The Aims of Education*

SOCIAL WORK

Addams, Jane   *Hull House*

The story of the settlement-house movement in Chicago by one of its greatest leaders.

Napier, Augustus   *The Family Crucible*
Satir, Virginia   *Conjoint Family Therapy*
Tratner, William   *From Poor Law to Welfare State*

SOCIOLOGY

Berger, Peter L. & Thomas   *The Social Construction of Reality*
  Luckmann

One of the most influential books in modern sociology, especially in the movement toward a sociology of knowledge perspective.

Bellah, Madsen, Sullivan,   *Habits of the Heart: Individualism and*
  Swidler, & Tipton   *Commitment in American Life*
Braverman, Harry   *Labor and Monopoly Capital*
Cloward, Richard & Francis   *Regulating the Poor*
  Fox Piven
Durkheim, Emile   *The Division of Labor in Society*
Erickson, Kai T.   *Wayward Puritans: A Study in the Sociology of Deviance*
Garfinkle, Harold   *Studies in Ethnomethodology*
Goffman, Erving   *The Presentation of Self in Everyday Life*
Mead, George Herbert   *Mind, Self, and Society*
Mills, C. Wright   *The Sociological Imagination; The Power Elite*
Weber, Max   *Economy and Society; The Protestant Ethic and the Spirit of Capitalism*
Whyte, William Foote   *Street Corner Society*

THEOLOGY

                                 The Holy Bible
Edwards, Jonathan   *Freedom of the Will*

Classic argument against freedom by one of the greatest American Protestant preachers and theologians.

Schweitzer, Albert   *The Quest for the Historical Jesus*

Classic example of historical-critical research.

Ahlstrom, Sydney   *A Religious History of the American People*
Anderson, Bernhard   *Understanding the Old Testament*
Aquinas, St. Thomas   *Summa Contra Gentiles*
Augustine, St. of Hippo   *The Confessions*

Bornkamm, Gunther	*Jesus of Nazareth*
Brown, Robert M.	*The Spirit of Protestantism*
Charpentier, Étienne	*How to Read the Old Testament*
Childs, Brevard	*The New Testament as Scripture*
Day, Dorothy	*The Long Loneliness*
De Vaux, Roland	*Ancient Israel*
Dulles, Avery	*A Church to Believe In*
Erickson, Erik	*Gandhi's Truth*
Hellwig, Monika	*Understanding Catholicism*
Heschel, Abraham	*God in Search of Man*
	The Interpreter's Dictionary of the Bible
	Jerome Biblical Commentary
Johnson, Paul	*History of Christianity*
Jerimias, J.	*The Parable of Jesus*
Kasper, Walter	*Jesus the Christ*
Kelly, J. N. D.	*Early Christian Doctrines*
Kierkegaard, Søren	*Fear and Trembling*
Kung, Hans	*On Being a Christian*
Latourelle	*Theology of Revelation*
Luther, Martin	*Christian Liberty*
Merton, Thomas	*Seeds of Contemplation*
Murray, John Courtney	*We Hold These Truths: Catholic Reflections on the American Proposition*
Niebuhr, H. Richard	*Christ and Culture; The Responsible Self*
Niebuhr, Reinhold	*The Nature and Destiny of Man*
Rahner, Karl	*Foundations of Christian Faith*
Ratzinger, Josef	*Introduction to Christianity*
Smith, John	*Experience and God*
Sobrino, Jon	*Christology at the Crossroads*
Teresa of Avila	*The Autobiography of Saint Teresa*
Chardin, P. Teilhard de	*The Divine Milieu*
Tillich, Paul	*Love, Power, and Justice*
Trevor, Meriol	*Newman (2 vols)*
Yoder, John Howard	*The Politics of Jesus*

Messiah College
Grantham, PA 17027
(717) 766-2511

Professor William Jolliff has listed several books that are used in Messiah's freshman Integrated Studies course Skill and Perceptions. "It is a one-semester course that integrates elements of traditional literature, composition, social psychology, and life skills courses." In it, students read a number of essays, short stories, and poems from **Carolyn Shrodes**, et al., eds., *The Conscious Reader*, and the following complete works:

Angelou, Maya	*I Know Why the Caged Bird Sings*
Conrad, Joseph	*Heart of Darkness*
Mauriac, François	*Vipers' Tangle*
O'Neill, Eugene	*Long Day's Journey Into Night*
Potok, Chaim	*The Chosen*

Miami University
GLOS Admission Center, Grey Gables
Oxford, OH 45056
(513) 529-2531

Miami has the following Suggested Reading List for High School Students:

Adams, Henry	*The Education of Henry Adams*
Adler, Irving	*How Life Began*
Aesop	*Fables*
Asimov, Isaac	*The Genetic Code*
Augustine, St.	*Confessions*
Aurelius, Marcus	*Meditations*
Austen, Jane	*Pride and Prejudice*
Ballou, Robert O., ed.	*The Portable World Bible*
Barnett, Lincoln	*The Universe and Dr. Einstein*
Beard, Charles A.	*The Rise of American Civilization*
Bellamy, Edward	*Looking Backward*
Benedict, Ruth	*Patterns of Culture*
Benet, Stephen Vincent	*John Brown's Body*
Boehm, G. A. W.	*The New World of Math*
Bowen, Catherine D.	*Yankee from Olympus*
Brogan, D. W.	*The American Character*
Brown, Harrison	*The Challenge of Man's Future*
Bulfinch, Thomas	*Mythology*
Bunyan, John	*The Pilgrim's Progress*
Carroll, Lewis	*Alice's Adventures in Wonderland*
Carson, Rachel	*The Sea Around Us*
Catton, Bruce	*A Stillness at Appomattox*
Ceram, C. W.	*Gods, Graves, and Scholars*
Cerf, Bennett, ed.	*Great Modern Short Stories*
Chase, Stuart	*Proper Study of Mankind*
Churchill, Winston	*A History of the English-Speaking Peoples*
Coleman, James A.	*Relativity for the Layman*
Commager and Nevins	*Freedom, Loyalty, and Dissent*
Conant, James B.	*Modern Science and Modern Man*
Conrad, Joseph	*Lord Jim*
Crane, Stephen	*The Red Badge of Courage*
Creekmore, Hubert, ed.	*A Little Treasury of World Poetry*

Curie, Eve	*Madame Curie*
Darwin, Charles	*Autobiography*
Davis, Elmer	*But We Were Born Free*
Day, Clarence	*Life with Father*
Dean, Vera M.	*The Culture of the Non-Western World*
Defoe, Daniel	*Moll Flanders*
Dickens, Charles	*David Copperfield*
Dostoevski, Feodor	*Crime and Punishment*
Doyle, Sir Arthur Conan	*The Adventures of Sherlock Holmes*
Dreiser, Theodore	*An American Tragedy*
Durant, Will	*The Story of Philosophy*
Epictetus	*Enchiridion*
Faulkner, William	*Three Famous Short Novels*
Franklin, Benjamin	*Autobiography*
Frazer, James George	*The Golden Bough*
Frost, Robert	*Poems*
Gamow, George	*The Creation of the Universe*
Gardner, Martin, ed.	*Great Essays on Science*
Hamilton, Madison, Jay	*On the Constitution* (Selections from *The Federalist Papers*)
Hamilton, Edith	*The Greek Way*
Hardy, Thomas	*The Return of the Native*
Hawthorne, Nathaniel	*The Scarlet Letter*
Heilbroner, Robert	*The Worldly Philosophers*
Hemingway, Ernest	*For Whom the Bell Tolls*
Hofstadter, Richard	*The American Political Tradition*
Homer	*The Iliad; The Odyssey*
Housman, A. E.	*A Shropshire Lad*
Huxley, Aldous	*Brave New World*
Huxley, Julian	*Man in the Modern World*
James, William	*The Varieties of Religious Experience*
Jean, James	*The Mysterious Universe*
Joyce, James	*A Portrait of the Artist as a Young Man*
Kasuer and Newman	*Mathematics and the Imagination*
Kennedy, John F.	*Profiles in Courage*
Kluckhohn, Clyde	*Mirror for Man*
Koestler, Arthur	*Darkness at Noon*
Loesser, Arthur	*Men, Women, and Pianos*
Lucretius	*On the Nature of Things*
Lynd and Lynd	*Middletown, U.S.A.*
Maeterlinck, Maurice	*The Life of the Bee*
Maugham, Somerset	*Of Human Bondage*
Mead, Margaret	*New Lives for Old*
Melville, Herman	*Moby-Dick*
Mill, John Stuart	*On Liberty*
Moore, Ruth	*Man, Time, and Fossils*
Muller, Herbert J.	*The Uses of the Past*
Orwell, George	*1984*
Parkman, Francis	*The Oregon Trail*
Poe, Edgar Allan	*Poems and Selected Tales*
St. Exupery, Antoine de	*The Little Prince*

Sandburg, Carl	*Harvest Poems*
Schweitzer, Albert	*Out of My Life and Thought*
Scientific American, eds.	*New Chemistry; The Planet Earth; The Physics and Chemistry of Life: The Universe*
Shakespeare, William	*Hamlet; Henry IV, Part I; Julius Caesar; MacBeth; Othello; Romeo and Juliet;* Selections from Sonnets
Shaw, George Bernard	*Arms and the Man; Caesar and Cleopatra; Candida; Major Barbara; Man and Superman; Pygmalion; St. Joan*
Steffens, Lincoln	*Autobiography*
Steinbeck, John	*The Grapes of Wrath*
Swift, Jonathan	*Gulliver's Travels*
Thackeray, William	*Vanity Fair*
Thoreau, Henry	*Civil Disobedience; Walden*
Tocqueville, Alexis de	*Democracy in America*
Twain, Mark	*The Adventures of Huckleberry Finn*
Van Loon, Hendrik	*The Story of Mankind*
Wells, H. G.	*An Outline of History*
Whitehead, Alfred North	*Science and the Modern World*
Whitman, Walt	*Leaves of Grass*
Wilder, Thornton	*Three Plays*
Williams, Oscar, ed.	*A Pocket Book of Modern Verse*
Yutang, Lin	*The Wisdom of China and India*
Zinsser, Hans	*Rats, Lice, and History*

The novel list for Miami's English 112 (freshman English) includes:

Amis, Kingsley	*Lucky Jim*
Anderson, Sherwood	*Winesburg, Ohio*
Angelou, Maya	*I Know Why the Caged Bird Sings*
Atwood, Margaret	*Surfacing*
Austen, Jane	*Pride and Prejudice*
Baldwin, James	*Go Tell It on the Mountain*
Barth, John	*The End of the Road*
Bellow, Saul	*Henderson the Rain King; Seize the Day*
Bradbury, Ray	*Dandelion Wine*
Brontë, Charlotte	*Jane Eyre*
Camus, Albert	*The Stranger*
Cather, Willa	*O Pioneers!*
Chopin, Kate	*The Awakening*
Conrad, Joseph	*Heart of Darkness* and *The Secret Sharer*
Ellison, Ralph	*Invisible Man*
Fitzgerald, F. Scott	*The Great Gatsby*
Fowles, John	*The Collector*
Greene, Graham	*Brighton Rock*
Hardy, Thomas	*Far from the Madding Crowd*
Hawkes, John	*Second Skin*
Hawthorne, Nathaniel	*The House of the Seven Gables*

Hemingway, Ernest	*A Farewell to Arms; The Sun Also Rises*
James, Henry	*The American*
Joyce, James	*A Portrait of the Artist as a Young Man; Dubliners*
Kesey, Ken	*One Flew over the Cuckoo's Nest*
Koestler, Arthur	*Darkness at Noon*
Lawrence, D. H.	*Sons and Lovers*
Malamud, Bernard	*The Assistant; The Fixer*
McCullers, Carson	*The Heart is a Lonely Hunter*
Melville, Herman	*Billy Budd*
O'Connor, Flannery	*Three by Flannery O'Connor (Wise Blood; The Violent Bear It Away; A Good Man is Hard to Find*
Orwell, George	*Animal Farm*
Pynchon, Thomas	*The Crying of Lot 49*
Salinger, J. D.	*The Catcher in the Rye*
Steinbeck, John	*Of Mice and Men*
Wallant, Edward Louis	*The Tenants of Moonbloom*
Wiesel, Elie	*Night*
West, Nathanael	*Day of the Locust; Miss Lonely-hearts*
Wilde, Oscar	*The Picture of Dorian Gray*
Wright, Richard	*Native Son*

Titles studied in English 112, a freshman drama class, are:

Albee, Edward	*Who's Afraid of Virginia Woolf?; The Zoo Story*
Anouilh, Jean	*Becket*
Aristophanes	*Lysistrata*
Baraka, Imamu Amiri (LeRoi Jones)	*Dutchman*
Beckett, Samuel	*Waiting for Godot*
Dryden, John	*All for Love*
Eliot, T. S.	*Murder in the Cathedral*
Ibsen, Henrik	*A Doll's House; An Enemy of the People; Hedda Gabler*
Ionesco, Eugene	*MacBett; Rhinoceros*
Kopit, Arthur	*Indians*
MacLeish, Archibald	*J. D.*
Miller, Arthur	*Death of a Salesman; The Crucible*
Molière	*The Misanthrope; Tartuffe*
O'Neill, Eugene	*Desire under the Elms; The Emperor Jones; The Hairy Ape*
Shakespeare, William	(any)
Shaw, George Bernard	*Arms and the Man; Candida; Pygmalion; St. Joan*
Sophocles	*Antigone; Oedipus Rex*
Stoppard, Tom	*Rosencrantz and Guildenstern Are Dead*
Synge, John	*The Playboy of the Western World*
Wilde, Oscar	*The Importance of Being Earnest*
Williams, Tennessee	*A Streetcar Named Desire*

Montana State University
120 Hamilton Hall
Bozeman, MT 59717-0024
(406) 994-2452

According to Dr. Michael Sexson, the 246 books on Montana State's English Department Reading List were compiled from suggestions from the university's English faculty.

Aucassin and Nicolette
Bhaghavad Gita
Beowulf
Bible
Eddas
Epic of Gilgamesh
Everyman
I Ching
Kojiki
Koran
Mahabharata
The Nibelungenlied
Piers Plowman
Ramayana
Sir Gawain and the Green Knight
Song of Roland
One Thousand and One Nights
Tristan and Iseult
Upanishads

Achebe, Chinua	*Things Fall Apart*
Aeschylus	*Oresteia*
Agee, James	*A Death in the Family*
Anderson, Sherwood	*Winesburg, Ohio*
Apuleius	*The Golden Ass*
Aquinas, Thomas	*Summa Theologica*
Aristophanes	*The Frogs*
Aristotle	*Poetics*
Arnold, Matthew	*On the Function of Criticism*
Auden, W. H.	Poems
Augustine, Saint	*Confessions*
Aurelius, Marcus	*Meditations*
Austen, Jane	*Pride and Prejudice*
Bacon, Francis	Essays
Baldwin, James	*Go Tell It on the Mountain*
Balzac, Honoré	*Human Comedy*
Barnes, Julian	*Flaubert's Parrot*
Baudelaire, Charles	*The Flowers of Evil*
Beauvoir, Simone de	*The Second Sex*
Beckett, Samuel	*Molloy*

Bellow, Saul	*Henderson the Rain King*
Bergson, Henri	*Creative Evolution*
Blake, William	*The Marriage of Heaven and Hell*
Boccaccio, Giovanni	*The Decameron*
Boethius	*The Consolation of Philosophy*
Borges, Jorge	*Labyrinth: Selected Stories and Other Writings*
Brecht, Bertolt	*Mother Courage*
Brontë, Emily	*Wuthering Heights*
Browning, Robert	Poems
Buber, Martin	*I and Thou*
Bunyan, John	*Pilgrim's Progress*
Byron, George Gordon	*Don Juan*
Calvino, Italo	*Cosmicomics*
Camus, Albert	*The Stranger*
Carroll, Lewis	*Alice in Wonderland*
Cassirer, Ernst	*Philosophy of Symbolic Forms*
Cather, Willa	*My Antonia*
Catullus	Poems to Lesbia
Cervantes, Miguel	*Don Quixote*
Chardin, P. Teilhard de	*Phenomenon of Man*
Chekhov, Anton	Stories
Chrètien de Troyes	*The Story of the Grail*
Christina de Pisan	*The City of Ladies*
Coleridge, Samuel T.	*Biographia Literaria*
Confucius	*Analects*
Conrad, Joseph	*Heart of Darkness*
Crane, Stephen	*The Red Badge of Courage*
Cusanus, Nicholas	Theological Writings
Dante Alighieri	*The Divine Comedy*
Darwin, Charles	*The Origin of Species*
Defoe, Daniel	*Robinson Crusoe*
Derridá, Jacques	Selections
Descartes, René	*Meditations*
Dewey, John	*Art as Experience*
Dickens, Charles	*Bleak House*
Dickinson, Emily	Poems
Dinesen, Isak	*Seven Gothic Tales*
Dogen (Joyo Daishi)	*Moon in a Dewdrop*
Donne, John	Poems
Dostoevski, Fyodor	*The Brothers Karamazov; The Idiot; The Possessed; Crime and Punishment*
Douglass, Frederick	*Narrative of the Life of Frederick Douglass*
Dreiser, Theodore	*Sister Carrie*
Eckhart, Johannes (Meister)	Theological Writings
Eliot, George	*Middlemarch*
Eliot, T. S.	*The Four Quartets*
Ellison, Ralph	*Invisible Man*
Emerson, Ralph	*On Nature*
Erasmus, Desiderius	*The Praise of Folly*

Euripides	*Medea*
Faulkner, William	*Absalom, Absalom!*
Ficino, Marsilio	Commentaries on Love
Fielding, Henry	*Tom Jones*
Fitzgerald, F. Scott	*The Great Gatsby*
Flaubert, Gustave	*Madame Bovary*
Fowles, John	*The Magus*
Frazer, James G.	*The Golden Bough*
Freud, Sigmund	*The Interpretation of Dreams*
Frost, Robert	Poems
Frye, Northrop	*The Secular Scripture*
Galeano, Eduardo	*Memory of Fire: Volume I Genesis*
García Lorca, Federico	*Blood Wedding*
García Márquez, Gabriel	*One Hundred Years of Solitude*
Gide, André	*The Immoralist*
Goethe, Johann W. von	*Faust*
Gogol, Nikolai Vasilievich	*Dead Souls*
Gorky, Maxim	Stories
Grahame, Kenneth	*Wind in the Willows*
Grass, Günter	*The Tin Drum*
Graves, Robert	*The White Goddess*
Grimm, Jacob and Wilhelm	*Grimms' Fairy Tales*
Hardy, Thomas	*Tess of the D'Urbervilles*
Hawthorne, Nathanial	*The Scarlet Letter*
Hegel, G. F.	*The Phenomenology of the Spirit*
Heidegger, Martin	*Being and Time*
Heller, Joseph	*Catch-22*
Hemingway, Ernest	*The Sun Also Rises*
Heraclitus	Fragments
Hesiod	*Theogony*
Hesse, Hermann	*Siddhartha*
Homer	*The Odyssey*
Hopkins, G. M.	Poems
Horace	*Ars Poetica*
Hume, David	Philosophical Writings
Hurston, Zora Neale	*Their Eyes Were Watching God*
Huxley, Aldous	*Brave New World*
Ibsen, Henrik	*A Doll's House*
James, Henry	*The Golden Bowl*
James, William	*Varieties of Religious Experience*
John of the Cross, St.	*Dark Night of the Soul*
Johnson, Samuel	*Lives of the Poets*
Jonson, Ben	*The Alchemist*
Joyce, James	*Finnegan's Wake*
Juliana of Norwich	*Revelations of Divine Love*
Jung, C. G.	*Memories, Dreams, and Reflections*
Kafka, Franz	*The Metamorphosis*
Kant, Immanuel	*Critique of Pure Reason*
Keats, John	Odes
Kierkegaard, Søren	*Philosophical Fragments*
Kristeva, Julia	Selections

Kundera, Milan	*The Unbearable Lightness of Being*
Lacan, Jacques	*The Works of Jacques Lacan*
Lao Tzu	*Tao Te Ching*
Lawrence, D. H.	*Women in Love*
Leskov, Nikolai	Stories
Lévi-Strauss, Claude	*Triste Tropiques*
Locke, John	*An Essay Concerning Understanding*
Longinus, Cassius	*On the Sublime*
Lorca, Frederico	*Blood Wedding*
Lowell, Robert	Poems
Lucretius	*On the Nature of the Universe*
Machiavelli, Niccolò	*The Prince*
Malamud, Bernard	*The Assistant*
Mallarmé, Stéphane	Poems
Malory, Thomas	*La Morte D'Arthur*
Mann, Thomas	*The Magic Mountain*
Marlowe, Christopher	*Dr. Faustus*
Marx, Karl	*Das Kapital*
Maugham, Somerset	*Of Human Bondage*
McCullers, Carson	*The Heart Is a Lonely Hunter*
Melville, Herman	*Moby-Dick*
Milton, John	*Paradise Lost*
Mirandola, Pico della	*Oration on the Dignity of Man*
Molière	*The Miser*
Montaigne, Michele de	*Essays*
Moore, Marianne	Poems
More, Thomas	*Utopia*
Morrison, Toni	*Beloved*
Nabokov, Vladimir	*Lolita*
Nietzsche, Friedrich	*Thus Spake Zarathustra*
O'Connor, Flannery	*A Good Man is Hard to Find*
O'Neill, Eugene	*A Long Day's Journey into Night*
Orwell, George	*1984*
Ovid	*Metamorphosis*
Pascal, Blaise	*Pensées*
Pater, Walter	*Studies in the History of the Renaissance*
Perrault, Charles	*Mother Goose Tales*
Petronius, Gaius	*Satyricon*
Pirandello, Luigi	*Six Characters in Search of an Author*
Plath, Sylvia	Poems
Plato	*Phaedrus*
Plautus	*Menaechmi*
Plotinus	Enneads
Plutarch	*Parallel Lives*
Poe, Edgar Allan	Poems
Pope, Alexander	*The Rape of the Lock*
Pound, Ezra	*Cantos*
Proust, Marcel	*Remembrance of Things Past*
Pushkin, Alexander	*Eugene Onegin*
Rabelais, François	*Gargantua and Pantagruel*
Racine	*Phèdre*

Richardson, Samuel	*Clarissa*
Rilke, Rainer Maria	*The Sonnets to Orpheus*
Rosenburg, Donna	*World Mythology*
Rousseau, Jean-Jacques	*Confessions*
Rushdie, Salman	*The Satanic Verses*
Salinger, J. D.	*The Catcher in the Rye*
Sankara	"Crest Jewel of Illumination"
Sappho	Love Poems
Sartre, Jean Paul	*Being and Nothingness*
Schopenhauer, Arthur	*The World As Will and Idea*
Seneca	*Thyestes*
Shakespeare, William	Complete Plays
Shelley, Percy Bysshe	Poems
Silko, Leslie	*Ceremony*
Singer, Isaac Bashevis	Stories
Smollett, Tobias	*Roderick Random*
Snyder, Gary	*Turtle Island*
Sophocles	The Theban Trilogy
Spenser, Edmund	*The Fairie Queen*
Spinoza, Baruch	Philosophical Writings
Steiner, George	*Real Presences*
Stendhal	*The Red and the Black*
Sterne, Laurence	*Tristram Shandy*
Stevens, Wallace	*Collected Poems*
Strindberg, August	*The Ghost Sonata*
Swift, Jonathan	*Gulliver's Travels*
Synge, John Millington	*Riders to the Sea*
Terence	*Eunuchus*
Thackeray, William M.	*Vanity Fair*
Thomas, Dylan	Poems
Thoreau, Henry David	*Walden*
Tolstoy, Leo	*Anna Karenina; War and Peace*
Toomer, Jean	*Cane*
Turgenev, Ivan	*Fathers and Sons*
Twain, Mark	*The Adventures of Huckleberry Finn*
Updike, John	The Rabbit Tetralogy
Vargas Llosa, Mario	*The Storyteller*
Vico, Giambattista	*The New Science*
Vergil	*The Aeneid*
Voltaire	*Candide*
Welty, Eudora	*Delta Wedding*
West, Nathanael	*Miss Lonelyhearts*
Wharton, Edith	*The Age of Innocence*
Whitman, Walt	*Leaves of Grass*
Wilde, Oscar	"The Decay of Lying"
Wilder, Thornton	*The Skin of Our Teeth*
Williams, W. C.	Poems
Wittgenstein, Ludwig	*Philosophical Investigations*
Wolfe, Thomas	*Look Homeward, Angel*

Wolfram von Eschenbach	*Parzival*
Woolf, Virginia	*To the Lighthouse*
Wordsworth, William	*Prelude*
Wright, Richard	*Native Son*
Yeats, William B.	*Collected Poems*

Mount Holyoke College
College Street
South Hadley, MA 01075-1488
(413) 538-2023

Elizabeth A. Green, Professor Emeritus of English at Mount Holyoke College, has written for the college a pamphlet of reading suggestions for college-bound high school students. More than a quarter of a million copies of the pamphlet have been distributed since it was first published in 1967. Although it is now in the process of another revision, the suggestions in the present issue are still relevant.

The list below is of the specific books mentioned in the pamphlet, but it should be viewed with reservations, its author states. She says the list "has grown out of the conversations of a number of Mount Holyoke students and faculty about what they read or wished they had read before college. It reflects a variety of individual enthusiasms, is offered as an aid to further personal discovery, and, by intention, is incomplete and unsystematic."

"Some of the best stories of love and separation come from the great age of the novel in the nineteenth century:

Austen, Jane	*Pride and Prejudice*
Brontë, Charlotte	*Jane Eyre*
Brontë, Emily	*Wuthering Heights*

"Twentieth-century love stories range just as widely:

| Bowen, Elizabeth | *The House in Paris* |
| Hemingway, Ernest | *A Farewell to Arms* |

"The relations between men and women that run counter to the standards of society have fascinated storytellers ever since the days of Helen of Troy. Three fine nineteenth-century instances are:

Eliot, George	*Adam Bede*
Hardy, Thomas	*Tess of the D'Urbervilles*
Hawthorne, Nathaniel	*The Scarlet Letter*

"The beginnings of a real feeling for the past can often be traced to the early reading of novels" such as:

Dickens, Charles	*Bleak House; David Copperfield; Great Expectations; The Pickwick Papers; A Tale of Two Cities*
Dostoevski, Feodor	*The Brothers Karamazov; Crime and Punishment*
Scott, Sir Walter	*Ivanhoe; Kenilworth; The Heart of Midlothian*
Tennyson, Alfred	*Idylls of the King*
Thackeray, Wm. M.	*Vanity Fair*
Tolstoy, Leo	*War and Peace*

"Among recent historical novelists worth knowing are:

Bryher, Winifred	*The Fourteenth of October*
Renault, Mary	*The Last of the Wine*
White, T. H.	*The Once and Future King*

"The problems of the sensitive young person growing up in an alien world have concerned many contemporary writers:

Faulkner, William	"The Bear"
Joyce, James	*A Portrait of the Artist as a Young Man*
Salinger, J. D.	*The Catcher in the Rye*

"From desegregation to atom bombs, the unsolved problems of society continue to rouse novelists and their readers." Examples can be found in:

Conrad, Joseph	*Heart of Darkness; Lord Jim*
Faulkner, William	*Intruder in the Dust*
Fitzgerald, F. Scott	*The Great Gatsby*
Golding, William	*Lord of the Flies*
Huxley, Aldous	*Brave New World*
Lewis, Sinclair	*Main Street*
Orwell, George	*Animal Farm*
Steinbeck, John	*The Grapes of Wrath*

"Some of the most stirring novels of the twentieth century deal with race relations:

Baldwin, James	*Go Tell It on the Mountain*
Forster, E. M.	*A Passage to India*
Lee, Harper	*To Kill a Mockingbird*
Paton, Alan	*Cry, The Beloved Country*
Wright, Richard	*Native Son*

"The best of English poetry is both unique and priceless, and high school readers are strongly urged to make special efforts to discover the poems that will give them immediate pleasure and those that will stay with them all their lives:

Arnold, Matthew	"Dover Beach"
Blake, William	Selections
Browning, Robert	Dramatic monologues
Byron, George Gordon	Selections

Coleridge, Samuel T.	Selections
Gray, Thomas	"Elegy Written in a Country Church-yard"
Keats, John	Selections
Milton, John	"L'Allegro" and "Il Penseroso"
Shakespeare, William	Songs and sonnets
Shelley, Percy Bysshe	Selections
Tennyson, Alfred	"The Lotos-Eaters"
Wordsworth, William	Selections

"Among the later nineteenth- and twentieth-century poets for whom many Mount Holyoke students and faculty developed enthusiasm before college are:

T. S. Eliot, "The Love Song of J. Alfred Prufrock," and selections from W. H. Auden, Emily Dickinson, e. e. cummings, Robert Frost, Gerard Manley Hopkins, A. E. Houseman, Theodore Roethke, Dylan Thomas, W. B. Yeats

"One of the treasures of the English-speaking world, which is in some danger of being lost to coming generations, is:

The Bible (King James edition)

"The plays of Shakespeare ought to be a part of everyone's education:

Shakespeare, William	*As You Like It; Hamlet; Julius Caesar; MacBeth; The Merchant of Venice; A Midsummer Night's Dream; Othello; Romeo and Juliet*

"The heritage of ancient Greece is increasingly accessible to high school students as good translations multiply:

Homer	*The Iliad* (Richmond Lattimore, tr.) *The Odyssey* (Robert Fitzgerald, tr.)

"Acquaintance with classical mythology is strongly urged:

Hamilton, Edith	*Mythology*

"Those ready to explore the great plays of the golden age of Greece frequently start with:

Sophocles	*Oedipus Rex* "

Among more recent plays, Professor Green mentions:

Hansberry, Lorraine	*A Raisin in the Sun*
Ibsen, Henrik	*A Doll's House*
Miller, Arthur	*Death of a Salesman*
O'Neill, Eugene	*Ah, Wilderness*
Shaw, George Bernard	*Androcles and the Lion; Major Barbara; Pygmalion; Saint Joan*
Wilder, Thornton	*Our Town; The Skin of Our Teeth*

Among other favorites that should be mentioned are:

Carroll, Lewis	*Alice's Adventures in Wonderland*
Doyle, Sir Arthur Conan	*The Hound of the Baskervilles*
Sayers, Dorothy	*The Nine Tailors*

In a postscript Professor Green commented on:

Hemingway, Ernest	his "chilling dialogue"
Malamud, Bernard	his "ironic studies of urban Jewish life"
O'Connor, Flannery	her "grim but fascinating pictures of the rural South"
Tolkien, J. R. R.	*The Lord of the Rings*
Updike, John	his "observations of high school mores"

She also wrote that "the omission of the large category called 'nonfiction' has left out older favorites as well as recent volumes, for instance:

Herriot, James	*All Creatures Great and Small*
Maxwell, Gavin	*Ring of Bright Water*
Thurber, James	Selected essays
Watson, James	*The Double Helix*
White, E. B.	Essays and letters"

Dr. Green reminds students that the pamphlet is "far from comprehensive—indeed, that entire categories have been omitted: short stories, biographies, essays, philosophy, history, interpretations of the contemporary scene." And she adds that "it is assumed that high school readers, like their elders before them, will also be exploring the ephemeral. From sampling best sellers, magazine fiction, and assorted trivia can come entertainment, a range of useful information, and a growing power to distinguish between what is short-lived and what is lasting .... The important thing for every high school reader to remember is that reading is fun. A catholic taste in books may produce all sorts of benefits, including an excellent background for college, but the fundamental advantage is to broaden and deepen one of the enduring pleasures of civilized men and women. Observing that the attitude that 'reading is work' seems to be held by numbers of students in both high school and college, one Mount Holyoke junior says, 'If I were preparing for college today, I would form two regular habits. Every morning I would take time to scan a newspaper and every night before I went to bed I would relax for a while with a book that I was reading for pure enjoyment.'

"Whatever a student's destination after high school, the habit of reading good books can enhance experience and open new possibilities for enjoyment throughout his or her lifetime."

Students contemplating applying to Mount Holyoke may obtain the revised pamphlet by writing The Office of Admissions, Mount Holyoke College, College Street, South Hadley, MA 01075-1488.

Mount Union College
Beeghly Hall
Alliance, OH 44601
(216) 821-5320

According to Dr. Gloria S. Malone, Chair of the Department of English, the recommended reading list for Mount Union's freshman English courses includes the following works:

Albee, Edward	*Who's Afraid of Virginia Woolf?*
Austen, Jane	*Pride and Prejudice*
Baldwin, James	*Go Tell It on the Mountain; Nobody Knows My Name*
Brontë, Charlotte	*Jane Eyre*
Brontë, Emily	*Wuthering Heights*
Camus, Albert	*The Stranger*
Chaucer, Geoffrey	*Canterbury Tales*
Chopin, Kate	*The Awakening*
Crane, Stephen	*The Red Badge of Courage*
Dickens, Charles	*Great Expectations; A Tale of Two Cities*
Ellison, Ralph	*Invisible Man*
Faulkner, William	*The Sound and the Fury*
Fitzgerald, F. Scott	*The Great Gatsby*
Haley, Arthur	*Roots*
Hawthorne, Nathaniel	*The Scarlet Letter*
Hemingway, Ernest	*A Farewell to Arms; The Sun Also Rises*
Hesse, Herman	*Siddhartha*
Hurston, Zora Neale	*Their Eyes Were Watching God*
Huxley, Aldous	*Brave New World*
Ibsen, Henrik	*A Doll's House*
Irving, Washington	*The Legend of Sleepy Hollow*
Joyce, James	*A Portrait of the Artist as a Young Man*
Kafka, Franz	*The Metamorphosis*
Marlowe, Christopher	*Dr. Faustus*
Miller, Arthur	*Death of a Salesman*
Morrison, Toni	*Song of Solomon*
Paton, Alan	*Cry, The Beloved Country*
Salinger, J. D.	*The Catcher in the Rye*
Shakespeare, William	*Hamlet; King Lear; Macbeth; The Merchant of Venice; Othello; Romeo and Juliet; The Taming of the Shrew*
Twain, Mark	*The Adventures of Huckleberry Finn; The Adventures of Tom Sawyer*
Walker, Alice	*The Color Purple*
Wilder, Thornton	*Our Town*
Wright, Richard	*Native Son*

Northeastern University
360 Huntington Avenue
Boston, MA 02115-9959
(617) 437-2200

Professor Kathleen Ann Kelly, Coordinator, Introductory Writing Programs at Northeastern, says the university has no recommended reading list. When students ask for reading suggestions, she tells them "to relax and read whatever it is they want to—use the summer to explore their own interests." She advises them "to read around in magazines and newspapers to get an idea of the variety available and a sense of different points of view, and to read through the journals and books of their chosen field in order to learn about how people 'do' biology or engineering, or whatever."

Occidental College
1600 Campus Road
Los Angeles, CA 90041-3393
(213) 259-2700

The lists below are some of the required readings in several of Occidental's introductory and survey courses.

INTRODUCTION TO LITERARY ANALYSIS

Abrams, M. H., ed.	*A Glossary of Literary Terms*
Bain, C. E., et al., eds.	*The Norton Introduction to Literature*
Bambara, Toni Cade	"My Man Bovanne"
Beaty, Jerome, ed.	*The Norton Introduction to Short Fiction*
Bierce, Ambrose	"Occurrence at Owl Creek Bridge"
Conrad, Joseph	*The Secret Sharer*
Hemingway, Ernest	"The Short Happy Life of Francis Macomber"
Jackson, Shirley	"The Lottery"
Joyce, James	"Araby"
Lawrence, D. H.	"Odour of Chrysanthemums"; "The Fox"
Lessing, Doris	"Our Friend Judith"
Morrison, Toni	*Sula*
Paley, Grace	"A Conversation with My Father"

AMERICAN LITERATURE FROM THE PURITANS TO THE MODERNS

Bradstreet, Anne	Selected poems
Cather, Willa	"Neighbor Rosicky"
Chopin, Kate	*The Awakening*
Crane, Stephen	"The Open Boat"
cummings, e. e.	Selected poems
Dickinson, Emily	Selected poems (including "Because I could not stop for Death–," "I like to see it lap the Miles,—")
Dreiser, Theodore	*Sister Carrie* (recommended)
Dubois, W. E. B.	"Of Mr. Booker T. Washington and Others"
Edwards, Jonathan	"Personal Narrative," "Sinners in the Hands of an Angry God"
Eliot, T. S.	"The Love Song of J. Alfred Prufrock," "Tradition and the Individual Talent," *The Waste Land*
Ellison, Ralph	*Invisible Man*
Emerson, Ralph Waldo	*Nature*, "The American Scholar," "Experience," "Self-Reliance"
Faulkner, William	"The Bear," "Delta Autumn," *Go Down Moses*
Fitzgerald, F. Scott	*The Great Gatsby*
Franklin, Benjamin	*Autobiography*
Frost, Robert	"Design," "The Oven Bird"
Gottesman, Ronald, et al.	*The Norton Anthology of American Literature*, Vols 1 & 2, 2nd ed.
Hawthorne, Nathaniel	Selected stories
Hemingway, Ernest	*In Our Time*
Melville, Herman	*Billy Budd*
Stevens, Wallace	"Anecdote of the Jar," "The Emperor of Ice-Cream," "The Idea of Order at Key West," "Sunday Morning," "A Study of Two Pears"
Taylor, Edward	Selected Poems
Thoreau, Henry	"Resistance to Civil Government," Selections from *Walden*
Washington, Booker T.	*Up from Slavery* (Selections)
Whitman, Walt	"Out of a Cradle Endlessly Rocking," "Preface to the 1855 edition of *Leaves of Grass*," "Song of Myself," "When Lilacs Last in the Dooryard Bloom'd"

EIGHTEENTH- AND NINETEENTH-CENTURY ENGLISH LITERATURE

Selected poetry from **Matthew Arnold, William Blake, Robert Browning, Lewis Carroll, Samuel Coleridge, William Collins, William Cowper, Thomas Gray, John Keats, Christina Rossetti, Alfred Tennyson, James Thomson,** and **William Wordsworth.**

Abrams, M. L., et al.	*The Norton Anthology of English Literature,* 5th ed. Vols. 1 and 2
Astell, Mary	"Some Reflections upon Marriage"
Brontë, Charlotte	*Jane Eyre*
Carlyle, Thomas	"Characteristics," and sections of "Industrialism," "The Woman Question"
Congreve, William	*The Way of the World*
Dickens, Charles	*Great Expectations*
Dryden, John	"Absalom and Achitophel"
Fielding, Henry	*Joseph Andrews*
Johnson, Samuel	*The History of Rasselas, Prince of Abyssinia*
Montague, Lady Mary W.	"The Lover: A Ballad," "Epistle from Mrs. Yonge to Her Husband"
Pope, Alexander	"An Essay on Man," "The Rape of the Lock," "Epistle to Dr. Arbuthnot"
Swift, Jonathan	*Gulliver's Travels*

Ohio State University
1800 Cannon Drive
Columbus, OH 43210-1230
(614) 292-3980

According to Professor Arnold Shapiro of the Ohio State English Department, anyone wishing to graduate with honors in English must take a three-hour written examination based on the department's list of major works. Since that examination "is intended to ensure representative coverage of major authors and works," it is an indication of the literature the department deems important. The list, therefore, is one that pre-college students considering Ohio State might consult as a guide to their own reading. Along with 19th- and 20th-century authors, it includes authors from the medieval, renaissance, and neoclassical periods: Fanny Burney, Geoffrey Chaucer, John Donne, John Dryden, John Gay, Samuel Johnson, Margery Kempe, Thomas Malory, John Milton, Alexander Pope, William Shakespeare, Sir Phillip Sidney, Edmund Spenser, and Jonathan Swift.

ROMANTICISM

Austen, Jane	*Pride and Prejudice*
Brontë, Emily	*Wuthering Heights*
Brontë, Charlotte	*Jane Eyre*
Coleridge, Samuel Taylor	*The Rime of the Ancient Mariner*
Shelley, Mary	*Frankenstein*
Shelley, Percy Bysshe	"Ode to the West Wind"
Keats, John	"Ode to a Nightingale," "Ode on a Grecian Urn"
Douglass, Frederick	*Narrative of the Life of Frederick Douglass*
Emerson, Ralph Waldo	"Nature" or "The Poet"
Hawthorne, Nathaniel	*The Scarlet Letter*
Melville, Herman	*Moby-Dick*
Thoreau, Henry David	*Walden* or "Civil Disobedience"
Wordsworth, William	"Tintern Abbey"

LATER NINETEENTH CENTURY

Arnold, Matthew	"The Function of Criticism at the Present Time"
Conrad, Joseph	*Heart of Darkness* or *Lord Jim*
Dickens, Charles	*Great Expectations* or *Bleak House*
Eliot, George	*Middlemarch*
Browning, Robert	"My Last Duchess"
Chesnutt, Charles W.	*The Conjure Woman*
Chopin, Kate	*The Awakening*
Dickinson, Emily	"I heard a Fly buzz," "Because I could not stop for Death"
Jacobs, Harriet	*Incidents in the Life of a Slave Girl*
James, Henry	*Portrait of a Lady*
Tennyson, Alfred Lord	"Ulysses"
Twain, Mark	*The Adventures of Huckleberry Finn*
Whitman, Walt	"Song of Myself"

MODERN LITERATURE

Eliot, T. S.	"The Love Song of J. Alfred Prufrock"
Ellison, Ralph	*Invisible Man*
Erdrich, Louise	*Love Medicine*
Faulkner, William	*The Sound and the Fury*
Fitzgerald, F. Scott	*The Great Gatsby*
Frost, Robert	"Design," "Birches"
Ginsberg, Alan	"Howl"
Hemingway, Ernest	*In Our Time; The Sun Also Rises*
Hurston, Zora Neale	*Their Eyes Were Watching God*
Joyce, James	*A Portrait of the Artist as a Young Man*
Lawrence, D. H.	*Sons and Lovers* or *Women in Love*
Miller, Arthur	*Death of a Salesman*

Moore, Marianne	Poetry
Morrison, Toni	*Sula* or *Beloved*
O'Neill, Eugene	*The Iceman Cometh*
Plath, Sylvia	"Lady Lazarus"
Pynchon, Thomas	*The Crying of Lot 49*
Rich, Adrienne	"Diving into the Wreck"
Sexton, Anne	"For My Lover, Returning to His Wife"
Stevens, Wallace	"Sunday Morning"
Woolf, Virginia	*To the Lighthouse* or *Mrs. Dalloway*
Yeats, William Butler	"The Second Coming," "Sailing to Byzantium," "Leda and the Swan"

Oral Roberts University
7777 South Lewis Avenue
Tulsa, OK 74171
(918) 495-6518

Oral Roberts provides two reading lists for students. The first of the lists is for the student who wishes to become a well-educated person. Dr. William R. Epperson, English Department chairman, precedes the list with the following comments:

To Be Well Read...
"The fundamental values men have traditionally espoused and lived by have been passed from one generation to another through the history of our race. One mode of this passage has been literature, in which, by conceptual and mimetic images, the relationship of values to life has been powerfully illustrated. . . .

"The books on this reading list form a literary core representing the orthodox values, called the *Tao* in C. S. Lewis's excellent book, *The Abolition of Man*. . . . The task of the educated person is to know the values, the *Tao*, the dimensions of humanness as traditionally conceived and imaged. . . . You will find yourself becoming educated only as you choose to engage personally in the dialogue of your race—the perennial, yet personal, formulation, clarification, actualization of the values that make you fully human.

"I hope this guide to selected readings will help you in this task. It is not a 'summer's reading list,' although I urge you to begin on it this summer. It is rather an essential foundation for your living, education, becoming process as a human person."

ANCIENT LITERATURE: GREEK, ROMAN, HEBREW, ORIENTAL

	Bible
Aeschylus	*Oresteia*
Aesop	*Fables*
Aristotle	*The Poetics*
Confucius	*The Analects* (selections)
Euripides	*Medea*
Hamilton, Edith	*Mythology*
Homer	*The Iliad; The Odyssey*
Lao Tse	*The Wisdom of Lao Tse*
Marcus Aurelius	*Meditations* (selections)
Plato	*Phaedrus; The Republic*
Plutarch	*The Makers of Rome*
Sophocles	*Antigone; Oedipus Rex*
Vergil	*The Aeneid*

MEDIEVAL LITERATURE

	Beowulf
	Sir Gawain and the Green Knight
Aquinas, Thomas	*Introduction to St. Thomas Aquinas* (Anton C. Pegis, Ed.)
Augustine, Saint	*The City of God*
Boccaccio, Giovanni	*The Decameron*
Chaucer, Geoffrey	*Canterbury Tales*
Dante	*The Divine Comedy*
Francis, Saint	*The Little Flowers*
Juliana of Norwich	*The Revelations of Divine Love*

RENAISSANCE LITERATURE

Bunyan, John	*The Pilgrim's Progress*
Cervantes, Miguel de	*Don Quixote*
Donne, John	Poems
Herbert, George	Poems
Jonson, Ben	*Volpone*
Machiavelli, Niccolò	*The Prince*
Milton, John	*Paradise Lost; Paradise Regained*
Montaigne, Michel de	Essays (selected)
Shakespeare, William	*Plays*

MODERN LITERATURE

18TH-CENTURY

Boswell, James	*Life of Johnson*

Fielding, Henry	*Tom Jones*
Franklin, Benjamin	*Autobiography*
Grimm, Jacob and Wilhelm	*Grimm's Fairy Tales*
Johnson, Samuel	"Preface" to *Shakespeare*
Pope, Alexander	"Essay on Man"
Swift, Jonathan	*Gulliver's Travels*
Voltaire	*Candide*

19TH-CENTURY

Austen, Jane	*Pride and Prejudice; Emma*
Brontë, Charlotte	*Jane Eyre*
Brontë, Emily	*Wuthering Heights*
Browning, Robert	Selected poetry
Coleridge, Samuel T.	Selected poetry
Dickens, Charles	*David Copperfield; Hard Times*
Dickinson, Emily	Poems
Dostoevski, Feodor	*The Brothers Karamazov*
Eliot, George	*Middlemarch*
Emerson, Ralph Waldo	"Nature" and "The Poet"
Hardy, Thomas	*Tess of the d'Urbervilles*
Hawthorne, Nathaniel	*The Scarlet Letter*
Keats, John	Selected Poetry
Melville, Herman	*Billy Budd; Moby-Dick*
Tennyson, Alfred	Selected poetry
Thoreau, Henry	*Walden*
Tolstoy, Leo	*The Death of Ivan Illych*
Whitman, Walt	*Song of Myself*
Wordsworth, William	Selections

20TH-CENTURY

Baldwin, James	"Sonny's Blues"
Beckett, Samuel	*Waiting for Godot*
Bellow, Saul	*Seize the Day*
Böll, Heinrich	*The Clown*
Bonhoeffer, Dietrich	*The Cost of Discipleship*
Borges, Jorge Luis	*Ficciones*
Buber, Martin	*I and Thou*
Camus, Albert	*The Fall; The Plague; The Stranger*
Cather, Willa	*Death Comes for the Archbishop*
Cela, Camilo José	*The Family of Pascual Duarte*
Chardin, P. Teilhard de	*The Phenomenon of Man*
Chekhov, Anton	*Three Sisters; The Cherry Orchard*
Conrad, Joseph	*Lord Jim; The Heart of Darkness; Nostromo*
Eliot, T. S.	*Four Quartets; The Waste Land*
Ellison, Ralph	*Invisible Man*
Faulkner, William	*The Sound and the Fury*
Frankel, Victor	*Man's Search for Meaning*
Freud, Sigmund	*General Introduction to Psychoanalysis*

García Márquez, Gabriel	*One Hundred Years of Solitude*
Heller, Joseph	*Catch-22*
Hemingway, Ernest	*For Whom the Bell Tolls*
Hesse, Herman	*Siddhartha*
James, Henry	*The Ambassadors*
Joyce, James	*A Portrait of the Artist as a Young Man*
Jung, Carl	*Modern Man in Search of a Soul*
Kafka, Franz	*The Trial; The Castle*
Lawrence, D. H.	*Sons and Lovers;* "The Blind Man"
Lewis, C. S.	*The Abolition of Man*
Mann, Thomas	*Death in Venice*
O'Connor, Flannery	Stories
Orwell, George	*Animal Farm; 1984*
Sartre, Jean-Paul	*Nausea; No Exit*
Silone, Ignazio	*Bread and Wine*
Solzhenitsyn, Alexander	*One Day in the Life of Ivan Denisovich*
Stevens, Wallace	Poems
Synge, J. Millington	*Riders to the Sea*
Unamuno, Miguel de	*Abel Sanchez*
Woolf, Virginia	*To the Lighthouse*

The second list ORU presents is for entering freshmen.

AMERICAN LITERATURE

Baldwin, James	*Go Tell It on the Mountain*
Cather, Willa	*Death Comes for the Archbishop*
Ellison, Ralph	*Invisible Man*
Emerson, Ralph W.	*The Essays of R. W. Emerson*
Franklin, Benjamin	*Autobiography*
Hawthorne, Nathaniel	*The Scarlet Letter*
Melville, Herman	*Billy Budd; Moby-Dick*
Miller, Arthur	*Death of a Salesman*
O'Connor, Flannery	Stories
Poe, Edgar Allan	Stories
Thoreau, Henry	*Walden*
Twain, Mark	*The Adventures of Huckleberry Finn*
Wright, Richard	*Black Boy*

ENGLISH LITERATURE

Austen, Jane	*Emma; Pride and Prejudice*
Brontë, Charlotte	*Jane Eyre*
Brontë, Emily	*Wuthering Heights*
Conrad, Joseph	*Lord Jim*
Fielding, Henry	*Joseph Andrews*
Hardy, Thomas	*The Return of the Native*

Huxley, Aldous	*Brave New World*
Joyce, James	*A Portrait of the Artist as a Young Man*
Milton, John	*Paradise Lost*
Orwell, George	*Animal Farm; 1984*
Shakespeare, William	*Hamlet; Julius Caesar; King Lear*

WORLD LITERATURE

Camus, Albert	*The Plague; The Fall*
Dostoevski, Feodor	*Crime and Punishment*
Hesse, Herman	*Siddhartha*
Homer	*The Iliad; The Odyssey*
Mann, Thomas	*Death in Venice*
Sophocles	*Antigone; Oedipus Rex*
Tolstoy, Leo	*The Death of Ivan Illych*
Vergil	*The Aeneid*

Oregon State University
Corvallis, OR 97331-2130
(503) 754-4411

Oregon State precedes its Readers' Guide for the Pre-college Student with the following statement:

"What is a great book?

"Obviously, some books are more significant and influential than others. Although many people have attempted to decide which are the truly great ones, our purpose here is more modest. This guide offers you some suggestions of widely appreciated books, arranged in eight subject categories. Within each category, we have subdivided the readings into two groups. First, listed with a brief description, are books that you, as an interested high school student, can read with both pleasure and profit. Second are those that help mark one as a member of the community of educated men and women.

"There are few better ways to prepare yourself for college than by gaining a familiarity with at least two or three of the works in each of the categories presented here. Indeed, your college experience would be enhanced significantly by continued reading of the books on this list—in addition to the texts required in your classes. We hope this guide will be useful both to those of you who are beginning your higher education and to all who realize that education is a lifelong process."

I. Adventure

Bradbury, Ray, *Fahrenheit 451:* This work is a distinctive contribution to the speculative science fiction of our time. Ultimately, the author probes, through symbolic terms, the nature of man as a creative and yet destructive creature.

Brown, Dee, *Bury My Heart at Wounded Knee:* The Indian perspective on the history of the relationship between Native Americans and the U. S. Government. Historically shaky at times, it nevertheless is a highly charged and emotional discussion, certain to prompt more thought.

Nordhoff, Charles & James Normal Hall, *Mutiny on the Bounty:* A gripping novel about life at sea, based on the 1787 mutiny against Captain William Bligh, commander of the British warship *H.M.S. Bounty.* The book is part of a trilogy that also includes *Men Against the Sea* and *Pitcairn's Island.*

Dana, Richard Henry	*Two Years Before the Mast*
Defoe, Daniel	*Robinson Crusoe*
Hemming, John	*The Conquest of Peru*
Heyerdahl, Thor	*Kon Tiki*
Hilton, James	*Lost Horizon*
London, Jack	*The Call of the Wild*
Prescott, William	*The Conquest of Mexico*
Roberts, Kenneth	*Northwest Passage*
Stevenson, Robert Louis	*Treasure Island*
St. Exupéry, Antoine de	*Night Flight*

II. Biography and Autobiography

Franklin, Benjamin, *Autobiography:* Scientist, statesman, inventor, and pragmatic philosopher, Franklin was a colonial intellectual and leader whose ideas helped shape American thought.

Haley, Alex and Malcolm X, *The Autobiography of Malcolm X:* An absorbing story of a man who rose from hoodlum, thief, dope peddler, and pimp to become a dynamic leader of the black revolution. It is filled with the power and passion of an entire people in their agonizing search for identity.

Keller, Helen, *The Story of My Life:* An inspiring account of the author's struggle against incredible odds. A moving testimony of the grandeur of the human spirit that bears rereading whenever one feels that one has been treated unfairly by an unjust fate.

Sandoz, Mari, *Crazy Horse: The Strange Man of the Oglalas:* The best biography of a Native American, this book deals with the life and achievements of the man who crushed Custer at Little Bighorn.

Washington, Booker T., *Up From Slavery:* Born on a Virginia plantation, the author records his own phenomenal rise from the inhuman institution of slavery. Simply and absorbingly written, the book is a significant document of how perseverance brings success even in the face of overwhelming odds.

Adams, Henry	*The Education of Henry Adams: An Autobiography*
Bainton, Roland	*Here I Stand: A Biography of Martin Luther*
Boswell, James	*Life of Johnson*
Bullock, Alan	*Hitler: A Study in Tyranny*
Clark, Robert	*Einstein: His Life and Times*
Erikson, Erik	*Gandhi's Truth on the Origins of Militant Nonviolence*
Lutz, Alma	*Susan B. Anthony: Rebel, Crusader, Humanitarian*
Sandburg, Carl	*Abraham Lincoln: The Prairie Years and the War Years*
Womack, John	*Zapata and the Mexican Revolution*
Wolfe, Thomas	*Look Homeward, Angel*

III. CLASSICAL, MEDIEVAL, AND RENAISSANCE WRITINGS

Bible

The basic sacred literature of Judaism and Christianity, the Bible is a treasure of religious ideas fundamental to an understanding of Western thought. Ecclesiastes: A philosopher reflects on man's fate, the vanity of human striving, and the search for a good life. Job: A profound literary analysis of the relationship between faith and suffering, this Old Testament book deals with such questions as "Why does a good man suffer?" and "If God is good, why does he permit suffering?" Matthew: A biography of Jesus emphasizing his teachings, including the Sermon on the Mount, and relating the idea of the Messiah to a Jewish audience. It reveals the view of the early church about Jesus as the Christ. Romans: A letter written by St. Paul to the Christian church at Rome explaining his understanding of the life and work of Christ and developing key concepts such as law, faith, grace, and salvation.

Chaucer, Geoffrey, *Canterbury Tales* (Nevill Coghill, tr.): Sometimes moral, sometimes ribald, always entertaining tales told by a fascinating variety of characters, presenting a panorama of medieval mind and culture.

Plato, *Apology:* Plato, perhaps the greatest of the Greek thinkers, pays tribute to his teacher Socrates, whose trial and death he here describes.

Crito: An excellent example of Plato's method of teaching through the use of dialogues. *The Republic*: Plato's vision of the ideal state and how to perpetuate it. Especially important is the alegory of the cave in Book VII.

Shakespeare, *Julius Caesar:* Political intrigue and assassination in ancient Rome containing some of the most quoted lines in world literature.

Aeschylus	*Prometheus Bound*
Aesop	*Fables*
Aristotle	*The Ethics; The Politics*
Cervantes, Miguel de	*Don Quixote*
Cicero	*On Friendship; On Old Age*
Herodotus	*The Persian Wars*
Homer	*The Iliad; The Odyssey*
Shakespeare, William	*Hamlet*
Sophocles	*Antigone; Oedipus Rex*

IV. CROSS-CULTURAL WRITINGS

Achebe, Chinua, *Things Fall Apart:* Set in Africa, this sensitive book deals with the trauma that occurs when traditional cultures come into conflict with the modern world.

Lao Tzu, *The Tao Te Ching:* A Chinese religious classic that describes the sacred in terms of the Tao (pronounced Dow) and inculcates passivity and a reverence for nature.

Leon-Portilla, Miguel, *The Broken Spears: The Aztec Account of the Conquest of Mexico:* The chronicle of an event comparable to an invasion from outer space by a superior alien race, this translation of writings by eyewitnesses of the Spaniards' destruction of a civilization is as exciting as it is unique.

Sembène, Ousmane, *God's Bits of Wood:* A classic novel about the independence struggle in Africa by one of Africa's leading novelists and the continent's foremost filmmaker. It reveals all the different levels of struggle for national independence: Africans vs. Europeans; elders vs. youth; males vs. females; tradition vs. modernity.

Benedict, Ruth	*The Chrysanthemum and the Sword: Patterns of Japanese Culture*
Boulding, Elise	*The Fifth World*
Confucius	*The Analects* (The LunYu)
Fanon, Franz	*The Wretched of the Earth*
Fitzgerald, Edward tr.	*The Rubaiyat of Omar Khayyam*
García Márquez, Gabriel	*One Hundred Years of Solitude*
Lappé, Frances Moore and Joseph Collins	*Food First: Beyond the Myth of Scarcity*
Lin Yutang	*The Importance of Understanding*
Muhammad	The Koran

Myrdal, Gunnar — *The Challenge of World Poverty: A World Anti-Poverty Program in Outline*

Snow, Edgar — *Red Star Over China*

V. IDEAS IN THE HUMANITIES

Frankl, Viktor, *Man's Search for Meaning:* After three grim years in a Nazi concentration camp, this psychiatrist writes of his life-affirming search for a higher meaning in human existence.

Huxley, Aldous, *Brave New World:* An imaginative vision of an assembly-line future where the state has learned that easy pleasure and comfort can more effectively control creativity and dissent than can torture and repression.

Josephson, Matthew, *The Robber Barons: The Great American Capitalists 1861–1901:* History that reads like a novel, *The Robber Barons* brings alive a pivotal epoch of the American past by describing the origins of the nation's great fortunes.

Mill, John Stuart, *On Liberty:* One of the finest and most eloquent essays on liberty in English, perhaps in any language, this slim volume was exceptionally farsighted in recognizing that social pressures toward conformity could constitute a tyranny more formidable than many kinds of political oppression.

Schumacher, E. F., *Small is Beautiful: Economics As If People Mattered:* One of the more important treatises of our times, this small book has planted seeds that may yet crack the foundations of modern economics. A wise, compassionate, and highly rewarding book.

Adams, Henry — *Mont-Saint-Michel and Chartres*
Beauvoir, Simone de — *The Second Sex*
Clark, Sir Kenneth — *Civilization*
Hamilton, Jay, Madison — *The Federalist Papers*
Machiavelli, Niccolò — *The Prince*
Marx, Karl and Friedrich Engels — *The Communist Manifesto*
Pirsig, Robert — *Zen and the Art of Motorcycle Maintenance*
Snow, C. P. — *The Two Cultures and the Scientific Revolution*
Toqueville, Alexis de — *Democracy in America*
Tuchman, Barbara — *A Distant Mirror: The Calamitous 14th Century*

VI. IDEAS IN THE SCIENCES

Asimov, Isaac, *Asimov on Astronomy:* From the moon's effects on tides through an exploration of the planets and onward to interstellar space,

supernovas, and exploding galaxies, astronomy with the sense of wonder preserved intact, engagingly presented by a master of both science
fact and science fiction.

Bronowski, Jacob, *Science and Human Values:* Three short essays on the
creative mind, the habit of truth, and the sense of human dignity by
one of the great scientist-humanists of our day.

Eiseley, Loren, *The Immense Journey:* In an unusual blend of scientific
knowledge and poetic vision, a famous naturalist explores the mysteries
of nature and mankind.

Mead, Margaret, *Coming of Age in Samoa:* The rites of passage in the
South Seas and what they tell us about young adults not only there but
the world over. A seminal work by a world-renowned anthropologist.

Benedict, Ruth	*Patterns of Culture*
Bronowski, Jacob	*The Ascent of Man*
Carson, Rachel	*Silent Spring*
Darwin, Charles	*The Descent of Man*
Dubos, René	*So Human an Animal*
Freud, Sigmund	*The Psychopathology of Everyday Life*
Hall, Edward	*The Hidden Dimension*
Kuhn, Thomas	*The Structure of Scientific Revolutions*
Thomas, Lewis	*Lives of a Cell: Notes of a Biology Watcher*
Whitehead, Alfred N.	*Science and the Modern World*

VII. MODERN LITERATURE: AMERICAN

Hemingway, Ernest, *The Old Man and the Sea:* Stubborn courage, rug-
ged strength, and marvelous skill sustain an aura of suspense in this
story until the tragic end. In many ways the book represents the struggle between man and nature and mankind's compulsion to destroy
those things of beauty—a human failure for which both the human
race and nature suffer.

Melville, Herman, *Billy Budd:* A short work by one of America's greatest writers, *Billy Budd* is on the one hand the suspenseful story of a
young man's unjust fate and at the same time a powerfully moving and
insightful statement about the relationships between good and evil, law
and justice, and individuals and institutions.

Miller, Arthur, *Death of a Salesman:* A modern tragedy of a failing, two-
martini salesman, his family, his loves, his end.

Twain, Mark, *The Adventures of Huckleberry Finn:* Termed a "joy forever
and an American masterpiece," this story deals with the reconciliation
of piety with human decency. Through wit and humor it considers
human hypocrisies, dishonesties, and cruelties and one character's deci-
sion to follow moral impulse rather than "village morality."

Crane, Stephen	*The Red Badge of Courage*
Faulkner, William	*Collected Stories*
Fitzgerald, F. Scott	*The Great Gatsby*
Hawthorne, Nathaniel	*The Scarlet Letter*
Melville, Herman	*Moby-Dick*
Poe, Edgar Allan	*Selected Poetry and Prose*
Steinbeck, John	*The Grapes of Wrath*
Thoreau, Henry David	*Walden*
Warren, Robert Penn	*All the King's Men*
Whitman, Walt	*Leaves of Grass*
Wilder, Thorton	*Our Town*

VIII. MODERN LITERATURE: EUROPEAN

Dickens, Charles, *David Copperfield:* As he progresses from boyhood and extremely hard times through school years to adulthood, love, marriage, and success, Dicken's most nearly autobiographical hero meets some of the most extraordinary characters in English literature.

Hugo, Victor, *Les Misérables:* In this epic of the masses Hugo paints a vast fresco of French society. His hero, Jean Valjean, spends twenty years in prison for stealing bread, and the rest of his life trying to become a member of "respectable" society.

Orwell, George, *1984:* Here is a vision of the future that portrays a nightmare rather than a paradise. The book is both a prophecy and a warning of what life might be if individuals allow themselves to be coerced into conformity by the state.

Remarque, Erich Maria, *All Quiet on the Western Front:* A searing indictment of war built around the experiences of a young German soldier in World War I.

Swift, Jonathan, *Gulliver's Travels:* A savage attack on human pride, ignorance, and perversity that has delighted readers of all ages for over 250 years.

Voltaire, *Candide:* A scathingly satirical attack on the fallacies of blind optimism and on human foibles in general.

Austen, Jane	*Pride and Prejudice*
Camus, Albert	*The Plague*
Carroll, Lewis	*Through the Looking-Glass*
Conrad, Joseph	*Heart of Darkness*
Dostoevski, Feodor	*Crime and Punishment*
Flaubert, Gustave	*Madame Bovary*
Forster, E. M.	*A Passage to India*
Golding, William	*Lord of the Flies*
Kafka, Franz	*The Trial*
Tolstoy, Leo	*War and Peace*
White, T. H.	*The Once and Future King*

IX. SOCIAL COMMENTARY

Barnet, Richard	*The Lean Years: Politics in the Age of Scarcity*
Boulding, Kenneth	*The Meaning of the 20th Century*
Braverman, Harry	*Labor and Monopoly Capital: The Degradation of Work in the 20th Century*
Commoner, Barry	*The Poverty of Power: Energy and the Economic Crisis*
Daly, Herman	*Steady-State Economics: The Economics of Biophysical Equilibrium and Moral Growth*
Fromm, Erich	*The Sane Society*
Galbraith, J. K.	*The Affluent Society*
Hayek, F. A.	*The Constitution of Liberty*
Heilbroner, Robert	*An Inquiry Into the Human Prospect*
Kahn, Herman	*Thinking about the Unthinkable*
Mumford, Lewis	*The Myth of the Machine*
Roszak, Theodore	*Where the Wasteland Ends: Politics and Transcendence in Post-Industrial Society*
Thompson, William Irwin	*The Edge of History: Speculations on the Transformation of Culture*
Thurow, Lester	*The Zero-Sum Society*

Pomona College
333 College Way
Claremont, CA 91711-6312
(714) 621-8134

All freshmen at Pomona take a writing-intensive course their first semester. As is true in many colleges and universities, the course combines writing with learning across the curriculum. The topics for writing vary from section to section according to the interests of the particular professors. In a section taught recently by Dr. Richard Barnes, for example, the students read and wrote about **Dante** and his world.

In their second semester, students may begin the first of a two-semester course, Major British Authors. In the second half of the course, instructors choose works from the 18th, 19th, and 20th centuries. Among the works studied in the first-semester survey are:

Chaucer, Geoffrey	*Canterbury Tales,* and the medieval lyric
Spenser, Edmund	*The Faerie Queen,* and the Elizabethan lyric
Milton, John	*Paradise Lost,* and the 17th-century lyric

Presbyterian College
South Broad Street
Clinton, SC 29325
(803) 833-2820

Presbyterian College's required freshman class in composition and literature focuses on a survey of world masterpieces. Dr. Neal Prater, Chair of the Department of English, says the major emphasis is on the following authors and types of literature:

A GREEK EPIC
Homer   *The Iliad; The Odyssey*

A GREEK TRAGEDY
Aeschylus   Any play
Euripides   Any play
Sophocles   Any play

A ROMAN EPIC
Vergil   *The Aeneid*

MEDIEVAL POETRY
Chaucer, Geoffrey   *Canterbury Tales*
Dante   *Inferno*

ELIZABETHAN DRAMA
Shakespeare, William   Any play

18TH-CENTURY SATIRE
Molière   *Tartuffe*
Voltaire   *Candide*

19TH-CENTURY POETRY AND DRAMA
A collection of English Romantic poems
Goethe, J. Wolfgang von   *Faust*

19TH-CENTURY NOVEL
Turgenev, Ivan   *Fathers and Sons*

20TH-CENTURY NOVEL

Faulkner, William   Any novel
Golding, William   *Lord of the Flies*

Princeton University
Box 430
Princeton, NJ 08544
(609) 452-3060

Freshmen students at Princeton are offered extra incentives in their pursuit of academic excellence. Two prizes are given each year to freshmen who excel in English:

The Class of 1883 English Prize for Academic Freshmen: This prize, the yearly income of $2300, is given to that freshman, a candidate for the degree of Bachelor of Arts, who has done the best work in the English studies of the year, and has submitted the best essay on a subject approved by the Department of English.

The Class of 1883 English Prize for Freshmen in the School of Engineering: This prize, the yearly income of $2300, is given to that freshman, a candidate for the degree of Bachelor of Engineering, who has done the best work in the English studies of the year, and has submitted the best essay on a subject approved by the Department of English.

The following list is of works recently studied in two of the freshman literature courses:

I. SHAKESPEARE

Shakespeare, William   *A Midsummer Night's Dream; Henry IV,
                           Part I; Twelfth Night; Hamlet; Corio-
                           lanus; King Lear; The Tempest*

II. MAJOR AMERICAN WRITERS

Cather, Willa   *A Lost Lady*
Chopin, Kate   *The Awakening*
Crane, Stephen   *The Red Badge of Courage;* "The Open
                           Boat," "The Blue Hotel"
Faulkner, William   "Red Leaves," "Wash," "The Bear,"
                           "Old Man"
Hemingway, Ernest   "Indian Camp," "The End of Some-
                           thing," "Three-Day Blow," "Big
                           Two-Hearted River," "Fathers and
                           Sons"
Melville, Herman   *Bartleby the Scrivener; Benito Cereno;
                           Billy Budd*

O'Neill, Eugene
Poe, Edgar Allan

Shepard, Sam
Twain, Mark
Walker, Alice
Also the poets:
Dickinson, Emily

Frost, Robert

Long Day's Journey into Night
"The Fall of the House of Usher,"
"The Tell-Tale Heart," "The
Raven," "The Philosophy of Com-
position," "The Purloined Letter"
True West
The Adventures of Huckleberry Finn
The Color Purple

"Success is counted sweetest," "I'm
'Wife'—I've finished that—," "I
taste a liquor never brewed," "Safe
in their Alabaster Chambers—,"
"There's a certain slant of light,"
"The Soul selects her own Society—," "He fumbles at your Soul,"
"A Bird came down the Walk—,"
"What Soft—Cherubic Creatures—,"
"This is my letter to the world," "I
heard a Fly buzz—when I died—,"
"This World is not Conclusion," "I
cannot live with You—," "I dwell in
Possibility—," "Because I could not
stop for Death," "My Life had
stood—a Loaded Gun," "A narrow
Fellow in the Grass," "Tell all the
Truth but tell it slant—," "A route
of Evanescence," "There is a solitude of space," "Elysium is as far
as to"

"Mending Wall," "After Apple-Pick-
ing," "The Wood-Pile," "The Road
Not Taken," "The Oven Bird,"
"Birches," "Out, Out" "Stopping
by the Woods on a Snowy Evening," "For Once, Then, Something," "Spring Pools," "Once by
the Pacific," "West-Running
Brook," "Two Tramps in Mud
Time," "Desert Places," "Design,"
"The Silken Tent"

Randolph-Macon Woman's College
2500 Rivermont Avenue
Lynchburg, VA 24503-1526
(804) 846-7392

At Randolph-Macon Woman's College all first-year students take a one-semester interdisciplinary writing and discussion course. The handbook used in the course is the *Harbrace College Handbook*. Dr. Carolyn Wilkerson Bell, Chair, Department of English, says some of the readings for the course vary from year to year, but the following have been recent choices:

Freud, Sigmund	*The Interpretation of Dreams*
Homer	*The Iliad* (Richmond Lattimore, tr.)
Kingston, Maxine Hong	*The Woman Warrior: Memoirs of a Girlhood among Ghosts*
Marx, Karl and Friedrich Engels	*The Communist Manifesto*
Plato	*The Symposium* (Walter Hamilton, tr.)
Shakespeare, William	*King Lear*
Sophocles	*The Theban Plays* (E. F. Watling, tr.)
Thucydides	*Peloponnesian War* (Walter Hamilton, tr.)
Voltaire	*Candide* (John Butt, tr.)
Vonnegut, Kurt, Jr.	*Slaughterhouse Five*
Wolfe, Tom	*The Painted Word*

St. John's College
PO Box 1651
Annapolis, MD 21404
(301) 263-2371

St. John's College
1160 Camino Cruz Blanca
Sante Fe, NM 87501
(505) 982-3691

The following quotations from St. John's "1987 Statement of Educational Policy" by Dr. Thomas J. Slakey, Dean, explain the uniqueness of the college whose curriculum is organized around great books. First, all students "follow a common curriculum throughout four years, embracing to the greatest extent possible the most important subject matters and methods of inquiry."

Second, the faculty "to the greatest extent possible teach throughout the curriculum, not confining themselves to any one subject matter or method."

Third, study centers around "the so-called 'great books,' those texts that over time have proved best at forcing their readers to rethink fundamental questions, and at helping them understand themselves and the world around them. The books [are] arranged roughly in chronological order so as to take beginning students completely out of their own familiar world, and so as to place them in the world of Homer, of Plato, of Ptolemy, and so on, so that when they arrive after four years at twentieth-century authors, they can read them with open eyes. The chronological order also profits from the remarkable degree to which the truly important authors draw upon their few truly important fellows from the past, as Vergil goes back to Homer, Dante to Vergil, Kant to Artistotle, Einstein to Newton, and so on. Thus occurs what Buchanan called 'the great conversation' among the authors, shared by the readers, shared especially in the discussion and questioning that follow careful reading."

The college believes that "students who develop habits of shared inquiry, turning to the best authors for help, but relying ultimately on their own imaginations and judgments, will grow as men and women and as responsible citizens." The St. John's program is symbolized by the fourfold Latin pun on its seal: *Facio liberos ex liberis, libris libraque*, "I make free men out of children by means of books and a balance."

The St. John's List of Great Books

Following is the list of books on which the St. John's program is based. The list is subject to constant review and revision. Some books are read only in part.

FRESHMAN YEAR

Homer	*Iliad; Odyssey*
Aeschylus	*Agamemnon; Choephoroe; Eumenides; Prometheus Bound*
Sophocles	*Oedipus Rex; Oedipus at Colonus; Antigone*
Thucydides	*Peloponnesian War*
Euripides	*Hippolytus; Medea; Bacchae*
Herodotus	*The Persian Wars*
Aristophanes	*The Clouds; The Birds*
Plato	*Apology; Crito; Gorgias; Ion; Meno; Parmenides; Phaedo; Phaedrus; Republic; Sophist; Symposium; Theaetetus; Timaeus*
Aristotle	*Poetics; Physics; Metaphysics; Ethics; On Generation and Corruption*
Euclid	*Elements*

Lucretius	*On the Nature of Things*
Plutarch	*Pericles; Alcibiades*
Marcus Aurelius	*Meditations*
Nicomachus	*Arithmetic*
Lavoisier, Antoine-Laurent	*Elements of Chemistry*

SOPHOMORE YEAR

	Bible
Aristotle	*De Anima; On Interpretation; Posterior Analytics; Categories; Parts of Animals; Generation of Animals*
Apollonius	*On Conic Sections*
Vergil	*The Aeneid*
Plutarch	*Caesar; Antony; Brutus; Cato the Younger; Pompey; Cicero*
Epictetus	*Discourses; Manual*
Tacitus	*Annals*
Ptolemy	*Almagest*
Galen	*On the Natural Faculties*
Plotinus	*Fifth Ennead*
Augustine, Saint	*Confessions; City of God*
Anselm, Saint	*Proslogium*
Aquinas, St. Thomas	*Summa Theologica; Summa Contra Gentiles*
Dante	*Divine Comedy*
Chaucer, Geoffrey	*Canterbury Tales*
Machiavelli, Niccolò	*The Prince; Discourses*
Copernicus, Nicolaus	*On the Revolution of the Spheres*
Luther, Martin	*The Freedom of a Christian; Secular Authority*
Rabelais, François	*Gargantua and Pantagruel*
Calvin, John	*Institutes of the Christian Religion*
Montaigne, Michel de	*Essays*
Viète, François	*Introduction to the Analytical Art*
Bacon, Francis	*Novum Organum*
Shakespeare, William	*Richard II; Henry IV; Henry V; The Tempest; As You Like It; Hamlet; Othello; Macbeth; King Lear; Coriolanus; Sonnets*
Kepler, Johannes	*Epitome of Copernican Astronomy*
Harvey, William	*Motion of the Heart and Blood*
Descartes, René	*Geometry*
Pascal, Blaise	*Generation of Conic Sections*
Darwin, Charles	*Origin of Species*
Mendel, Gregor Johann	*Experiments in Plant Hybridization*

JUNIOR YEAR

Cervantes, Miguel de	*Don Quixote*
Galilei, Galileo	*Two New Sciences*
Hobbes, Thomas	*Leviathan*
Descartes, René	*Discourse on Method; Meditations; Rules for the Direction of the Mind*
Milton, John	*Paradise Lost; Samson Agonistes*
La Rochefoucauld, François de	*Maxims*
La Fontaine, Jean de	*Fables*
Pascal, Blaise	*Pensées*
Huygens, Christiaan	*Treatise on Light; On the Movement of Bodies by Impact*
Spinoza, Benedictus de	*Theologico-Political Treatise*
Locke, John	*Second Treatise of Government*
Racine, Jean	*Phèdre*
Newton, Sir Isaac	*Principia Mathematica*
Leibniz, Gottfried	*Monadology; Discourse on Metaphysics; Principles of Nature and Grace Founded on Reason; Essay on Dynamics*
Swift, Jonathan	*Gulliver's Travels*
Berkeley, George	*Principles of Human Knowledge*
Fielding, Henry	*Tom Jones*
Hume, David	*Treatise of Human Nature; Dialogues Concerning Natural Religion; Enquiry Concerning Human Understanding*
Rousseau, Jean-Jacques	*Social Contract*
Smith, Adam	*Wealth of Nations*
Kant, Immanuel	*Critique of Pure Reason; Fundamental Principles of Metaphysics of Morals*
Mozart, Wolfgang Amadeus	*Don Giovanni* (opera)
Austen, Jane	*Pride and Prejudice*
Hamilton, Jay Madison	*The Federalist Papers*
Melville, Herman	*Billy Budd; Benito Cereno; Moby-Dick*
Dedekind, Julius Wilhelm	*Essay on the Theory of Numbers*

SENIOR YEAR

Shakespeare, William	*Antony and Cleopatra*
Molière	*The Misanthrope; Tartuffe*
Goethe, Johann von	*Faust*
Hegel, Georg W. F.	*Phenomenology of Mind; Logic* (from the Encyclopedia)
Woolf, Virginia	*To the Lighthouse*
Douglass, Frederick	*The Constitution and Slavery*
O'Connor, Flannery	*Everything That Rises Must Converge*
Lobachevsky, Nikolai	*Theory of Parallels*

Tocqueville, Alexis de	*Democracy in America*
Lincoln, Abraham	Speeches
Kierkegaard, Søren A.	*Philosophical Fragments; Fear and Trembling*
Wagner, Richard	*Tristan and Isolde* (opera)
Thoreau, Henry David	*Walden*
Marx, Karl	*Communist Manifesto; Capital; The Economic and Philosophic Manuscripts of 1844*
Dostoevski, Feodor	*Brothers Karamazov; The Possessed*
Tolstoy, Leo	*War and Peace*
Twain, Mark	*The Adventures of Huckleberry Finn*
James, William	*Psychology, Briefer Course*
Nietzsche, Friedrich W.	*Birth of Tragedy; Thus Spake Zarathustra; Beyond Good and Evil*
Freud, Sigmund	*General Introduction to Psychoanalysis; Civilization and Its Discontents; Beyond the Pleasure Principle*
Valéry, Paul	Poems
Jung, Carl	*Two Essays in Analytic Psychology*
Mann, Thomas	*Death in Venice*
Kafka, Franz	*The Trial*
Heidegger, Martin	*What is Philosophy?*
Heisenberg, Werner Karl	*The Physical Principles of the Quantum Theory*
Millikan, Robert Andrews	*The Electron*

Siena College
Route 9
Loudonville, NY 12211
(518) 783-2423

The Siena Research Institute surveyed 126 faculty members from 126 colleges and universities to determine what books they felt entering college students should have read. The faculty members thought that on the average students should have read at least 15 of the following books. Siena's list of the most frequently mentioned works follows and includes the percentage of those faculty surveyed who recommended each book. The percentages in parentheses represent the share of 1138 entering freshmen at 37 colleges in 25 states who said they had read each book. The average number was 10 books per student.

	Declaration of Independence	91%	(58%)
	Bible	80%	(55%)
Aristotle	*Politics*	10%	(4%)
Austen, Jane	*Pride and Prejudice*	49%	(14%)
Chaucer, Geoffrey	*Canterbury Tales*	48%	(52%)
Dickens, Charles	*Great Expectations* and *A Tale of Two Cities*	83%	(55%)
Dickinson, Emily	Poems	68%	(53%)
Dostoevski, Feodor	*Crime and Punishment*	21%	(10%)
Emerson, Ralph Waldo	Essays and poems	44%	(42%)
Faulkner, William	Novels	29%	(23%)
Fitzgerald, F. Scott	*The Great Gatsby*	65%	(41%)
Frost, Robert	Poems	87%	(55%)
Hawthorne, Nathaniel	*The Scarlet Letter*	81%	(59%)
Homer	*The Iliad* or *The Odyssey*	72%	(43%)
Machiavelli, Niccolò	*The Prince*	14%	(8%)
Marx, Karl and Friedrich Engels	*Communist Manifesto*	31%	(11%)
Melville, Herman	*Moby-Dick*	29%	(30%)
Milton, John	*Paradise Lost*	20%	(21%)
Orwell, George	*1984*	59%	(38%)
Plato	*The Republic*	30%	(7%)
Salinger, J. D.	*The Catcher in the Rye*	62%	(32%)
Shakespeare, William	Works	91%	(68%)
Sophocles	*Oedipus Rex*	60%	(29%)
Steinbeck, John	*The Grapes of Wrath*	62%	(37%)
Thoreau, Henry	*Walden*	64%	(28%)
Tocqueville, Alexis de	*Democracy in America*	26%	(3%)
Tolstoy, Leo	*War and Peace*	6%	(6%)
Twain, Mark	*The Adventures of Huckleberry Finn*	96%	(68%)
Vergil	*The Aeneid*	25%	(8%)
Whitman, Walt	*Leaves of Grass*	45%	(9%)

Smith College
Northampton, MA 01063
(413) 584-0515

Among the works in Smith's list of "Suggested Reading For Students Planning To Enter Smith College" are:

	Bible (King James Version: "the best preparation for literary studies")
Aeschylus	*Prometheus Bound*
Euripides	*The Trojan Women*
Homer	*The Odyssey*

Sophocles   *Antigone; Oedipus Rex* (these four works "invite study of Greek mythology")

Shakespeare, William   *Julius Caesar; Macbeth; Richard II* (or perhaps *Henry V* in connection with Olivier's film); *Twelfth Night*

NOVELS:

Austen, Jane	*Pride and Prejudice; Emma*
Brontë, Charlotte	*Jane Eyre*
Brontë, Emily	*Wuthering Heights*
Conrad, Joseph	*Heart of Darkness; The Secret Sharer*
Dickens, Charles	*Great Expectations*
Dreiser, Theodore	*Sister Carrie*
Eliot, George	*The Mill on the Floss*
Ellison, Ralph	*Invisible Man*
Faulkner, William	*As I Lay Dying; Light in August*
Hardy, Thomas	*The Mayor of Casterbridge; Tess of the D'Urbervilles*
Hawthorne, Nathaniel	*The Scarlet Letter* or some of the tales
Hemingway, Ernest	*A Farewell to Arms*
James, Henry	*The Turn of the Screw* or *Washington Square*
Joyce, James	*A Portrait of the Artist as a Young Man; Dubliners*
Lawrence, D. H.	*The Fox* or *Sons and Lovers* or any collection of short stories
Melville, Herman	*Billy Budd*
Poe, Edgar Allan	Selected tales
Waugh, Evelyn	*Decline and Fall* or *A Handful of Dust*
Wharton, Edith	*Ethan Frome* or *The House of Mirth*

The author of the list also would include "a couple of novels by contemporary writers currently esteemed (twenty years ago I would have said **Salinger**, ten years ago **Vonnegut**): **Ann Beattie, Bobbie Ann Mason, Alice Munro.**"

The author also feels that pre-college reading should include "poetry in a good anthology" with "substantial samples of the major British and American poets. Students would do well to study two or three poets, one of them twentieth century, 'in depth.' " Plays by **Anton Chekov, Henrik Ibsen, Arthur Miller, Harold Pinter, George Bernard Shaw** are also highly recommended.

South Dakota State University
Box 2275A
Brookings, SD 57007-1397
(605) 688-5191

Dr. George West, Head of the Department of English at South Dakota State, suggests the following "to high school teachers or to anyone who writes in for a list of recommended readings."

A Very Selective Reading List

CLASSICS

	Bible
Hamilton, Edith	*Mythology*
Homer	*The Iliad; The Odyssey*
Sophocles	*Oedipus Rex*
Vergil	*The Aeneid*

ENGLISH

MIDDLE AGES

Chaucer, Geoffrey	Prologue to *The Canterbury Tales* and a tale or two

RENAISSANCE

Shakespeare, William	*Julius Caesar; Macbeth; The Merchant of Venice; Romeo and Juliet*

17TH CENTURY

Milton, John	*Paradise Lost* (selections)

18TH CENTURY

Pope, Alexander	*The Rape of the Lock*

ROMANTICS

Poetry: **Samuel Taylor Coleridge, John Keats, William Wordsworth**

VICTORIANS

Austen, Jane	*Pride and Prejudice*
Brontë, Charlotte	*Jane Eyre*
Brontë, Emily	*Wuthering Heights*
Dickens, Charles	Anything
Tennyson, Alfred Lord	Poems

20TH CENTURY

Conrad, Joseph	A short story or novel
Golding, William	*Lord of the Flies*
Hardy, Thomas	Poems or a novel
Housman, A. E.	Poems

AMERICAN

Cather, Willa	*My Antonia*
Crane, Stephen	*The Red Badge of Courage*
Ellison, Ralph	*The Invisible Man*
Emerson, Ralph Waldo	Selections
Faulkner, William	*As I Lay Dying*
Fitzgerald, F. Scott	*The Great Gatsby*
Franklin, Benjamin	Selections
Hawthorne, Nathaniel	*The Scarlet Letter*
Hemingway, Ernest	*The Sun Also Rises*
Lewis, Sinclair	*Main Street*
London, Jack	*The Call of the Wild*
Melville, Herman	*Moby-Dick*
Neihardt, John G.	*Black Elk Speaks*
Salinger, J. D.	*The Catcher in the Rye*
Steinbeck, John	*The Grapes of Wrath*
Thoreau, Henry David	Selections
Twain, Mark	*The Adventures of Huckleberry Finn*
Wright, Richard	*Native Son*

Poetry: Emily Dickinson, T. S. Eliot, Robert Frost, Edgar Allan Poe, E. A. Robinson, Carl Sandburg, Wallace Stevens, Walt Whitman, William Carlos Williams

Drama: Edward Albee, Arthur Miller, Tennessee Williams

Short Stories: Sherwood Anderson, Willa Cather, Stephen Crane, William Faulkner, F. Scott Fitzgerald, Nathaniel Hawthorne, Ernest Hemingway, Washington Irving, Jack London, Sinclair Lewis, Herman Melville, Flannery O'Connor, Edgar Allan Poe, Katherine Ann Porter, John Steinbeck

Some highly regarded contemporary fiction writers: Ann Beattie, E. L. Doctorow, Louise Erdrich, John Gardner, Gail Godwin, John Irving, Ursula Le Guin, Toni Morrison, Joyce Carol Oates, Thomas Pynchon, Philip Roth, Leslie Marmon Silko, Anne Tyler, John Updike, Alice Walker, James Welch

Spelman College
350 Spelman Lane Southwest
Atlanta, GA 30314-4399
(404) 681-3643

According to Dr. J. M. Aldridge, Chair of the Department of English at Spelman, the following list was developed by a faculty committee to send to incoming freshmen. One custom has been for the books to be discussed in group sessions in dormitories as a part of freshman orientation.

Freshman Reading List

Theme: The Significance of Black Culture

Baldwin, James	*The Fire Next Time* (1963)
Baraka, Imamu Amiri (LeRoi Jones)	*Blues People* (1965)
Cole, Johnnetta B., ed.	*All American Women* (1986)
Dubois, W. E. B.	*The Souls of Black Folk* (1903)
Franklin, John Hope	*From Slavery to Freedom* (6th ed.)
Giddings, Paula J.	*When and Where I Enter: The Impact of Black Women on Race and Sex in America* (1984)
Hughes, Langston	*The Best of Simple* (1961)
Hurston, Zora Neale	*Their Eyes Were Watching God* (1937)
King, Martin Luther, Jr.	*Why We Can't Wait* (1964)
Maynard, Olga	*Judith Jamison: Aspects of a Dancer* (1982)
Shange, Ntosake	*for colored girls who have considered suicide when the rainbow is enuf; a choreopoem* (1971)
Walker, Alice	*Meridian* (1976)
Washington, Mary Helen	*Invented Lives: Narratives of Black Women 1860–1960* (1987)
Woodson, Carter G.	*The Mis-Education of the Negro* (1933)

State University of New York at Albany
1400 Washington Avenue
Albany, NY 12222
(518) 442-5435

Professor David C. Redding, Summer Chairman of the English Department, states that the University at Albany has no reading lists for pre-college students, but "if anyone asks me what I recommend, I say the Bible: it's basic to literature and culture." He also says that there are no fixed lists of readings for freshman courses. "For the last several years incoming students have been asked to read two books and discuss them when they come, but the books are simply ones of current interest and change each year."

Stetson University
DeLand, FL 32720
(904) 734-4121

Freshmen at Stetson take three required courses: two in English and one in religion. The required text for the English course is **J. W. Corder** and **John Jay Ruszkiewicz**, *Handbook of Current English*, 8th edition. For the religion course, students read **J. Benton White**'s *From Adam to Armageddon* and **Olive A. Burns**' *Cold Sassy Tree*.

Swarthmore College
Swarthmore, PA 19081
(215) 328-8300

The following is a partial list of works included in the Freshman English syllabi at Swarthmore:

Aristotle	Essays
Atwood, Margaret	*Bodily Harm*
Blake, William	Selected Poems and Letters
Brontë, Charlotte	*Jane Eyre*
Coetzee, J. M.	*Foe*
Crane, Stephen	Stories and Tales
Defoe, Daniel	*Robinson Crusoe*
Dickinson, Emily	*Final Harvest*

Eagleton, Terry	*Literary Theory*
Eliot, George	*Middlemarch*
Ellison, Ralph	*Invisible Man*
Emerson, Gloria	*Winners and Losers*
Euripides	*The Complete Greek Tragedies V*
Fielding, Henry	*Joseph Andrews*
Forster, E. M.	*A Passage to India*
Freud, Sigmund	*Dora: An Analysis of a Case of Hysteria*
Hardy, Thomas	*Jude the Obscure*
Hwang, David Henry	*M. Butterfly*
Herr, Michael	*Dispatches*
Irigaray, Luce	Essays
James, Henry	*Daisy Miller and Other Stories*
Kessler, Lyle	*Orphans*
Lawrence, D. H.	*Lady Chatterley's Lover; Sons and Lovers*
Minot, Susan	*Monkeys*
Olds, Sharon	*The Dead and the Living*
Olsen, Tillie	*Tell Me a Riddle*
Puccini, Giacomo	*Madame Butterfly*
Rhys, Jean	*Wide Sargasso Sea*
Shakespeare, William	*Hamlet; Henry IV*, Part I; *King Lear; Much Ado About Nothing; Othello; Richard II; The Tempest*
Shaw, George Bernard	Plays
Shelley, Mary	*Frankenstein*
Stoppard, Tom	*Rosenkrantz and Guildenstern Are Dead*
Swift, Jonathan	*Gulliver's Travels*
Terry, Wallace	*Bloods*
Trimble, John	*Writing with Style*
Wharton, Edith	*Ethan Frome*
Woolf, Virginia	*Mrs. Dalloway; A Room of One's Own*
Wright, Richard	*Native Son*

Temple University
Conwell Hall
Philadelphia, PA 19122-1803
(215) 787-7200

The Undergraduate Division of the English Department at Temple chaired by W. Ben Crane lists in its pamphlet The Green Bag II the works read in its various courses. In their first year students usually take a composition course and "Introduction to Literature." The following lists include the works often read in other courses open to underclassmen.

AMERICAN/AFRO-AMERICAN LITERATURE

Brooks, Gwendolyn	Poetry
Brown, William Wells	*Clotel*
Chesnutt, Charles W.	*The Marrow of Tradition*
Chopin, Kate	*The Awakening*
Crane, Stephen	*The Red Badge of Courage*
Delany, Martin	*Blake*
Dickinson, Emily	Various poems
Douglass, Frederick	*Narrative of the Life of an American Slave*
Dreiser, Theodore	*Sister Carrie*
Dubois, W. W. B.	*The Souls of Black Folk*
Eliot, T. S.	*The Waste Land*
Ellison, Ralph	*Invisible Man*
Emerson, Ralph Waldo	*Essays*
Equiano, Olaudah	Slave narrative
Faulkner, William	*The Sound and the Fury*
Fitzgerald, F. Scott	*The Great Gatsby*
Franklin, Benjamin	*Autobiography*
H. D. (Hilde Doolittle)	Poems
Hawthorne, Nathaniel	*The Scarlet Letter*
Hemingway, Ernest	*The Sun Also Rises*
Hughes and Bontemps	*The Book of Negro Folklore*
Hughes, Langston	Poetry
Hurston, Zora Neale	*Their Eyes Were Watching God*
Jacobs, Harriet	"Linda Brent"
James, Henry	*The Portrait of a Lady*
Johnson, James Weldon	*Autobiography of an Ex-Colored Man*
Larsen, Nella	*Passing*
Lorde, Audrey	Poetry
Melville, Herman	*Moby-Dick*
Morrison, Toni	*Beloved; Sula*
Nabokov, Vladimir	*Lolita*
O'Neill, Eugene	*Desire under the Elms*
Poe, Edgar Allan	"The Fall of the House of Usher"
Pound, Ezra	*Hugh Selwyn Mauberley*
Sanchez, Sonia	Poetry
Toomer, Jean	*Cane*
Twain, Mark	*The Adventures of Huckleberry Finn*
Walker, Alice	*Meridan; The Color Purple*
Walker, Margaret	*Jubilee*
Wharton, Edith	*The House of Mirth*
Whitman, Walt	*Song of Myself*
Wilson, Harriet	*Our Nig*
Wright, Richard	*Native Son*

DRAMA

Beckett, Samuel	*Waiting for Godot*
Brecht, Bertolt	*Mother Courage and Her Children*

Buchner, Georg	*Woyzeck*
Calderon, Pedro	*Life Is a Dream*
Congreve, William	*The Way of the World*
Ibsen, Henrik	*A Doll's House*
Miller, Arthur	*Death of a Salesman*
Molière	*The Misanthrope*
Pirandello, Luigi	*Six Characters in Search of an Author*
Shakespeare, William	Tragedies, comedies, romances, and historical plays
Shaw, George Bernard	*Major Barbara*

ENGLISH LITERATURE

	Beowulf
	Everyman
	Sir Gawain and the Green Knight
	The Seafarer
	The Wanderer
Auden, W. H.	*Selected Poems, 1930–1955*
Austen, Jane	*Emma; Sense and Sensibility*
Beckett, Samuel	*Happy Days; Murphy*
Blake, William	*The Songs of Innocence and Experience*
Boswell, James	*The Life of Johnson*
Burns, Robert	*The Poetry of Burns*
Byron, George Gordon	"Childe Harold's Pilgrimage"
Chaucer, Geoffrey	*Troilus and Criseyde; Canterbury Tales*
Coleridge, S. T.	"Kubla Khan"
Congreve, William	*The Way of the World*
Conrad, Joseph	*Heart of Darkness; Lord Jim*
De Quincey, Thomas	*Confessions of an English Opium-Eater*
Eliot, T. S.	*Prufrock and Other Observations; The Waste Land*
Fielding, Henry	*Joseph Andrews*
Ford, Ford Maddox	*The Good Soldier*
Forster, E. M.	*A Passage to India*
Gay, John	*The Beggar's Opera*
Johnson, Samuel	*Rasselas*
Joyce, James	*A Portrait of the Artist as a Young Man; Ulysses*
Keats, John	"Ode on a Grecian Urn"
Langland, William	*Piers Plowman*
Lawrence, D. H.	*Lady Chatterley's Lover; Women in Love*
Lewis, Matthew	*The Monk*
Malory, Sir Thomas	*Morte D'Arthur*
Pope, Alexander	"The Rape of the Lock"
Shaw, G. B.	*Heartbreak House; Man and Superman*
Shelley, Mary	*Frankenstein*
Shelley, P. B.	"Mont Blanc"
Swift, Jonathan	*Gulliver's Travel's*
Wollstonecraft, Mary	*A Vindication of the Rights of Women*
Woolf, Virginia	*To the Lighthouse*

| Wordsworth, William | "Tintern Abbey" |
| Yeats, W. B. | *The Tower* and *The Winding Stair* |

CONTEMPORARY LITERATURE

Achebe, Chinua	*Things Fall Apart*
Barth, John	*Lost in the Funhouse*
Barthelme, Donald	*City Life*
Calvino, Italo	*t zero*
Fuentos, Carlos	*The Death of Artemio Cruz*
García Márquez, Gabriel	*One Hundred Years of Solitude*
Grass, Günter	*The Tin Drum*
Pinter, Harold	*The Homecoming*
Pynchon, Thomas	*Gravity's Rainbow*
Simon, Claude	*The Flanders Road*

The University of Alabama
PO Box AU
Tuscaloosa, AL 35487-9787
(205) 348-5666

In a letter to college-bound students planning to attend the university, Professor Robert W. Halli, Jr., Director of Undergraduate English Studies, writes that he hopes the following list will be "interesting and helpful." But he offers it with "a fistful of warnings," saying "it is not complete or definitive because it is deliberately short enough to be feasible."

Reading the books on the list, he says "won't automatically make you into an educated or cultured person, nor will it guarantee you an A in Freshman English. So, what *is* it good for? Reading the works on this list, mostly drawn from English and American literature, will give you a background, a direction, a springboard that will be of value to you in a number of ways, some related to your academic course work and some not.

"But, perhaps most of all, reading literature, such as the works on this list, should help establish a life-long pleasure in reading. And those who read effectively and with enjoyment tend to 'do' well and 'live' well (not necessarily the same thing)."

Suggested Reading List for High School Students

Poetry anthology with selections from **W. H. Auden, William Blake, Robert Browning, S. T. Coleridge, Emily Dickinson, John Donne, T. S. Eliot, Robert Frost, Thomas Hardy, George Her-**

bert, Robert Herrick, John Keats, Robert Lowell, Edgar Allan Poe, Alexander Pope, Theodore Roethke, William Shakespeare (sonnets), P. B. Shelley, Wallace Stevens, Sir Philip Sydney, Alfred, Lord Tennyson, Walt Whitman, William Wordsworth, Sir Thomas Wyatt, W. B. Yeats

Austen, Jane	*Pride and Prejudice*
Bellow, Saul	*Humboldt's Gift*
Chaucer, Geoffrey	*Canterbury Tales* (Selections, perhaps in translation)
Conrad, Joseph	*Heart of Darkness*
Defoe, Daniel	*Robinson Crusoe*
Dickens, Charles	*Great Expectations* or *Hard Times*
Faulkner, William	"The Bear"
Fielding, Henry	*Joseph Andrews* or *Tom Jones*
Fitzgerald, F. Scott	*The Great Gatsby*
Fowles, John	*The French Lieutenant's Woman*
Hardy, Thomas	*The Return of the Native*
Hawthorne, Nathaniel	*The Scarlet Letter*
Hemingway, Ernest	*A Farewell to Arms*
Homer	*The Iliad* and/or *The Odyssey*
James, Henry	*The American* or *The Portrait of a Lady*
Joyce, James	*Dubliners*
Lewis, Sinclair	*Babbitt* or *Main Street*
Miller, Arthur	*Death of a Salesman*
Milton, John	*Paradise Lost* (Selections)
Paton, Alan	*Cry, The Beloved Country*
Shakespeare, William	A comedy such as *Midsummer Night's Dream;* a history such as *Richard II*; a tragedy such as *Hamlet* or *King Lear*
Shaw, George Bernard	*Arms and the Man*
Sophocles	*Oedipus Rex*
Thoreau, Henry	*Walden*
Twain, Mark	*The Adventures of Huckleberry Finn*
Vergil	*The Aeneid*
Vonnegut, Kurt	*Slaughterhouse Five*
Waugh, Evelyn	*A Handful of Dust*
Wright, Richard	*Native Son*

University of California, Davis
175 Mark Hall
Davis, CA 95616
(916) 752-2971

Pre-college students interested in attending the University of California can get some idea of which literary works the Department of English considers important by scanning the minimum reading list for English majors. The list is preceded by the statement that "twelve centuries separate the writer of *Beowulf* from Robert Frost; despite the many differences between these two poets, there is still at base at least one thing they have in common: both composed their verse in English. The titles suggested in the Reading List attempt to represent in some fair way those twelve centuries of literature in the English tongue."

THE BEGINNINGS TO SHAKESPEARE

POETRY:

> *Beowulf*; English and Scottish Popular Ballads, *Sir Gawain and the Green Knight*, Geoffrey Chaucer, Henry Howard, Earl of Surrey, Walter Raleigh, Christopher Marlowe, William Shakespeare (Sonnets), Sir Philip Sidney, John Skelton, Edmund Spenser, Sir Thomas Wyatt

PROSE:

	The King James Bible: Genesis, Exodus, Ruth, Job, Ecclesiastes, The Song of Solomon, The Gospels, I Corinthians
Hooker, Richard	*Of the Laws of Ecclesiastical Politie*, Bk. I, chs. 1–8
Lyly, John	*Euphues:* First half of Book I
Malory, Sir Thomas	*Morte d'Arthur:* the stories of Sir Tristram and of the death of Arthur
More, Sir Thomas	*Utopia* (Robinson, tr.)
Nashe, Thomas	*The Unfortunate Traveler*
Sidney, Sir Philip	*A Defense of Poesie*

DRAMA:

	The Brome Abraham and Isaac
	Everyman
	Gammer Gurton's Needle
	The Wakefield Noah
	The Wakefield Second Shepherds' Play
Kyd, Thomas	*The Spanish Tragedy*

Marlowe, Christopher	*Dr. Faustus; Edward II*
Norton, Thomas & Thomas Sackville	*Gorboduc*
Shakespeare, William	Plays

DONNE TO MARVELL

POETRY:

Richard Crashaw, John Donne, George Herbert, Robert Herrick, Ben Jonson, Richard Lovelace, Andrew Marvell, John Milton, Sir John Suckling, Henry Vaughan

PROSE:

Bacon, Francis	Selected essays
Browne, Sir Thomas	Selections from *Religio Medici* and *Hydriotaphia*
Burton, Robert	Selections from *The Anatomy of Melancholy*
Donne, John	*Meditations* 16, 17, 18
Hobbes, Thomas	*Leviathan,* Part I: 1, 2, 3, 14
Jonson, Ben	*Timber* or *Discoveries* (Selections)
Milton, John	*Areopagitica*
Taylor, Jeremy	Selections from *The Rule and Exercises of Holy Living/Holy Dying*

DRAMA:

Beaumont, Francis	*The Knight of the Burning Pestle*
Beaumont and John Fletcher	*The Maid's Tragedy* or *Philaster*
Dekker, Thomas	*The Shoemakers' Holiday*
Ford, John	*The Broken Heart* or *'Tis Pity She's a Whore*
Heywood, Thomas	*A Woman Killed with Kindness*
Jonson, Ben	*The Alchemist; Volpone*
Massinger, Philip	*A New Way to Pay Old Debts*
Webster, John	*The Duchess of Malfi; The White Devil*

DRYDEN TO BURNS

POETRY:

William Blake, Anne Bradstreet, Robert Burns, William Collins, William Cowper, George Crabbe, John Dryden, Philip Freneau, Oliver Goldsmith, Thomas Gray, Samuel Johnson, Alexander Pope, Matthew Prior, Edward Taylor, James Thompson, John Wilmot, Earl of Rochester

PROSE:

Addison, Joseph & Richard Steele	Selections from *The Spectator; The Tatler*
Boswell, James	*The Life of Johnson* and *The London Journal* (Selections)
Bunyan, John	*The Pilgrim's Progress,* Part I
Burke, Edmund	*Reflections on the Revolution in France* (Selections)
Cooper, Anthony Ashley	*Men, Manners, Opinions, Times,* Book I
Crèvecoeur, St. Jean de	*Letters from an American Farmer: What is an American?*
Dryden, John	*An Essay of Dramatic Poesy;* Preface to *Fables*
Edwards, Jonathan	*Personal Narrative; Sinners in the Hands of an Angry God; Sarah Pierrepont*
Franklin, Benjamin	*An Edict by the King of Prussia; The Ephemera; The Way to Wealth*
Gibbon, Edward	*The History of the Decline and Fall of the Roman Empire,* Ch. XXXI
Johnson, Samuel	*Lives of the Poets;* Preface to *Shakespeare; Rasselas* (Selections)
Locke, John	Selections from *Second Treatise of Civil Government & An Essay Concerning Human Understanding*
Pepys, Samuel	*Diary* (Selections)
Swift, Jonathan	*The Battle of the Books; Gulliver's Travels;* "A Modest Proposal"

NOVEL:

Austen, Jane	*Emma* or *Pride and Prejudice*
Defoe, Daniel	*Moll Flanders*
Fielding, Henry	*Tom Jones*
Richardson, Samuel	*Clarissa* (Selections)
Smollett, Tobias	*Humphry Clinker* or *Roderick Random*
Sterne, Laurence	*Tristram Shandy*

DRAMA:

Congreve, William	*The Way of the World*
Dryden, John	*All for Love*
Etherege, George	*The Man of Mode*
Goldsmith, Oliver	*She Stoops to Conquer*
Sheridan, R. B.	*The Rivals* or *The School for Scandal*
Steele, Richard	*The Conscious Lovers*
Wycherley, William	*The Country Wife*

THE NINETEENTH CENTURY

POETRY:

Matthew Arnold, Robert Browning, George Gordon, Lord Byron, Samuel Taylor Coleridge, Emily Dickinson, Ralph Waldo Emerson, Thomas Hardy, Gerard Manley Hopkins, John Keats, Edgar Allan Poe, Dante Gabriel Rossetti, Percy Bysshe Shelley, Algernon Charles Swinburne, Alfred, Lord Tennyson, Walt Whitman, William Wordsworth

PROSE:

Arnold, Matthew	Selections from *Culture and Anarchy; Essay on Wordsworth*
Carlyle, Thomas	*The Everlasting Yea; Heroes and Hero Worship; The Hero as Poet; Sartor Resartus*
Coleridge, Samuel Taylor	*Biographia Literaria,* Ch. XIV
Emerson, Ralph Waldo	"The American Scholar," "Nature," "Self-Reliance"
Hazlitt, William	Selected essays
Lamb, Charles	*The Essays of Elia* (Selections)
Macaulay, Thomas B.	*Essay on Clive*
Pater, Walter	*The Renaissance:* Conclusion
Ruskin, John	Selections from *The Stones of Venice* and *Modern Painters*
Thoreau, Henry David	"Civil Disobedience," *Walden* (Selections)
Wordsworth, William	Preface to *Lyrical Ballads*

FICTION:

Brontë, Emily	*Wuthering Heights*
Cooper, James Fenimore	*The Deerslayer* or *Last of the Mohicans*
Dickens, Charles	*Bleak House* or *David Copperfield* or *Great Expectations*
Eliot, George	*Middlemarch*
Hardy, Thomas	*The Return of the Native*
Hawthorne, Nathaniel	*The Scarlet Letter*
Melville, Herman	*Moby-Dick*
Meredith, George	*The Egoist* or *The Ordeal of Richard Feveral*
Poe, Edgar Allan	"The Fall of the House of Usher"
Scott, Sir Walter	*The Heart of Midlothian*
Thackeray, W. M.	*Vanity Fair*
Twain, Mark	*The Adventures of Huckleberry Finn*

DRAMA:

Wilde, Oscar	*The Importance of Being Earnest*

THE TWENTIETH CENTURY TO 1950

POETRY:

W. H. Auden, Hart Crane, T. S. Eliot, Robert Frost, A. E. Housman, Ezra Pound, John Crowe Ransom, Edwin Arlington Robinson, Wallace Stevens, Dylan Thomas, William Butler Yeats

PROSE:

Adams, Henry	*The Education of Henry Adams; The Dynamo and the Virgin*
Eliot, T. S.	*Tradition and the Individual Talent*
Richards, I. A.	*Practical Criticism*

FICTION:

Conrad, Joseph	*Lord Jim; Nostromo*
Faulkner, William	*Light in August; The Sound and the Fury*
Fitzgerald, F. Scott	*The Great Gatsby*
Forster, E. M.	*A Passage to India*
Hemingway, Ernest	*The Sun Also Rises*
James, Henry	*The Portrait of a Lady*
Joyce, James	*Dubliners* (Selections); *A Portrait of the Artist as a Young Man*
Lawrence, D. H.	*Sons and Lovers*

DRAMA:

Eliot, T. S.	*Murder in the Cathedral*
Miller, Arthur	*Death of a Salesman*
O'Neill, Eugene	*Desire Under the Elms*
Shaw, George Bernard	*Pygmalion*
Synge, J. M.	*Riders to the Sea*
Wilder, Thornton	*Our Town*
Williams, Tennessee	*The Glass Menagerie*

SINCE 1950

POETRY:

Gwendolyn Brooks, Allen Ginsberg, Robert Lowell, Sylvia Plath, Theodore Roethke, Karl Shapiro, Gary Snyder

OTHER LITERATURE:

Baldwin, James	*The Fire Next Time*
Bellow, Saul	*Seize the Day*
Ellison, Ralph	*Invisible Man*
Kerouac, Jack	*On the Road*
O'Connor, Flannery	"A Good Man is Hard to Find"

RECOMMENDED READINGS IN
LITERATURES OTHER THAN ENGLISH AND
AMERICAN

	Old Testament (King James): Genesis, Exodus, Job, Ruth, Psalms, Isaiah
	New Testament: Luke, Corinthians, Revelation
Aristotle	*Poetics*
Cervantes, Miguel de	*Don Quixote*
Dante	*The Divine Comedy*
Dostoevski, Feodor	*Crime and Punishment*
Flaubert, Gustave	*Madame Bovary*
Goethe, Johann von	*Faust,* Part I; *Sorrows of Young Werther*
Homer	*The Iliad; The Odyssey*
Ibsen, Henrik	*Hedda Gabler*
Montaigne, Michel	*Essays* (Selections)
Ovid	*The Metamorphosis*
Plato	*The Republic* (Bk. 10, alegory of the cave); *Symposium*
Proust, Marcel	*Swann's Way*
Tolstoy, Leo	*War and Peace*
Voltaire	*Candide*
Vergil	*The Aeneid*

University of Delaware
116 Hullihen Hall
Newark, DE 19716
(302) 451-8123

The University of Delaware has a recommended reading list for pre-college students. According to Professor Philip Flynn, "students are asked to read three books (of their choice) from this list during the summer before they enter the University and during their freshman year." The lists, which are annotated, vary from year to year. Recently the following works were recommended:

Dubois, W. E. B., *The Souls of Black Folk:* A book of essays on the study of the problem of race in America. Written in 1903, it is one of the first scholarly attempts to explain "blackness." When first published, the Nashville *Banner* commented that "this book is dangerous for the Negro to read, for it will only excite discontent and fill his imagination with things that do not exist."

192 / *University of Delaware*

Dubos, René, *Mirage of Health: Utopias, Progress, and Biological Change:*
From biological adaptation to social evolution, René Dubos presents a
panoramic vista of the individual's quest for health and happiness, with
some detours along the way. Drawing upon relationships among the
fields of biology, geography, history, ecology, mythology, and anthropology, the author reveals humankind's unified trajectory in a universe
filled with both predictabilities and surprises. The desire for change for
change's sake, the urge for progress and independence, the restless
search for freedom are presented as motivators for a dynamic life of adventure and transcendence beyond survival, beyond utopias, and beyond
any static concept of health and happiness.

Friedman, Milton and **Rose Friedman,** *Free to Choose:* The Friedmans
explore the paradox of intentions involved in the production and dis-
tribution of numerous goods and services in today's society and con-
clude that economic freedom is a requisite for political freedom.

Gilligan, Carol, *In a Different Voice:* This book explores the theme of
moral development by examining the modes of thought associated with
"male and female voices" and, as one reviewer commented, turning
"old prejudices against women on their ears."

Marx, Karl and **Friedrich Engels,** *Manifesto of the Communist Party:* The
classic analysis by Karl Marx and Friedrich Engels of the modern conditions produced by capitalist economic systems, and the solution to those
conditions.

Pirsig, Robert, *Zen and the Art of Motorcycle Maintenance:* A spiritual odyssey in the guise of a motorcycle journey. Pirsig's hero finds hope in
the pursuit of Quality as a way of combatting the shoddy workmanship
that so often infects people in every walk of life in our technological
world. Though Pirsig's conclusion is ambivalent, the book is a challenging fable about the difficulty of being authentic in the modern age.

Raup, David M., *The Nemesis Affair: A Story of the Death of Dinosaurs and
the Ways of Science:* A renowned scientist discusses the birth and controversial life of a recent theory. This is a wonderful insider's view of
scientists at work.

Shipman, Harry L., *Space 2000: Meeting the Challenge of A New Era:* A
University of Delaware astronomer and NASA consultant reveals the ex-
citement and the scientific and technical challenges of the American
space program. Shipman gives real insight into topics ranging from "Ma-
terials Processing in Space" to "Exploration of the Distant Universe."

Tolstoy, Leo, "The Death of Ivan Ilych": The description of an ordinary death of an ordinary man, this is a meditation on the mystery of
human life.

Tuchman, Barbara, *The Guns of August:* Barbara Tuchman's unforgettable account of how the great powers of Europe stumbled into war in
August 1914. It is a cautionary tale about how the momentum of the

war took hold of statesmen and began to destroy the very national values they had sought to protect.

Wright, Richard, *Native Son:* A grim story of racism in America.

University of Denver
Mary Reed Building #107
Denver, CO 80208-0132
(303) 871-2036

Dr. Margaret E. Whitt, Director of Freshman English at Denver, has compiled a list that is not meant "to be conclusive or definitive; it is only suggestive." The authors she says "may very well appear and re-appear on our freshman course syllabi in English-related classes, [but] a rather unknown name is just as likely to appear." Works by the following writers have been taught in Denver's freshman classes:

Aristotle
Arnold, Matthew
Atwood, Margaret
Auden, W. H.
Bambara, Toni Cade
Brontë, Charlotte
Byron, Lord
Capote, Truman
Cather, Willa
Chopin, Kate
Coleridge, Samuel Taylor
Conrad, Joseph
Dickinson, Emily
Dinesen, Isak
Eliot, T. S.
Emerson, Ralph Waldo
Faulkner, William
Fitzgerald, F. Scott
Freud, Sigmund
Frost, Robert
García Márquez, Gabriel
Hawthorne, Nathaniel
Hemingway, Ernest
Henley, Beth
Hughes, Langston
Hurston, Zora Neale
Ibsen, Henrik
Jackson, Shirley
Joyce, James
Keats, John

King, Martin Luther Jr.
Lawrence, D. H.
LeGuin, Ursula
Miller, Arthur
Milton, John
Morrison, Toni
Munro, Alice
Naylor, Gloria
Oates, Joyce Carol
O'Connor, Flannery
Olsen, Tillie
Plath, Sylvia
Plato
Poe, Edgar Allan
Rich, Adrienne
Robinson, Edwin Arlington
Shakespeare, William
Shelley, Percy Bysshe
Sophocles
Steinbeck, John
Thomas, Dylan
Thoreau, Henry David
Thurber, James
Twain, Mark
Walker, Alice
Welty, Eudora
Wharton, Edith
White, E. B.
Whitman, Walt
Williams, Tennessee

Williams, William Carlos
Woolf, Virginia
Wordsworth, William

Wright, Richard
Yeats, William Butler

University of Florida
Gainesville, FL 32611
(904) 392-1365

In one of the sections of the University of Florida's freshman English composition-literature course, Professor Chris Coates states his objective for the course: "to make [the student] comfortable with forming ideas and assumptions about literature, and with transforming those ideas and assumptions into sophisticated and coherent written arguments." The following are among the anthologies and critical analyses studied in the various sections: **Abcarian** and **Klotz**, eds., *Literature: A Personal Experience*; **Sylvan Barnet**, *A Short Guide to Writing About Literature*; **Biddle** and **Fulwiler**, *Reading, Writing, and Study of Literature*; **R. V. Cassill**, *The Norton Anthology of Short Fiction*; **Donald Hall**, *To Read Literature*; **Alice S. Landy**, *The Heath Introduction to Literature*; **Litzinger & Oates**, eds., *Story: Fictions Past and Present*; **James Moffett** and **K. R. McElheny**, eds., *Points of View*; **Nadell & Langan**, *The Macmillan Reader*; **Edgar V. Roberts**, *Writing Themes About Literature: Brief 6th ed.*; **E. B. White**, *Elements of Style*.
Other works include:

Agee, James	*A Death in the Family*
Albee, Edward	*The Zoo Story*
Anderson, Sherwood	"Unlighted Lamps," "The Egg"
Baldwin, James	"Sonny's Blues"
Bellow, Saul	*The Adventures of Augie March;* "A Father to Be "
Bierce, Ambrose	"Jupiter Doke, Brigadier General"
Calvino, Italo	*If on a Winter's Night a Traveler*
Capote, Truman	"My Side of the Matter"
Carter, Angela	*Nights at the Circus*
Cheever, John	"The Five-Forty-Eight"
Chekov, Anton	"The Lady with the Dog"
Chopin, Kate	*The Awakening*
Crane, Stephen	"The Open Boat"
Duras, Marguerite	*The Lover*
Erdrich, Louise	*The Beet Queen*
Faulkner, William	*Go Down, Moses;* "A Rose for Emily"
Fitzgerald, F. Scott	*The Great Gatsby,* "Babylon Revisited"
Frost, Robert	"Birches"
García Márquez, Gabriel	"A Very Old Man with Enormous Wings"

Gardner, John	*Grendel*
Gibbons, Kaye	*Ellen Foster*
Hawthorne, Nathaniel	"Young Goodman Brown"
Hayden, Robert	"Those Winter Sundays"
Heinemann, Larry	*Paco's Story*
Hemingway, Ernest	"The Short Happy Life of Francis Macomber"
Henley, Beth	*Crimes of the Heart*
Jackson, Shirley	"The Lottery"
Joyce, James	"Araby"
Justice, Donald	*Selected Poems of Donald Justice*
Keats, John	"Ode on a Grecian Urn," "When I Have Fears"
Kennedy, William	*Ironweed*
Kafka, Franz	"The Hunger Artist"
Lawrence, D. H.	"The Horse Dealer's Daughter," "The Rocking Horse Winner," "Piano"
Macleish, Archibald	"Ars Poetica"
Malamud, Bernard	"The Prison"
Mamet, David	*American Buffalo*
Mansfield, Katherine	"Her First Ball"
Marvell, Andrew	"To His Coy Mistress"
McCullers, Carson	"A Tree, A Rock, A Cloud"
McGuane, Thomas	*Something to Be Desired*
McInerney, Jay	*Bright Lights, Big City*
Medoff, Mark	*When You Comin' Back Red Ryder?*
Melville, Herman	"Bartleby the Scrivener"
Moffett, James	"The Suicides of Private Greaves"
Morrison, Toni	*Beloved; Sula; Song of Solomon*
O'Connor, Flannery	"The Artificial Nigger," "A Good Man is Hard to Find," "Good Country People"
Plath, Sylvia	"Metaphors"
Poe, Edgar Allan	"The Cask of Amontillado," "The Fall of the House of Usher"
Porter, Katherine Anne	"Flowering Judas"
Pound, Ezra	"In a Station of the Metro"
Powell, Padgett	*Edisto*
Rich, Adrienne	"Diving into the Wreck"
Roethke, Theodore	"My Papa's Waltz"
Salinger, J. D.	*The Catcher in the Rye*
Shakespeare, William	*King Lear*
Shaw, Irwin	*Act of Faith*
Shepard, Sam	*Buried Child*
Spender, Stephen	"Irish Airman"
Steinbeck, John	*East of Eden;* "Johnny Bear"
Stock, Gregory	*The Book of Questions*
Thomas, Dylan	"Patricia, Edith, and Arnold"
Twain, Mark	*The Adventures of Huckleberry Finn*
Updike, John	"A and P"

| Welty, Eudora | "Powerhouse," "Why I Live at the P.O." |
| Wordsworth, William | "Westminster Bridge" |

University of Indianapolis
1400 East Hanna Avenue
Indianapolis, IN 46227
(317) 788-3216

According to Dr. Charlotte Templin, English Department chair, "the University of Indianapolis booklist, which is offered to students preparing for college and to readers of all ages, includes works modern and ancient, short and long. The list, a compilation of works selected by seven faculty members, represents a variety of tastes. We did not intend this booklist to include all significant books printed in English, nor do we expect students to read every work listed. In Robert Herrick's words, 'If thou dislik'st the piece thou light'st on first,' select another."

CLASSICS

	Bible: Genesis, Exodus, Joshua, Judges, Ruth, Esther, Mark, Acts, Romans, I & II Corinthians
Chaucer, Geoffrey	*Canterbury Tales*
Grimm, Jakob and Wilhelm	*Fairy Tales*
Homer	*The Iliad and The Odyssey*
Malory, Sir Thomas	*Morte d'Arthur*

DRAMA

	Everyman
Aristophanes	*Lysistrata*
Beckett, Samuel	*Waiting for Godot*
Fugard, Athol	*"Master Harold" . . . and the Boys*
Ibsen, Henrik	*A Doll's House*
Hansberry, Lorraine	*A Raisin in the Sun*
Jonson, Ben	*Volpone*
Miller, Arthur	*Death of a Salesman*
Shakespeare, William	*Midsummer Night's Dream; Hamlet*
Sophocles	*Oedipus Rex*
Wilde, Oscar	*The Importance of Being Earnest*

Wilder, Thornton	*Our Town*
Williams, Tennessee	*The Glass Menagerie*

FICTION

Achebe, Chinua	*Things Fall Apart*
Anderson, Sherwood	*Winesburg, Ohio*
Arnow, Harriet	*The Dollmaker*
Atwood, Margaret	*The Handmaid's Tale*
Austen, Jane	*Pride and Prejudice*
Baldwin, James	*Go Tell It on the Mountain; Blues for Mister Charlie*
Brontë, Charlotte	*Jane Eyre*
Brontë, Emily	*Wuthering Heights*
Cather, Willa	*My Antonia*
Chopin, Kate	*The Awakening*
Conrad, Joseph	*Heart of Darkness*
Crane, Stephen	*The Red Badge of Courage*
Dickens, Charles	*Great Expectations*
Dostoevski, Feodor	*Crime and Punishment*
Dumas, Alexandre	*The Count of Monte Cristo*
Eliot, George	*The Mill on the Floss*
Ellison, Ralph	*Invisible Man*
Faulkner, William	"Barn Burning," "The Bear"
Fitzgerald, F. Scott	*The Great Gatsby*
Flaubert, Gustave	*Madame Bovary*
Frank, Anne	*The Diary of Anne Frank*
Gaines, Ernest	*The Autobiography of Miss Jane Pittman*
Gardiner, Nadine	*My Son's Story*
Golding, William	*Lord of the Flies*
Hawthorne, Nathaniel	*The House of the Seven Gables*
Hemingway, Ernest	*The Old Man and the Sea*
Hugo, Victor	*Lés Misérables; Notre Dame de Paris*
Hurston, Zora Neale	*Their Eyes Were Watching God*
Huxley, Aldous	*Brave New World*
James, Henry	*The Portrait of a Lady*
Knowles, John	*A Separate Peace*
Lee, Harper	*To Kill a Mockingbird*
Lewis, Sinclair	*Babbitt*
London, Jack	*The Sea Wolf*
Malamud, Bernard	*The Assistant*
Mason, Bobbie Ann	*Shiloh and Other Stories*
Maugham, W. Somerset	*Of Human Bondage*
McCullers, Carson	*The Heart Is a Lonely Hunter*
Morrison, Toni	*The Bluest Eye; Song of Solomon*
Munro, Alice	*Lives of Girls and Women*
Naylor, Gloria	*The Women of Brewster Place*
Orwell, George	*Animal Farm; 1984*
O'Connor, Flannery	"A Good Man Is Hard to Find," "Everything That Rises Must Converge"

Plath, Sylvia	*The Bell Jar*
Poe, Edgar Allan	*Complete Tales and Poems*
Porter, William Sydney	*Tales of O. Henry*
Rawlings, Marjorie Kinnan	*The Yearling*
Remarque, Erich Maria	*All Quiet on the Western Front*
Salinger, J. D.	*The Catcher in the Rye*
Shange, Ntozake	*Betsy Brown*
Silko, Leslie	*Ceremony*
Solzhenitsyn, Aleksandr	*One Day in the Life of Ivan Denisovich*
Spark, Muriel	*The Prime of Miss Jean Brodie*
Steinbeck, John	*The Grapes of Wrath;The Red Pony*
Stowe, Harriet	*Uncle Tom's Cabin*
Tolkien, J. R. R.	*The Hobbit; The Lord of the Rings*
Twain, Mark	*Pudd'nhead Wilson; The Adventures of Huckleberry Finn*
Voltaire	*Candide*
Vonnegut, Kurt	*Slaughterhouse Five*
Walker, Alice	*The Color Purple*
Wells, H. G.	*The War of the Worlds*
Welty, Eudora	"Petrified Man," "The Wide Net," "Why I Live at a P.O."
Wharton, Edith	*The House of Mirth*
Wolfe, Thomas	*Look Homeward, Angel*
Wright, Richard	*Native Son*

NONFICTION

Angelou, Maya	*I Know Why the Caged Bird Sings*
Dillard, Annie	*Pilgrim at Tinker Creek*
Earhart, Amelia	*For the Fun of It*
Fenelon, Fania	*Playing for Time*
Frank, Anne	*The Diary of Anne Frank*
Hamilton, Edith	*Greek Mythology*
Hellman, Lillian	*Pentimento*
Kahn, Roger	*The Boys of Summer*
Shirer, William	*The Rise and Fall of the Third Reich*
Thoreau, Henry David	*Walden*
Tuchman, Barbara	*The Guns of August*
Twin, Stephanie, ed.	*Out of the Bleachers: Writing on Women and Sports*
Wright, Richard	*Black Boy*
Welty, Eudora	*One Writer's Beginnings*

POETRY

The poetry of **William Blake; Gwendolyn Brooks; George Gordon; Lord Byron; e.e. cummings; Emily Dickinson; T. S. Eliot; Robert Frost; Allen Ginsberg; Thomas Hardy; H. D. (Hilda Doolittle); Seamus Heaney; Langston Hughes; Ted Hughes; Maxine Kumin; Claude McKay; Edna St. Vincent Millay; Ogden Nash; Pablo Neruda; Mary Oliver; Sylvia Plath; Adrienne Rich;**

Rainer Maria Rilke; Theodore Roethke; Muriel Rukeyser; Anne Sexton; Wallace Stevens; Alfred, Lord Tennyson; Walt Whitman; William Wordsworth; James Wright; William B. Yeats

University of Iowa
Calvin Hall
Iowa City, IA 52242
(319) 335-3847

Freshmen at the University of Iowa must take a rhetoric course. After that, they may choose from courses offered in The General Education in Literature Program. The following are two courses from a recent publication of "Course Descriptions and Readings" for that program. The first is a prerequisite for the other fourteen courses in the program. Students may test out of it as indicated by the instructions at the end of the Iowa listings.

THE INTERPRETATION OF LITERATURE

The purpose of this course is "to introduce students to a wide range of literature; we want students to improve their ability to read, to write about, and to discuss literary texts with confidence and enjoyment. The course explores a variety of literary forms, in part to acquaint students with major works in different genres, in part to serve as a background for and anticipation of the more specialized elective courses. The course concentrates on poetry, drama, and prose fiction, although other forms (e.g., film, autobiography, essay) might be included."

Anthologies and books about critical analyses for each section are selected from the following: **C. E. Bain**, et al., *Norton Introduction to Literature*; **David Bergman** and **David Epstein**, *Heath Guide to Poetry*; **R. V. Cassill**, *Norton Anthology of Short Fiction*; **John J. Clayton**, *Heath Introduction to Fiction*; **Joseph DeRoche**, ed., *Heath Introduction to Poetry*; **Daniel F. Howard**, ed., *The Modern Tradition*; **Paul Hunter**, ed., *Norton Introduction to Poetry*; **X. J. Kennedy**, ed., *Introduction to Poetry*; **Alton C. Morris**, ed., *Imaginative Literature*; **Robert Scholes**, et al., *Elements of Literature*, 3rd ed. Other book choices are:

Achebe, Chinua	*Things Fall Apart*
Austen, Jane	*Pride and Prejudice*
Beckett, Samuel	*Waiting for Godot*
Brecht, Bertolt	*The Caucasian Chalk Circle*
Camus, Albert	*The Stranger*

Chekhov, Anton	*The Major Plays*
Chopin, Kate	*The Awakening*
Dickens, Charles	*Hard Times*
Fitzgerald, F. Scott	*The Great Gatsby*
Flaubert, Gustave	*Madame Bovary*
García Márquez, Gabriel	*One Hundred Years of Solitude*
Ibsen, Henrik	*Four Major Plays*, Vol. 1
Kesey, Ken	*One Flew Over the Cuckoo's Nest*
Miller, Arthur	*Death of a Salesman*
Morrison, Toni	*Sula*
Reinert & Arnott, eds.	*Thirteen Plays*
Shaffer, Peter	*Amadeus; Equus*
Shakespeare, William	*Hamlet; King Lear; Macbeth; A Mid-summer Night's Dream; Othello*
Shaw, George Bernard	*Pygmalion*
Steinbeck, John	*The Grapes of Wrath*
Stoppard, Tom	*Rosencrantz and Guildenstern Are Dead*
Walker, Alice	*The Color Purple*
Wilde, Oscar	*The Importance of Being Earnest*
Williams, Tennessee	*Cat on a Hot Tin Roof*
Woolf, Virginia	*Mrs. Dalloway*

BIBLICAL AND CLASSICAL LITERATURE

The course description states that "many of the literary, ethical, and intellectual values of Western civilization derive from biblical, Greek, and Roman literature. This course examines the greatness of the literatures, *as literature*, and the richness of its ideas about the human condition. Every class includes, at least, readings from the Bible, dialogues of Plato, classical drama, lyrical poetry, and an epic or two. Under study will be myth, folk-tale, history, biography, tragedy, epic, oratory, epistle, and lyric. Students have the opportunity to extend their skill in speaking, writing, and literary analysis."

Books for each section are selected from the following list:

	Bible
	Epic of Gilgamesh
Aeschylus	*The Oresteia* (Fagles, tr.)
Aristophanes	*Lysistrata; The Complete Plays*
Euripides	*Euripides* (Grene, tr.)
Grene, ed.	*Greek Tragedies*, Vol. 1
Homer	*The Iliad; The Odyssey*
Ovid	*Metamorphoses*
Plato	*The Last Days of Socrates; The Symposium*
Sophocles	*Sophocles*, Vol. 1 (Grene, tr.)
Vergil	*The Aeneid*

THE INTERPRETATION OF LITERATURE
CREDIT BY EXAMINATION

Upon application to the Liberal Arts Office of Academic Programs or the Evaluation and Examination Service, students may take CLEP (College-Level Examination Program) exams for exemption from the College's 8G:1 [The Interpretation of Literature] requirement. For especially high performance, students may receive 3 semester hours of academic credit as well as exemption.

The exam package for 8G:1 is:

1. "The Analysis and Interpretation of Literature"—a 90-minute, objective examination, made and machine-graded by Educational Testing Service in Princeton, New Jersey
2. "The Essay Exam in the Analysis and Interpretation of Literature"—a 90-minute written exam evaluated by the General Education in Literature Program staff.

University of Kansas
126 Strong Hall
Lawrence, KS 66045-0215
(913) 864-3911

According to Dr. Albert B. Cook, Coordinator of Undergraduate Studies, University of Kansas, the following list of recommended reading is sent on request to teachers and to their college-preparatory students for some "systematic sampling." Divided into two parts, the list was compiled from suggestions by the Kansas faculty. It is preceded by the following caveats:

Recommended Reading

"They're on'y three books in th' wurruld worth readin',—Shakespeare, th' Bible, an' Mike Ahearn's histhry iv Chicago." —Mr. Dooley

1. This is not meant to be a magic list that will guarantee success at the University of Kansas, or anywhere else.

2. This is not intended to be a definitive list. We are not saying that a reading of these works and nothing else will make a student an educated person.

3. This list is not meant to have universal appeal. Most students will find at least some of it hard going. They may have to put a book down and come back to it later—sometimes much later, and just possibly not at all! Some of these books may be read several times, and all of them

improve with rereading. But the point is, that the list will affect each interested student differently.

4. Nothing will replace the entire, unabridged work. The substitution of *Reader's Digest* abridgements or of outlines like *Cliff's Notes* should be treated as abominations. Still, many paperback editions of entire works are widely available with helpful notes and introductions.

5. Students should be encouraged to pursue reading interests of their own, whether or not these interests are based on this list. This wider reading can include newspapers, magazines, current bestsellers, and "light summer reading." The fact is that almost all young people do not read nearly enough, maybe because outside of English classes it is not encouraged either by precept or example.

6. Our experience is that young people are woefully ignorant of the specific contents of the Bible, of classical mythology (both a fertile source of literary allusion), of American history, and even of contemporary culture, broadly interpreted, apart from television shows and popular music lyrics. We don't pretend to know why this is so, or how to reverse this trend, but any efforts you can exert to alter this state of affairs would be much appreciated.

With these qualifications in mind, then, we pass these recommended works on to you. . . ."

WORKS MOST FREQUENTLY MENTIONED:

The Bible: The so-called "King James Version" is the traditional "literary" one, but such modern translations as the Revised Standard Version, the New English Bible, or the Jerusalem Bible are certainly acceptable. Specific books of the Bible mentioned are Genesis, Exodus, Judges, I & II Samuel, Job, Jonah, selected Psalms, and the Gospels, particularly Mark.

A collection or compendium of *Classical Mythology*: **Edith Hamilton's** *Mythology* or **Thomas Keightley's** collections are both good. **Robert Graves'** collection makes exciting reading, but his interpretations have been questioned.

Brontë, Charlotte	*Jane Eyre* or
Brontë, Emily	*Wuthering Heights*
Dickens, Charles	A novel—probably *David Copperfield* or *Great Expectations*—and again the student is warned away from abridgements.
Fitzgerald, F. Scott	*The Great Gatsby* (also short stories)
Hardy, Thomas	A novel, probably *Far from the Madding Crowd, Return of the Native,* or *Tess of the D'Urbervilles*
Hawthorne, Nathaniel	*The Scarlet Letter* (also short stories)
Hemingway, Ernest	*A Farewell to Arms; The Old Man and the Sea; The Sun Also Rises* (also short stories)

Homer	*The Iliad* and *The Odyssey* (Robert Fitzgerald or Richmond Lattimore, tr.)
Shakespeare, William	*As You Like It; Hamlet; Henry IV, Part I; Julius Caesar; King Lear; Macbeth; The Merchant of Venice; A Midsummer Night's Dream; Othello; Richard II; Romeo and Juliet; The Tempest; Twelfth Night* (Students should note particularly that we recommend here the entire play, in each instance, not a cut version or abridgement.)
Sophocles	*Antigone; Oedipus Rex; Oedipus at Colonus* (Robert Fitzgerald, tr.)
Thoreau, Henry David	*Walden* (also "Civil Disobedience")
Twain, Mark	*The Adventures of Huckleberry Finn* (also *The Adventures of Tom Sawyer*, if you haven't already read it)

OTHER WORKS MENTIONED

PRE-HISTORY AND CLASSICAL ANTIQUITY

	The Arabian Nights (especially "Sinbad," "Ali Baba," "Aladdin")
Aeschylus	Selected plays
Durant, Will	*The Story of Philosophy* or **Zeller's** *Outline of the History of Greek Philosophy*
Euripides	Selected plays
Grimm, Jakob and Wilhelm	*Fairy Tales* or **Keightley's** *Fairy Mythology*
Vergil	*The Aeneid* (Robert Fitzgerald or Allen Mandelbaum, tr.)

MIDDLE AGES AND RENAISSANCE

Dante	*The Divine Comedy,* especially *The Inferno* (John Ciardi or Allen Mandelbaum, tr.)
Cervantes, Don Miguel de	*Don Quixote* (Samuel Putnam, tr.)
Chaucer, Geoffrey	*Canterbury Tales* (The Middle English text makes for difficult reading, but most college-level editions have handy and helpful glossaries and notes)
Jonson, Ben	*The Alchemist; Volpone*
Marlowe, Christopher	*Doctor Faustus*
Milton, John	*Areopagitica; Paradise Lost* (Book I for starters); Selected sonnets

Spenser, Edmund	*The Faerie Queene,* Book I (inclusion questioned by some)
Webster, John	*The Duchess of Malfi*

SEVENTEENTH AND EIGHTEENTH CENTURIES

Blake, William	*Songs of Innocence and Experience*
Bunyan, John	*The Pilgrim's Progress,* Book I
Defoe, Daniel	A novel, probably *Moll Flanders* or *Robinson Crusoe*
Fielding, Henry	A novel, probably *Tom Jones*
Franklin, Benjamin	*Autobiography*

Some authentic historical documents, like **Lewis and Clark**'s *Journals,* **Francis Parkman**, etc. A close reading of the Declaration of Independence, the Constitution, and the Bill of Rights wouldn't hurt, either.

NINETEENTH CENTURY

Austen, Jane	A novel, probably *Pride and Prejudice*
Carlyle, Thomas	*Heroes and Hero Worship*
Dickinson, Emily	The *Final Harvest* poems
Dostoevski, Feodor	*Crime and Punishment* (David Magarshack, tr.) and/or **Leo Tolstoy,** *War and Peace* (Maudes, tr.). The latter, though a "blockbuster," is probably more manageable than the former.
Eliot, George	A novel, probably *Middlemarch* or *Adam Bede* (several professors warned against including *Silas Marner)*
Emerson, Ralph Waldo	*Essays* (especially "The American Scholar" and "Self-Reliance")
Flaubert, Gustave	*Madame Bovary* (Francis Steegmuller, tr.)
Keats, John	Selected poetry, especially "Eve of St. Agnes," the odes, the sonnets. One professor suggested that **George Gordon, Lord Byron,** being a perennial adolescent, is particulary good for high school and college students.
Melville, Herman	*Moby-Dick*
Scott, Sir Walter	*Ivanhoe* (or better, one of the Scottish novels, such as *The Heart of Midlothian)*
Stowe, Harriet Beecher	*Uncle Tom's Cabin* (everyone "remembers" the "Tom Show," but few have read the novel. It is far greater than its reputation.)
Whitman, Walt	*Leaves of Grass*

Wordsworth, William	Selected poetry (especially "Ode: Intimations of Immortality" and such obvious classics)

TWENTIETH CENTURY AND MODERN TIMES

Agee, James	*Let Us Now Praise Famous Men*
Anderson, Kurt	*The Real Thing*
Bierce, Ambrose	*The Devil's Dictionary;* also short stories
Berger, Thomas	*Little Big Man*
Cather, Willa	*My Antonia; O Pioneers!*
Conrad, Joseph	*Lord Jim; The Nigger of the "Narcissus"*
Cormier, Robert	*The Chocolate War*
Dinesen, Isak	*Out of Africa* (perhaps one should be careful about the influence of the film upon one's understanding of the book)
Faulkner, William	*Intruder in the Dust; The Unvanquished*
Frost, Robert	Selected poetry
Gage, Nicholas	*Eleni*
Golding, William	*Lord of the Flies*
Graves, Robert	*I, Claudius*
Grubb, David	*The Night of the Hunter*
Heller, Joseph	*Catch-22*
Hughes, Langston	*Not Without Laughter* or **Gordon Parks,** *The Learning Tree,* two autobiographical novels about growing up black in Kansas
Kafka, Franz	Selected short stories
Joyce, James	*Dubliners; A Portrait of the Artist as a Young Man*
McCullers, Carson	*The Member of the Wedding;* short stories
Meltzer, Milton	Any books (This is a good place to mention outstanding books for adolescents by such writers as **S. E. Hinton.**)
Paton, Alan	*Cry, the Beloved Country*
Pirsig, Robert	*Zen and the Art of Motorcycle Maintenance*
Salinger, J. D.	*The Catcher in the Rye*
Wharton, Edith	*The Age of Innocence; The House of Mirth*
White, E. B.	*Charlotte's Web;* also selected essays
Wilder, Thornton	*The Bridge of San Luis Rey; Heaven's My Destination; The Ides of March*
Woolf, Virginia	*A Room of One's Own; To the Lighthouse*
Wright, Richard	*Native Son*

High school students don't read nearly enough plays, beyond the mandatory Shakespeare. (Students should likewise make use of every opportunity to see significant dramas performed, either on the stage or on television.) We recommmend in particular such contemporary playwrights as:

Inge, William	*Bus Stop* or *Come Back, Little Sheba*
Miller, Arthur	*Death of a Salesman*
O'Neill, Eugene	*Desire under the Elms; The Hairy Ape;* the *S. S. Glencairn* plays
Saroyan, William	*The Time of Your Life*
Williams, Tennessee	*The Glass Menagerie* or *A Streetcar Named Desire*
Wilder, Thornton	*The Skin of Our Teeth*

MISCELLANEOUS

A collection of contemporary short stories: in addition to such authors as **Fitzgerald** or **Hemingway**, already mentioned before, the student should be aware of significant contemporary writers who specialized in this genre—**John Cheever, Frank O'Conner, Flannery O'Connor, Tillie Olsen, John Updike,** to name only a few.

Some good modern essays: even a regular reading of *Time* or *Newsweek*—or the editorial and op-ed columns of a daily newspaper—would be useful. Particularly recommended is *The Penguin Book of Contemporary American Essays* (Maureen Howard, ed.)

Allen, Woody	*Getting Even*
Edel, Leon	*Writing Lives*
Fischer, Louis	*Life of Mahatma Gandhi*
Hayakawa, S. I.	*Language in Thought and Action*
Potter, Stephen	*The Complete Upmanship*
Strunk and White	*Elements of Style* (but take the usage dicta with a grain of salt)
Wodehouse, P. G.	Any of the Jeeves novels or the Mr. Mulliner stories.

University of Kentucky
100 Funkhouser Building
Lexington, KY 40506-0054
(606) 257-7148

According to Dr. William R. Campbell, Director of the Writing Program, the Department of English has "no list of readings suggested for entering students. . . . No syllabus here is based on the assumption that certain works are already in the background of entering students, even the Bible." The content of the entrance level courses varies, but UK freshmen study a novel in their required writing course. Recently-assigned novels have included:

Chopin, Kate	*The Awakening*
Fitzgerald, F. Scott	*The Great Gatsby*
Orwell, George	*Animal Farm*
Steinbeck, John	*Of Mice and Men*
Twain, Mark	*The Adventures of Huckleberry Finn*

University of Louisville
2211 South Brook Street
Louisville, KY 40292
(502) 588-6166

According to Professor Lucy M. Freibert, Director of Undergraduate English at the University of Louisville, the department advises its undergraduates to "review the *Norton Anthology of English Literature*, and the *Norton Anthology of American Literature*, and to study **Hugh Holman**, *A Handbook to Literature*." In the list that follows, all the authors but not all the specific works have been included from the university's Undergraduate Reading List.

I. CLASSICAL BACKGROUNDS

Aeschylus	*Agamemnon*
Aristotle	*The Poetics*
Euripides	*Medea*
Homer	*The Iliad* and *The Odyssey* (E. V. Rieu, tr.)
Longinus	"On the Sublime"
Sappho	Selected poems and fragments
Sophocles	*Oedipus Rex, Antigone*
Vergil	*The Aeneid*

II. ENGLISH LITERATURE

OLD ENGLISH

Battle of Maldon (selections in *Norton Anthology of English Literature*)
Beowulf
The Dream of the Rood
The Seafarer (C. W. Kennedy, tr.)
The Wanderer

MIDDLE ENGLISH

	Ballads
	The Cloud of Unknowing (selections)
	Everyman
	Middle English Lyrics
Langland, William	*Piers Plowman* (Selections in *Norton Anthology of English Literature*)
	The Second Shepherd's Play
	Sir Gawain and the Green Knight (James L. Rosenberg, tr.)
Chaucer, Geoffrey	*Canterbury Tales* (except tales of the Cook, the Squire, the Physician, the Shipman, Melibee, the Monk, the Second Nun, and the Manciple)
Julian Of Norwich	*Revelations of Divine Love*
Kempe, Margery	*The Book of Margery Kempe* (Selections in *Norton Anthology of English Literature*)
Malory, Thomas	*Le Morte d'Arthur*, Book XXI

RENAISSANCE

Bacon, Francis	*Essays*
Browne, Thomas	*Religion Medici*, first section
Earle, John	*Micro-Cosmographie;* poetry
Hooker, Richard	*Of The Laws of Ecclesiastical Polity*, Book I, Sections 1–8
Jonson, Ben	*The Alchemist; Volpone;* poetry
Lyly, John	*Euphues*—up to mention of Philautus
Marlowe, Christopher	*Doctor Faustus; Tamburlaine the Great*, Part I
Milton, John	"Lycidas," *Paradise Lost*, Books I–V, IX, X, XIII; *Samson Agonistes; Sonnets:* "Avenge, O Lord, Thy Slaughtered Saints," "Cromwell, our Chief of Men," "Cyriak, this three year's day," "How soon hath time," "Lady, that in the prime of earliest youth," "On the Morning of Christ's Nativity," "When I consider how my light is spent"
More, Thomas	*Utopia*, Edward Surtz, tr.
Shakespeare, William	*Antony and Cleopatra; As You Like It; Hamlet; Henry IV*, Parts 1 & 2; *Henry V; Julius Caesar; Othello; Richard II; Richard III; The Tempest; Twelfth Night; The Winter's Tale*

Spenser, Edmund	*Amoretti,* selected sonnets; *The Faerie Queene;* "Epithalamion"; Letter to Raleigh; *Shepheardes Calender:* "April," "October," "November"

And the poetry of **Richard Crashaw, John Donne, George Herbert, Robert Herrick, Andrew Marvell, Philip Sidney, Thomas Wyatt,** and **H. H. Surrey.**

RESTORATION AND EIGHTEENTH CENTURY

Addison and **Steele**	*The Spectator*
Austen, Jane	*Emma* or *Pride and Prejudice*
Blake, William	*Songs of Innocence* and *Songs of Experience* (Selections)
Boswell, James	*The Life of Samuel Johnson* (from May 16, 1763)
Congreve, William	*The Way of the World*
Cowper, William	*Retirement*
Crabbe, George	*The Village*
Dryden, John	*Absalom and Achitophel; All for Love; The Hind and the Panther; Mac-Flecknoe;* "Preface to the Fables"; *Religio Laici*
Goldsmith, Oliver	*The Deserted Village*
Johnson, Samuel	*The Idler* (16, 61); *Life of Addison; The Rambler* (4, 25); *Rasselas; The Vanity of Human Wishes*
Pope, Alexander	*The Dunciad (IV);* "An Essay on Man"; "The Rape of the Lock"; *Windsor Forest;* and other selections
Sheridan, Richard B.	*The School for Scandal*
Swift, Jonathan	"An Argument Against Abolishing Christianity"; "A Description of the Morning"; *Gulliver's Travels;* "A Modest Proposal"
Walpole, Horace	*The Castle of Otranto*
Wollstonecraft, Mary	*Vindication of the Rights of Women*
Wycherley, William	*The Plain Dealer*

And the poets **Robert Burns** and **Thomas Gray.**

EARLY NINETEENTH CENTURY

Hazlitt, William	"On Familiar Style"
Lamb, Charles	"Old China"
Peacock, Raymond L.	*Nightmare Abbey*
Scott, Sir Walter	*Quentin Durward* or *Waverley*
Shelley, Mary	*Frankenstein*

And the poets **George Gordon, Lord Byron, Samuel Taylor Coleridge, John Keats, Percy Bysshe Shelley, William Wordsworth.**

VICTORIAN PERIOD

Arnold, Matthew	*Culture and Anarchy; The Function of Criticism at the Present Time;* poetry
Brontë, Charlotte	*Jane Eyre*
Brontë, Emily	*Wuthering Heights*
Butler, Samuel	*The Way of All Flesh*
Carlyle, Thomas	*Heroes and Hero-Worship,* I; *Past and Present,* II, III; *Sartor Resartus,* II
Dickens, Charles	*David Copperfield*
Eliot, George	*Adam Bede* or *Middlemarch* or *The Mill on the Floss*
Hardy, Thomas	*The Return of the Native*
Huxley, Thomas	*Science and Culture*
Meredith, George	*The Egoist*
Mill, John Stuart	*On Liberty*
Newman, Cardinal J. H.	*The Idea of a University*
Pater, Walter	*The Renaissance* (Conclusion)
Stevenson, Robert L.	*The Master of Ballantrae*
Thackeray, Wm. Makepeace	*Vanity Fair*
Wilde, Oscar	*The Importance of Being Earnest*

And the poets **Robert Browning, Gerard Manley Hopkins, Alfred, Lord Tennyson.**

THE MODERN PERIOD, 1890 TO THE PRESENT

Beckett, Samuel	*Waiting for Godot*
Conrad, Joseph	*Heart of Darkness* or *Lord Jim*
Eliot, T. S.	*Burnt Norton;* "Hamlet and His Problems"; "The Love Song of J. Alfred Prufrock"; "Preludes"; "Tradition and the Individual Talent"; "The Waste Land"
Forster, E. M.	*A Passage to India*
Greene, Graham	*The Power and the Glory*
Joyce, James	*Dubliners; A Portrait of the Artist as a Young Man; Ulysses*
Lawrence, D. H.	"Bavarian Gentians," "The Horse Dealer's Daughter," "Piano," "Snake"; *Sons and Lovers* or *Women in Love*
Mansfield, Katherine	"The Garden Party," "Her First Ball"
Pinter, Harold	*The Birthday Party* or *Caretaker* or *Homecoming*
Shaw, George Bernard	*Candida;* Preface to *Back to Methuselah*
Synge, J. M.	*The Playboy of the Western World*
Thomas, Dylan	*Fern Hill*
Waugh, Evelyn	*A Handful of Dust*
Woolf, Virginia	*To the Lighthouse*

And selected poetry from **W. H. Auden, Philip Larkin, John Masefield, Wilfred Owen, William Butler Yeats.**

III. AMERICAN LITERATURE

Adams, Henry	*The Education of Henry Adams,* Chs. XXV, LIII; *Mont-Saint-Michel and Chartres,* Ch. VI
Anderson, Sherwood	*Winesburg, Ohio* (selections)
Ashbery, John	"Self-Portrait on a Convex Mirror"
Baldwin, James	*Go Tell It on the Mountain*
Barth, John	"The Literature of Exhaustion"; Selected short stories
Bellow, Saul	*Seize the Day*
Brooks, Gwendolyn	*Maud Martha* (optional); Selected poems
Chopin, Kate	*The Awakening*
Cooper, James Fenimore	*The Pioneers* or *The Last of the Mohicans*
Crane, Hart	*The Bridge*
Crane, Stephen	*Maggie;* "The Open Boat"; *The Red Badge of Courage*
Douglass, Frederick	*Narrative of the Life of Frederick Douglass*
Dreiser, Theodore	*Jennie Gearhardt* or *Sister Carrie;* "Nigger Jeff"
Edwards, Jonathan	*Personal Narrative;* "Sinners in the Hands of an Angry God"
Emerson, Ralph Waldo	Essays—"The American Scholar," "Nature," "Self-Reliance"; Selected Poems
Faulkner, William	"The Bear"; *Light in August; Absalom Absalom* or *As I Lay Dying* or *The Sound and the Fury*
Fitzgerald, F. Scott	*The Great Gatsby*
Franklin, Benjamin	*The Autobiography of Benjamin Franklin,* first 50 pp.
Hawthorne, Nathaniel	Short stories and *The Scarlet Letter*
Hellman, Lillian	*Another Part of the Forest; The Little Foxes*
Hemingway, Ernest	*A Farewell to Arms; The Nick Adams Stories; The Sun Also Rises*
Howells, William Dean	*A Hazard of New Fortunes* or *The Rise of Silas Lapham*
Hurston, Zora Neale	*Their Eyes Were Watching God*
Irving, Washington	"The Legend of Sleepy Hollow"; *Rip Van Winkle*
Jacobs, Harriet A.	*Incidents in the Life of a Slave Girl*
James, Henry	*The American;* "Art of Fiction," "The Beast in the Jungle"; *Daisy Miller*
Lewis, Sinclair	*Main Street*

Mailer, Norman	*Armies of the Night; The Naked and the Dead*
Melville, Herman	*Benito Cereno* or *Billy Budd; Moby-Dick;* Poems—"Art," "The Maldive Shark"
Miller, Arthur	*Death of a Salesman*
Morrison, Toni	*Beloved; The Bluest Eye* or *Sula*
O'Connor, Flannery	"The Artificial Nigger," "Good Country People"
O'Neill, Eugene	*Desire under the Elms; Mourning Becomes Electra*
Paine, Thomas	*Common Sense* (selections); *The Crisis I* (selections in *Norton Anthology of American Literature*)
Poe, Edgar Allan	Critical essay—"The Philosophy of Composition"; selected poems and short stories.
Porter, K. A.	"The Jilting of Granny Weatherall"
Rowlandson, Mary	"Narrative of the Captivity of Mary Rowlandson"
Stein, Gertrude	"Melanctha"
Stowe, Harriet Beecher	*Uncle Tom's Cabin*
Thoreau, Henry	*Civil Disobedience; Walden,* chs. I, II, III
Toomer, Jean	*Cane*
Twain, Mark	"The Celebrated Jumping Frog of Calaveras County," *The Adventures of Huckleberry Finn*
Walker, Alice	*The Color Purple*
Wharton, Edith	*Ethan Frome; The House of Mirth* (optional); "Roman Fever"
Whitman, Walt	"Crossing Brooklyn Ferry"; 1855 Preface to *Leaves of Grass;* "Out of the Cradle Endlessly Rocking"; *Song of Myself* (1855 ed.); "When Lilacs Last in the Dooryard Bloom'd"
Wilder, Thornton	*Our Town*
Williams, Tennessee	*The Glass Menagerie*
Wright, Richard	*Black Boy* or *Native Son*

And selected poems from Anne Bradstreet, Emily Dickinson, Robert Frost, H. D. (Hilde Doolittle), Langston Hughes, Robert Lowell, Audrey Lorde, Adrienne Rich, E. A. Robinson, Wallace Stevens, Edward Taylor, William Carlos Williams.

University of Maine
Chadbourne Hall
Orono, ME 04469-0113
(207) 581-1561

Although the University of Maine at Orono has no specific reading list for the pre-college student, its pamphlet "What to Study in High School" makes several comments about reading and reading skills:

In their recommendations for specific course work in English the authors of the pamphlet state that they expect that "all entering freshmen will be active and critical readers as well as fluent and flexible writers." With regard to reading they stress that the student should have (1) "learned how to participate in literature: how to follow textual clues to genre, tone, and context in reliving poetic, narrative, and dramatic texts," (2) "learned how to read critically both literary and non-literary texts by knowing how to recognize their constituents, and by knowing how to discover a text's assumption and implications," and (3) "studied some classic literary texts in depth and have come to understand those texts as embodying beliefs and values central to human experience."

The pamphlet makes specific recommendations for "a more rigorous college preparatory curriculum," also noting that "the quality of high school course work is more important than its quantity." It stresses "the importance of the senior year in the transition to college-level work [saying] students who choose undemanding courses in the senior year will find difficulty adjusting to work at UMO."

Anyone interested in learning more about Maine's recommendations for pre-college high school study in the fields of English, history, science, mathematics and the arts may obtain the pamphlet from the Office of the Vice President for Academic Affairs, 201 Alumni Hall, University of Maine at Orono, Orono, Maine 04469, telephone 207 581-1547.

University of Maryland, College Park
North Administration Building
College Park, MD 20742
(301) 454-5550

Core reading for students majoring in English at the University of Maryland includes the following required works:

Arnold, Matthew

Beowulf
Sir Gawain and the Green Knight
Selected essays and lyrics

Austen, Jane	*Emma*
Beckett, Samuel	*Waiting for Godot*
Chaucer, Geoffrey	*Canterbury Tales:* General Prologue and Retraction; two tales read in Middle English
Dickens, Charles	*Bleak House*
Dickinson, Emily	Poems
Donne, John	Selected poetry
Dryden, John	"Absalom and Achitophel," Part 1
Eliot, T. S.	*The Waste Land*
Emerson, R. W.	An Essay
Faulkner, William	*As I Lay Dying*
Fielding, Henry	*Tom Jones*
Franklin, Benjamin	*Autobiography*
Hurston, Zora Neale	*Their Eyes Were Watching God*
James, Henry	*The Bostonians* or *The Portrait of a Lady*
Jonson, Ben	"To Penshurst," *Volpone*
Marlowe, Christopher	*Dr. Faustus*
Melville, Herman	Short novels
Milton, John	"Lycidas," *Paradise Lost* (1, 2, 4, 9)
Pope, Alexander	"Essay on Criticism," "The Rape of the Lock"
Spenser, Edmund	*The Faerie Queen* (Book 1 and selections from 2 and 3); "Letter to Raleigh"
Swift, Jonathan	*Gulliver's Travels* (1, 2, 4)
Williams, Tennessee	*A Streetcar Named Desire*
Whitman, Walt	Selected poetry
Woolf, Virginia	*Mrs. Dalloway*
Wordsworth, William	Selected poetry

University of Michigan
1220 Student Activities Building
Ann Arbor, MI 48109-1316
(313) 764-7433

Students in the University of Michigan's Undergraduate English Association advise pre-college students, especially those planning a concentration in English, to have a knowledge of the Bible and of Greek mythology, "for many concepts and plots throughout literature are drawn from these sources." They add, "exposure to some works by **Shakespeare** and a **Dickens** novel would be helpful in developing the necessary skill of analyzing and comparing different authors' styles." And they also suggest high school students "expand their reading beyond the traditional English and American works to include writers from various parts of thc world." The English faculty of the university have compiled an "unofficial reading list," which suggests some of the works they consider important.

Department of English Language and Literature Unofficial Reading List

	Sir Gawain and the Green Knight
Anderson, Sherwood	*Winesburg, Ohio*
Austen, Jane	*Emma; Northanger Abbey; Pride and Prejudice*
Baldwin, James	*Notes of a Native Son*
Barth, John	Selections
Beckett, Samuel	*Waiting for Godot*
Behn, Aphra	*Oroonoko, or The Royal Slave*
Brontë, Charlotte	*Jane Eyre*
Chaucer, Geoffrey	*Canterbury Tales*
Congreve, William	Plays
Conrad, Joseph	*Heart of Darkness*
Defoe, Daniel	*The Fortunate Mistress* or *Roxanna*
Dickens, Charles	*Great Expectations; Hard Times*
Dickinson, Emily	Poems and Letters
Dryden, John	*All for Love*
Eliot, T. S.	*The Waste Land and Other Poems*
Faulkner, William	*As I Lay Dying;* "The Bear"; *Go Down Moses*
Fielding, Henry	*Joseph Andrews; Tom Jones*
Fitzgerald, F. Scott	*The Last Tycoon*
Greene, Graham	*The Quiet American*
Hardy, Thomas	*Jude the Obscure; Tess of the D'Urbervilles*
Hawthorne, Nathaniel	*The Scarlet Letter*
Hemingway, Ernest	*African Stories; In Our Time; The Snows of Kilamanjaro and Other Stories*
James, Henry	*The Turn of the Screw; The Wings of the Dove*
Jonson, Ben	*Bartholomew Fayre; Volpone;* Selected poetry
Joyce, James	*Dubliners*
Kafka, Franz	*In the Penal Colony*
Kyd, Thomas	*The Spanish Tragedy*
Lawrence, D. H.	*Lady Chatterley's Lover*
Mann, Thomas	*Mario the Magician*
Marlowe, Christopher	*Dr. Faustus; Jew of Malta*
Miller, Arthur	Plays
Milton, John	*Paradise Lost*
More, Thomas	*Utopia*
Orwell, George	*Keep the Aspidistra Flying*
Pinter, Harold	Plays

Pynchon, Thomas	*The Crying of Lot 49*
Shakespeare, William	*Richard III*
Shaw, George Bernard	*Pygmalion*
Shelley, Mary	*Frankenstein*
Shepard, Sam	*Seven Plays*
Spenser, Edmund	*The Faerie Queene*
Sterne, Laurence	Selections
Stowe, Harriet	*Uncle Tom's Cabin*
Swift, Jonathan	*Gulliver's Travels* and other writings
Thoreau, Henry	*Civil Disobedience; Walden*
Trollope, Anthony	*The Warden*
Twain, Mark	*A Connecticut Yankee in King Arthur's Court; The Adventures of Huckleberry Finn*
Updike, John	*Rabbit, Run*
Walker, Alice	*The Color Purple*
Webster, John	*The Duchess of Malfi*
West, Nathanael	*Day of the Locust*
Wilde, Oscar	Plays
Wollstonecraft, Mary	Selections
Woolf, Virginia	*A Room of One's Own; To the Lighthouse*
Wordsworth, Dorothy	Selections
Wycherly, William	*The Country Wife*
Yearsley, MacLeod	Selections

And selected poetry from **Matthew Arnold, William Blake, Samuel Taylor Coleridge, John Donne, Ralph Waldo Emerson, Peter Finch, Robert Frost, George Herbert, John Keats, Andrew Marvell, Alexander Pope, Sir Walter Raleigh, Percy Bysshe Shelley, Philip Sidney, Alfred, Lord Tennyson, Walt Whitman, William Wordsworth, Thomas Wyatt,** and **William Butler Yeats.**

University of Minnesota
230 Williamson Hall, 231 Pillsbury Drive S. E.
Minneapolis, MN 55455
(612) 625-5880

The Associate Director of Undergraduate Studies at the University of Minnesota, Beverley M. Atkinson, suggests a list of "fifteen works of literature . . . most important to incoming freshmen" with the following reservations: that it is "by no means the one and only list," because "the content would continue to change according to the point of view of the compiler."

She said the following list is based on the assumptions "one, that the work of literature should be widely representative of both the form in which it is written and the culture; two, that any anthology included should teach the reader methods and techniques for understanding the literature."

	Bible (King James)
Brontë, Charlotte	*Jane Eyre*
Dickens, Charles	*Great Expectations*
Dickinson, Emily	Poems
Dostoevski, Feodor	A novel (or one by Tolstoy)
Drew, Elizabeth	*Understanding Poetry*
Ellmann, Richard and Robert O'Clair	*The Norton Anthology of Modern Poetry*
Ellison, Ralph	*Invisible Man*
Homer	*The Iliad; The Odyssey*
Ibsen, Henrik	*A Doll's House*
Melville, Herman	*Moby-Dick*
Milton, John	"L'Allegro" and "Il Penseroso"
Scholes, Robert, ed.	*Elements of Fiction* (1981)
Shakespeare, William	*As You Like It; Hamlet; King Lear; Richard III*
Synge, John	*Riders to the Sea*
Tolstoy, Leo	A novel (or one by Dostoevski)
Whitman, Walt	*Leaves of Grass*

Dr. Atkinson adds that "unrepresented on this list are many, many authors and many other forms of literature—notably, the essay (**Ralph Waldo Emerson, Henry Thoreau, Virginia Woolf, Joan Didion, E. B. White, James Thurber, Adrienne Rich,** etc.) and the journal or memoir (**Anaïs Nin, Anne Frank, Dorothy Wordsworth, Patricia Hampl, James Boswell,** etc.). Women authors are noticeably few on the list but are more represented in the anthologies."

Dr. Atkinson also has recommended the following two reading lists of American fiction and nonfiction:

AMERICAN FICTION

Baldwin, James	*Go Tell It on the Mountain*
Cather, Willa	*My Antonia*
Faulkner, William	*The Hamlet*
Hawthorne, Nathaniel	*The Scarlet Letter*
Hemingway, Ernest	*In Our Time; The Sun Also Rises*
Kingston, Maxine Hong	*The Woman Warrior*
Melville, Herman	*Moby-Dick*
Petry, Ann	*The Street*
Stowe, Harriet Beecher	*Uncle Tom's Cabin*
Twain, Mark	*The Adventures of Huckleberry Finn*
Wolfe, Thomas	*Look Homeward, Angel*

AMERICAN NONFICTION

Didion, Joan	Essays
Emerson, Ralph Waldo	Essays

Franklin, Benjamin	*Autobiography*
Goodman, Ellen	Essays
James, Henry	*The Art of Fiction*
Thoreau, Henry	*Walden*
Wheatley, Phillis	Essays

In addition to J. J. Clayton, *The Heath Introduction to Fiction* (2nd ed., 1984), the following is a sample of the texts that have been required for University of Minnesota's English 1018: Introduction to Modern Fiction:

Conrad, Joseph	*Heart of Darkness*
Erdrich, Louise	*Love Medicine*
Fitzgerald, F. Scott	*The Great Gatsby*
Hemingway, Ernest	*The Sun Also Rises*
Olsen, Tillie	*Tell Me a Riddle*
Roth, Philip	*Goodbye, Columbus*

University of Montana
Lodge 101
Missoula, MT 59812
(406) 243-6266

Montana offers beginning students a number of introductory courses. Explorations in Literature, for example, is designed to help the student develop "critical thinking about, and strong responses to: the signs, signals, political messages, news stories, essays, poems, fiction, film, TV, and popular song." The texts used in this class are:

McCormick, Waller & Flower	*Reading, Writing, Responding*
Scholes, Robert, et al.	*An Introduction to Literary Language*
Waller, Gary F., et al.	*The Lexington Introduction to Literature*
Scholes, R., et al.	*An Introduction to Literary Language*

In other introductory courses, the following texts are used: **R. V. Cassill**, *Norton Anthology of Short Fiction; Heath Introduction to Drama;* **J. H. Pickering**, *Fiction 100: An Anthology of Short Stories* and

	Sir Gawain and the Green Knight
Donne, John	*John Donne's Poetry*
Dostoevski, Feodor	*The Brothers Karamazov*
Erdrich, Louise	*Love Medicine*
Ferlinghetti, Lawrence	*A Coney Island of the Mind*
Keats, John	Selected Poems
Lawrence, D. H.	Selected Poems
Leslie, Craig	*Winterkill*
Milton, John	*Paradise Lost*

Nims, John	*Western Wind*
Olds, Sharon	*The Dead and the Living*
Oliver, Mary	*American Primitive*
Ransom, J. C., ed.	*Selected Poems of Thomas Hardy*
Robinson, Marilynne	*Housekeeping*
Shakespeare, William	*Julius Caesar*, Sonnets
Stevenson, R. L.	*Dr. Jekyll and Mr. Hyde*

University of Nebraska
Room 106 Administration Building
Lincoln, NE 68588-0415
(402) 472-2023

University of Nebraska's Introduction to Literature course for beginning college students is designed to meet the university's general education humanities requirements. The core list comprises "about 50% of the minimum reading for each section, the rest of the reading being chosen by the individual instructors." The required list is planned to ensure "some reasonable balance among the genres, with attention paid to literature from various times and places, including literature that addressed issues of special concern to women and minorities."

In accordance with "the college standards for general education courses, approximately ten pages of formal writing, upon which the instructor comments in writing, is expected from each student, in addition to any in-class writing, examinations, journals, and the like that the instructor might assign." Dr. R. V. Stock, Acting Chairman of the Department of English, says this is the only course Nebraska has at any level that has a core reading list.

The anthology used in the course is **Bain, Carl E.**, et al., eds., *The Norton Introduction to Literature*. Other readings are:

FICTION

Baldwin, Richard	"Sonny's Blues"
Chopin, Kate	*The Awakening*
Conrad, Joseph	*The Secret Sharer*
Fitzgerald, F. Scott	"Babylon Revisited"
Faulkner, William	"Barn Burning"
Hawthorne, Nathaniel	"Young Goodman Brown"
Hemingway, Ernest	"The Short Happy Life of Francis Macomber"
Lawrence, D. H.	"Odour of Chrysanthemums"
Munro, Alice	"Boys and Girls"
Walker, Alice	"The Revenge of Hannah Kemhuff"

POETRY

Arnold, Matthew	"Dover Beach"
Browning, Robert	"My Last Duchess"
cummings, e. e.	"anyone lived in a pretty how town"
Dickinson, Emily	"Because I could Not Stop for Death"
Donne, John	"The Flea"
Eliot, T. S.	"The Love Song of J. Alfred Prufrock"
Frost, Robert	"Range-Finding"
Hughes, Ted	"Theme for English B"
Keats, John	"Ode on a Grecian Urn"
Knight, Etheridge	"Hard Rock Returns to Prison from the Hospital for the Criminal Insane"
Lorde, Audrey	"Recreation"
Marvell, Andrew	"To His Coy Mistress"
McKay, Claude	"America"
Milton, John	(Before the Fall)
Okara, Gabriel	"Piano and Drums"
Piercy, Marge	"Barbie Doll"
Rich, Adrienne	"Orion"
Roethke, Theodore	"I Knew a Woman"
Shakespeare, William	"Sonnet X"
Shelley, Percy Bysshe	"Ozymandias"
Stevens, Wallace	"Sunday Morning"
Thomas, Dylan	"Fern Hill"
Tennyson, Alfred Lord	"Ulysses"
Wakoski, Diane	"Uneasy Rider"
Whitman, Walt	"When Lilacs Last in the Dooryard Bloom'd"
Yeats, William Butler	"Leda and the Swan"

DRAMA

Ibsen, Henrik	*Hedda Gabler*
Sophocles	*Oedipus Rex*

University of Notre Dame
Office of Admissions
Notre Dame, IN 46556
(219) 239-7505

Notre Dame has two Reading Lists For College-Bound Students: I, compiled by the undergraduate director aided by some of the graduate students, and II, compiled from a questionnaire sent to college and university teachers.

I.

	Everyman
	Selections from Romantic poetry
Brontë, Emily	*Wuthering Heights*
Dante	*Inferno*
Dickens, Charles	*Great Expectations*
Dickinson, Emily	Poetry
Faulkner, William	"The Bear"
Fitzgerald, F. Scott	*The Great Gatsby*
Hawthorne, Nathaniel	*The Scarlet Letter*
Homer	*The Odyssey*
Miller, Arthur	*Death of a Salesman*
Shakespeare, William	*Hamlet; King Lear*
Twain, Mark	*The Adventures of Huckleberry Finn*

II.

The authors of this second list asked the teachers "to consider what books they would most like their students to have read before coming to college." They ask that you "notice that this is a very limited list. It is taken for granted, for example, that students would read several plays of Shakespeare, certain selections from major English poets, etc."

A. VERY HIGHLY RECOMMENDED

	Arthurian Tales "Important as background for college reading."
	Bible "A student without knowledge of the Bible is lost."
	Robin Hood tales
Cervantes, Miguel de	*Don Quixote*
Defoe, Daniel	*Robinson Crusoe*
Dickens, Charles	*David Copperfield* "An enjoyable acquaintance with Dickens is a 'must.'"

Homer	*The Iliad* and *The Odyssey* "Necessary background for understanding much of English and American literature."
Melville, Herman	*Moby-Dick*
Twain, Mark	*The Adventures of Huckleberry Finn*
Swift, Jonathan	*Gulliver's Travels* "The best introduction to satire."
Vergil	*The Aeneid* "Not sufficient to read only what you have in Latin class!"

B. HIGHLY RECOMMENDED

Brontë, Charlotte	*Jane Eyre*
Brontë, Emily	*Wuthering Heights*
Buck, Pearl	*The Good Earth*
Cather, Willa	*My Antonia*
Conrad, Joseph	*Lord Jim*
Cooper, James Fenimore	*Leatherstocking Tales*
Crane, Stephen	*The Red Badge of Courage*
Dickens, Charles	*Great Expectations; Oliver Twist; A Tale of Two Cities*
Dostoevski, Feodor	*Crime and Punishment*
Doyle, Sir Arthur Conan	*Sherlock Holmes*
Eliot, George	*The Mill on the Floss*
Emerson, Ralph Waldo	*Essays*
Fitzgerald, F. Scott	*The Great Gatsby*
Hawthorne, Nathaniel	*The House of the Seven Gables*
Hemingway, Ernest	*For Whom the Bell Tolls; The Old Man and the Sea*
Huxley, Aldous	*Brave New World*
Lewis, Sinclair	*Main Street; Babbit*
London, Jack	*The Call of the Wild*
Miller, Arthur	*Death of a Salesman*
Nordhoff and Hall	*Mutiny on the Bounty*
O'Neill, Eugene	*The Emperor Jones*
Parkman, Francis	*Oregon Trail*
Paton, Alan	*Cry, The Beloved Country*
Poe, Edgar Allan	*Tales*
Remarque, Erich Maria	*All Quiet on the Western Front*
Roberts, Kenneth	*Northwest Passage*
Rostand, Edmond	*Cyrano de Bergerac*
Scott, Sir Walter	*Quentin Durward*
Shaw, George Bernard	*Pygmalion; Saint Joan*
Sheridan, Richard	*The Rivals*
Sienkiewicz, Henryk	*Quo Vadis*
Steinbeck, John	*The Grapes of Wrath*
Thackeray, Wm. M.	*Vanity Fair*
Tolstoy, Leo	*War and Peace*
Verne, Jules	*Around the World in Eighty Days*
Wilder, Thornton	*Our Town*

C. RECOMMENDED

Adler, Mortimer	*How to Read a Book*
Allen, Frederich L.	*Only Yesterday*
Austen, Jane	*Mansfield Park*
Carroll, Lewis	*Alice's Adventures in Wonderland*
Cather, Willa	*Death Comes for the Archbishop*
Chesterton, G. K.	*Father Brown Stories*
Clark, Walter V.	*The Ox-Bow Incident*
Dante	*Inferno*
Dumas, Alexandre	*The Three Musketeers; The Count of Monte Cristo*
Fermi, Laura	*Atoms in the Family: My Life With Enrico Fermi*
Galsworthy, John	*Man of Property*
Greene, Graham	*The Power and the Glory*
Hudson, W. H.	*Green Mansions*
Kipling, Rudyard	*Jungle Books*
Lewis, C. S.	*Out of the Silent Planet*
Plato	*Dialogues*
Sandburg, Carl	*Lincoln*
Scott, Sir Walter	*Ivanhoe*
Stevenson, R. L.	*Treasure Island*
Twain, Mark	*Life on the Mississippi*
White, E. B.	*One Man's Meat*

University of the Pacific
Stockton, CA 95211
(209) 946-2211

The following list is "quite unofficial and chatty," according to Professor Arlen J. Hansen, Chair of the University of the Pacific's Department of English. It is what the department sends out when high school students, teachers, or counselors ask for their recommendations for pre-college reading.

The list is entitled:

Something to Read

SERIOUS STUFF:

Brontë, Emily, *Wuthering Heights:* The whole cycle: affection, love, and heartbreak. Almost as good as the 1939 movie.

Crane, Stephen, *The Red Badge of Courage:* A young soldier rationalizes that he's not a coward, war's not bloody, and nature's not cruel.

Defoe, Daniel, *Robinson Crusoe:* Desert island tale about having to reinvent civilization, not to mention the wheel.

Dickens, Charles, *Great Expectations:* Don't let the title fool you. The 19th-century English disillusionment novel.

A Tale of Two Cities: Opens with one of the all-time greatest lines and keeps the beat to the very end.

Faulkner, William, *Intruder in the Dust:* About racism and resistance to change; probably the most accessible of Faulkner's novels.

Fitzgerald, F. Scott, *The Great Gatsby:* The American dream fails to deliver the goods and yet ennobles the dreamer.

Hawthorne, Nathaniel, *The Scarlet Letter:* Good old American subjects: sex, guilt, sin, love, hypocrisy, and self-torture.

Hemingway, Ernest, *The Nick Adams Stories:* Covers all kinds of "initiation"—a boy gets burned in just about every way possible.

Lewis, Sinclair, *Arrowsmith:* Implicates the ambitious doctors and the phonies around them.

Poe, Edgar Allan, "The Tell-Tale Heart" (a guy's guilt-ridden imagination gives him away), "The Black Cat" (a guy hates his cat and kills his wife, or is it the other way around?), "The Cask of Amontillado" (a guy buries his rival alive), and "The Pit and the Pendulum" (a guy trapped by time [the pendulum] and by space [the pit]).

Scott, Sir Walter, *Ivanhoe:* A sentimental romance filled with historical inaccuracies makes a lively adventure.

Shakespeare, William, *Hamlet:* What would *you* do if your uncle killed your father and married your mother?

Julius Caesar: Maybe the easiest play by Shakespeare but has some great lines. Your basic betrayal story.

Macbeth: A wife gets carried away in her ambition for her husband. Don't miss the "sound and fury" speech.

Stevenson, Robert Louis, *Dr. Jekyll and Mr. Hyde:* Assumes we're all evil underneath but lack the chemistry to release that side of us.

Twain, Mark, *The Adventures of Huckleberry Finn:* Don't let *Tom Sawyer* fool you, this is an angry book. Hilarious too, of course.

Innocents Abroad: This'll be one of the funniest books you'll ever get to read.

JUST FOR THE FUN OF IT:

Beckett, Samuel, *Waiting for Godot:* A play in which nothing much happens but it makes a lot of sense anyway. Like life that way.

Didion, Joan, *Slouching Towards Bethlehem:* Some absolutely unforgettable examples of "the new journalism" or whatever you call it.

Ellison, Ralph, *Invisible Man:* A reflective, intelligent novel loaded with poignant incidents from the life of a black man.

Heller, Joseph, *Catch-22:* Out-MASHes M.A.S.H. in hilarity and contempt for war.

Mailer, Norman, *The Armies of the Night:* This "history as a novel" is about a 1967 anti-war march. But mostly, of course, about Mailer.

Malamud, Bernhard, *The Magic Barrel:* Curious but rich stories about urban life and man's tendency to deceive himself and others.

Salinger, J. D., *The Catcher in the Rye:* Lays into phoniness.

Vonnegut, Kurt Jr., *Slaughterhouse-Five:* Billy Pilgrim, the Dresden bombing, and a time-warp loop.

Williams, Tennessee, *The Glass Menagerie:* You can't help loving—and even, at times, admiring—these pathetic, dear dreamers.

Wolfe, Tom, *The Right Stuff:* Unabashed hero-worship, but loaded with solid cultural analysis and insights into human nature.

University of Pennsylvania
1 College Hall
Philadelphia, PA 19104-6376
(215) 898-7507

The Department of English at Pennsylvania has compiled the following Pre-College Reading List:

Austen, Jane	*Pride and Prejudice*
Brontë, Charlotte	*Jane Eyre* or
Brontë, Emily	*Wuthering Heights*
Browning, Robert	Selections: "My Last Duchess," "The Bishop Orders his Tomb...," "Fra Lippo Lippi"
Cervantes, Miguel de	*Don Quixote*
Chaucer, Geoffrey	A taste of Chaucer, some in Middle English, if possible (say, The Prologue to the *Canterbury Tales* and the Wife of Bath's Prologue and Tale)
Chopin, Kate	*The Awakening*
Conrad, Joseph	*Heart of Darkness*
Dante	Selections

Defoe, Daniel	One novel (or one by Fielding)
Dickens, Charles	One novel (perhaps *A Tale of Two Cities*)
Dickinson, Emily	Selections
Donne, John	Selections
Eliot, T. S.	"The Love Song of J. Alfred Prufrock"
Ellison, Ralph	*Invisible Man*
Faulkner, William	"The Bear"
Fielding, Henry	One novel (or one by Defoe)
Fitzgerald, F. Scott	*The Great Gatsby*
Flaubert, Gustave	*Madame Bovary*
Golding, William	*Lord of the Flies*
Hawthorne, Nathaniel	*The Scarlet Letter*
Hemingway, Ernest	*A Farewell to Arms* or *The Sun Also Rises*
Homer	*The Iliad* or *The Odyssey*
James, Henry	*Daisy Miller*
Joyce, James	*Dubliners*
Keats, John	"Ode on a Grecian Urn"
Lawrence, D. H.	*Sons and Lovers*
Melville, Herman	*Billy Budd*
Milton, John	Selections from *Paradise Lost* and "L'Allegro and Il Penserosa," "Lycidas"
Poe, Edgar Allan	Selections
Pope, Alexander	"The Rape of the Lock"
Shakespeare, William	*As You Like It*; *Hamlet*; *Macbeth*; *Midsummer Night's Dream*; *Romeo and Juliet*; Sonnets, selections
Spenser, Edmund	A little Spenser (perhaps "Epithalamion")
Stevens, Wallace	Selections: "Sunday Morning" or "The Idea of Order at Key West" or "Thirteen Ways of Looking at a Blackbird"
Swift, Jonathan	"A Modest Proposal"; *Gulliver's Travels*
Tennyson, Alfred Lord	Selections from *Idylls of the King*, and "Ulysses," "Tithonas," "The Lotos-Eaters"
Twain, Mark	*The Adventures of Huckleberry Finn*
Whitman, Walt	Selections from *Leaves of Grass*
Wordsworth, William	Selections from *Lyrical Ballads* and "Tintern Abbey"
Yeats, William Butler	"Sailing to Byzantium" or other selection

University of Rochester
Meliora Hall
Rochester, NY 14627
(716) 275-3221

According to Dr. Morris Eaves, Chairman of the Department of English, "all freshmen at Rochester are required to take one basic writing course and two upper-level writing courses. The basic course is taught in the English department, and the upper-level courses in almost all departments; therefore, students may receive instruction geared specifically to their discipline." In all of these courses, the writing is based on reading and subsequent discussion. Almost all freshmen take one of the three following courses:

I. VENTURES:

Approximately half of the freshman course work is included in each segment of this program. Each Venture "organizes popular freshman courses around an important question so that you can examine this question from the perspectives of different disciplines." Freshmen interested in Ventures must apply for admission. Texts vary greatly depending on the theme of the particular course. The themes are Foundations of Western Culture; Ourselves and Others; The Organizing Mind: Science, Music, and Writing; Social and Biological Determinants of Behavior; Resources, Environment, and Political Choice; Personality and Human Development.

II. FICTIONS AND REALITIES:

This course analyzes some of the fictions that have been offered to explain reality. Instructors choose from these books:

Berger, John	*Ways of Seeing*
Freud, Sigmund	*Three Case Histories*
Goffman, Erving	*Presentation of Self*
Gould, Stephen Jay	*The Mismeasure of Man*
Horney, Karen	*Our Inner Conflicts*
Kingston, M. H.	*The Woman Warrior*
Mailer, Norman	*The Armies of the Night*
Underhill, Ruther	*Papago Woman*
Watson, James	*The Double Helix*

III. WRITING AND THINKING:

This course combines the analysis of fiction, poetry, and nonfiction prose with instruction in expository and persuasive writing. Instructors most frequently use one of the following anthologies of readings:

| Booth and Marshall, eds. | *The Harper & Row Reader* |
| Shrodes, Carolyn, et al. | *The Conscious Reader* |

They also have included the following novels or long prose works in their courses:

Barth, John	*Lost in the Funhouse*
Brontë, Charlotte	*Jane Eyre*
Brontë, Emily	*Wuthering Heights*
Camus, Albert	*The Plague*
Hardy, Thomas	*Jude the Obscure*
Hawthorne, Nathaniel	*The Scarlet Letter*
Hurston, Zora Neale	*Their Eyes Were Watching God*
Kafka, Franz	*The Trial*
Lewis, C. S.	*Till We Have Faces*
Melville, Herman	*Billy Budd and Other Stories*
Morrison, Toni	*Song of Solomon*
Naylor, Gloria	*The Women of Brewster Place*
Roth, Philip	*The Ghost Writer*
Sayers, Dorothy	*Murder Must Advertise*
Shelley, Mary	*Frankenstein*
Sontag, Susan	*Illness as Metaphor*
Warren, Robert Penn	*All the King's Men*
Wharton, Edith	*The Age of Innocence; The House of Mirth*
Waugh, Evelyn	*A Handful of Dust*

The University of the South
Sewanee, TN 37375
(615) 598-5931

According to Dr. Edwin Stirling, Chairman of the Department of English, no reading list *per se* is sent out to prospective students, but a list is provided for those interested in majoring in English to "help [them] begin [their] reading in a particular period or author."

General texts include *The Norton Anthology of English Literature* (2 vols) and the *Macmillan Anthology of American Literature*. Also suggested are **Albert C. Baugh's** *A Literary History of England* and a "useful popular history," *The Land and Literature of England* by **Robert M. Adams**. Other recommendations are **Robert E. Spiller** et al., *Literary History of the United States* and **Marcus Cunliffe's** *Literature of the United States* "short, perceptive, and readable." **C. Hugh Holman's** *A Handbook to Literature* is also mentioned. Authors and some of the titles on the reading list follow:

BACKGROUND

Aeschylus	*The Oresteia*
	The Bible: especially Genesis, Job, The Psalms, and the Gospels (King James Authorized Version)
Aristotle	*Poetics*
Boethius	*The Consolation of Philosophy*
Dante	*The Divine Comedy*
Homer	*The Iliad; The Odyssey*
Sophocles	*Antigone; Oedipus Rex*
Vergil	*The Aeneid*

MEDIEVAL

	Beowulf
	"The Battle of Maldon," "The Dream of the Rood," "The Seafarer," "The Wanderer"
	Everyman
	Pearl; Sir Gawain and the Green Knight
	The Wakefield Second Shepherd's Play
Chaucer, Geoffrey	*Canterbury Tales; Troilus and Criseyde*
Malory, Sir Thomas	*Morte d'Arthur* (I, VII, VIII)

RENAISSANCE

Lyric poets: Thomas Campion, Samuel Daniel, John Donne, Michael Drayton, George Herbert, Robert Herrick, Henry Howard, Earl of Surrey, Andrew Marvell, John Milton, Sir Philip Sidney, Edmund Spenser, Sir Thomas Wyatt

Jonson, Ben	*The Alchemist; Volpone;* poetry
Kyd, Thomas	*The Spanish Tragedy*
Marlowe, Christopher	*Doctor Faustus*
Milton, John	*Paradise Lost; Samson Agonistes;* other poetry
More, Sir Thomas	*Utopia*
Shakespeare, William	Plays and sonnets
Spenser, Edmund	*The Faerie Queene; The Shepheardes Calendar* ("October"); "Epithalamion"
Webster, John	*The Duchess of Malfi*

RESTORATION AND EIGHTEENTH-CENTURY

Bunyan, John	*The Pilgrim's Progress*
Boswell, James	*Life of Johnson*
Congreve, William	*The Way of the World*

Defoe, Daniel	*Moll Flanders*
Dryden, John	*Absalom and Achitophel* and other works
Fielding, Henry	*Joseph Andrews; Tom Jones*
Goldsmith, Oliver	*She Stoops to Conquer;* "The Deserted Village"
Gray, Thomas	"Elegy Written in a Country Church-yard," and other poetry
Johnson, Samuel	Preface to *Dictionary* and other works
Pope, Alexander	*An Essay on Criticism* and other works
Richardson, Samuel	*Pamela*
Sheridan, R. B.	*The Rivals*
Sterne, Laurence	*A Sentimental Journey*
Swift, Jonathan	*Gulliver's Travels* and other works
Wycherley, William	*The Country Wife*

NINETEENTH-CENTURY

Lyric poets: Matthew Arnold, William Blake, Robert Browning, Robert Burns, George Gordon, Lord Byron, Samuel Taylor Coleridge, Gerard Manley Hopkins, John Keats, Percy Bysshe Shelley, Alfred, Lord Tennyson, William Wordsworth

Austen, Jane	*Pride and Prejudice*
Brontë, Charlotte	*Jane Eyre*
Brontë, Emily	*Wuthering Heights*
Dickens, Charles	*Bleak House; Hard Times*
Eliot, George	*Middlemarch*
Hardy, Thomas	*Tess of the D'Urbervilles*
Pater, Walter	Conclusion to *The Renaissance*
Scott, Sir Walter	*The Heart of Midlothian*
Trollope, Anthony	*Barchester Towers*
Wilde, Oscar	*The Picture of Dorian Gray*

AMERICAN LITERATURE

Crane, Stephen	*The Red Badge of Courage;* "The Open Boat"
Dickinson, Emily	Selected poems
Edwards, Jonathan	*Personal Narrative;* "Sinners in the Hands of an Angry God"
Emerson, Ralph Waldo	"Nature," "The Poet," "Self-Reliance"
Franklin, Benjamin	*Autobiography*
Hawthorne, Nathaniel	*The Scarlet Letter* and short stories
James, Henry	*The Portrait of a Lady* and short stories
Melville, Herman	*Benito Cereno, Moby-Dick*
Poe, Edgar Allan	Tales
Thoreau, Henry David	"Civil Disobedience," *Walden*
Twain, Mark	*The Adventures of Huckleberry Finn*
Whitman, Walt	Selected poetry

TWENTIETH-CENTURY

Lyric poets: W. H. Auden, T. S. Eliot, Robert Frost, Thomas Hardy, Robert Lowell, Ezra Pound, John Crowe Ransom, Wallace Stevens, Allen Tate, Dylan Thomas, William Carlos Williams, William Butler Yeats

Conrad, Joseph	*Heart of Darkness; Lord Jim*
Faulkner, William	*Absalom, Absalom!; Go Down Moses; The Sound and the Fury*
Fitzgerald, F. Scott	*The Great Gatsby*
Hemingway, Ernest	*For Whom the Bell Tolls*
Joyce, James	*Dubliners; A Portrait of the Artist as a Young Man; Ulysses*
Lawrence, D. H.	*Women in Love*
O'Neill, Eugene	*Long Day's Journey Into Night*
O'Connor, Flannery	"Good Country People," "A Good Man Is Hard To Find"
Shaw, George Bernard	*Heartbreak House*; *Major Barbara*
Welty, Eudora	"The Petrified Man," "A Worn Path," "Why I Live at the P.O."
Woolf, Virginia	*To the Lighthouse*

The University of Texas at Austin
Austin, TX 78712-1159
(512) 471-7601

The Texas List of Unrequired Reading

The University of Texas has compiled lists of twelve books and twelve alternates for each of the four college undergraduate years. The Unrequired Reading List Committee includes in its brochure the following note: "This is not a list of the books we think every student should read. Rather, its purpose is to encourage reading and to provide a good starting point and plan for future reading. Alternate titles are provided, because we recognize the vast differences among individuals in reading experience and taste. We encourage you to start by following your own inclinations.

"The topics covered in these volumes are a good sampling of the most important ideas and events responsible for intellectual life and struggle in Western Civilization. A serious effort to examine at least selected topics in history, literature, philosophy, and science is an essential beginning in your education beyond secondary school. And this effort does not have to constitute a great burden. Only one book per month completes the reading program."

FRESHMAN

PHILOSOPHY AND OTHER TOPICS

Heilbroner, Robert	*The Worldly Philosophers*
Russell, Bertrand	*The Problems of Philosophy*
Smith, Huston	*The Religions of Man*

[Alternates]

Plato	*The Republic*
Rousseau, J. J.	*The Social Contract*
Russell, Bertrand	*A History of Western Philosophy*

SCIENCE

Sacks, Oliver	*Awakenings*
Thomas, Lewis	*The Lives of a Cell*
Watson, James	*The Double Helix*

[Alternates]

Boorstin, D. J.	*The Discoverers*
Gould, Stephen Jay	*The Panda's Thumb*
Lorenz, Konrad	*King Solomon's Ring*

LITERATURE

Hemingway, Ernest	*The Sun Also Rises*
Homer	*The Odyssey* (Lawrence, tr.)
Twain, Mark	*The Adventures of Huckleberry Finn*

[Alternates]

Austen, Jane	*Pride and Prejudice*
Conrad, Joseph	*Heart of Darkness*
Sophocles	*Antigone; Oedipus Rex*

HISTORY

Bloch, Marc	*The Historian's Craft*
Erikson, Erik H.	*Young Man Luther*
Hofstadter, Richard	*The American Political Tradition*

[Alternates]

Franklin, Benjamin	*The Autobiography of Benjamin Franklin*
Southern, R. W.	*The Making of the Middle Ages*
Wain, John, ed.	*Samuel Johnson*

SOPHOMORE

PHILOSOPHY AND OTHER TOPICS

Aristotle	*The Nicomachean Ethics*
Bible:	Old Testament: Genesis, Exodus, Job, Proverbs, Ecclesiastes, Isaiah, Amos, New Testament: Luke, John, Acts, Galatians, Ephesians
Tocqueville, Alexis de	*Democracy in America*

[Alternates]

Hallie, Phillip P.	*Lest Innocent Blood Be Shed*
Machiavelli, Niccolò	*The Prince*
Weber, Max	*The Theory of Social and Economic Organization*

SCIENCE

De Kruif, Paul	*Microbe Hunters*
Weinberg, Steven	*The First Three Minutes*
Whitehead, A. N.	*Science and the Modern World*

[Alternates]

Bernstein, Jeremy	*Einstein*
Pfeiffer, John E.	*The Creative Explosion*
Weisskopf, Victor F.	*Knowledge and Wonder*

LITERATURE

Carroll, Lewis	*Alice's Adventures in Wonderland* and *Through the Looking Glass*
Melville, Herman	*Moby-Dick*
Shakespeare, William	*Richard II*

[Alternates]

Fielding, Henry	*Tom Jones*
Milton, John	*Paradise Lost*
Waugh, Evelyn	*Brideshead Revisited*

HISTORY

Catton, Bruce	*This Hallowed Ground*
Cecil, David	*Melbourne*
Mattingly, Garrett	*The Defeat of the Spanish Armada*

[Alternates]

Adams, Henry	*The Education of Henry Adams*
Prescott, William H.	*History of the Conquest of Mexico*
Woodward, C. Vann	*Origins of the New South*

JUNIOR

PHILOSOPHY AND OTHER TOPICS

Elsen, A. E.	*Purposes of Art,* second ed.
James, William	*The Varieties of Religious Experience*
Mill, J. S.	*Utilitarianism; On Liberty*

[Alternates]

Chambers, Whitaker	*Witness*
James, William	*Pragmatism*
Norberg-Schulz, C.	*Meaning in Western Architecture*

SCIENCE

Hardy, G. H.	*A Mathematician's Apology*
Pagels, Heinz	*The Cosmic Code*
Reichenbach, Hans	*The Rise of Scientific Philosophy*

[Alternates]

Ravetz, Jerome R.	*Scientific Knowledge and Its Social Problems*
Snow, C. P.	*The Two Cultures and the Scientific Revolution*
Wilson, E. O.	*On Human Nature*

LITERATURE

	The Norton Anthology of Poetry, third edition
Shakespeare, William	*Hamlet*
Voltaire	*Candide*

[Alternates]

Cervantes, Miguel de	*Don Quixote*
Dickens, Charles	*Hard Times*
Woolf, Virginia	*To the Lighthouse*

HISTORY

Bullock, Alan	*Hitler: A Study in Tyranny*
Moorehead, Alan	*The White Nile*
Schlesinger, Arthur	*The Crisis of the Old Order*

[Alternates]

Tocqueville, Alexis de	*The Old Regime and the French Revolution*
James, Marquis	*The Raven*
Williams, T. H.	*Huey Long*

SENIOR

PHILOSOPHY AND OTHER TOPICS

Hamilton, Madison, Jay — *The Federalist Papers* (B. F. Wright, ed.)
Kant, Immanuel — *Groundwork of the Metaphysic of Morals*
Lewis, C. S. — *The Screwtape Letters*

[Alternates]

Hayek, Friedrich A. — *The Road to Serfdom*
Marx, Karl — *A Contribution to the Critique of Political Economy*
Orwell, George — *The Road to Wigan Pier*

SCIENCE

Dobzhansky, Theodosius — *Mankind Evolving*
Gardner, Martin — *Science: Good, Bad, and Bogus*
Kuhn, Thomas S. — *The Structure of Scientific Revolutions*

[Alternates]

Mayr, Ernst — *The Growth of Biological Thought*
Minnaert, M. — *The Nature of Light and Color in the Open Air*
Monod, Jacques — *Chance and Necessity*

LITERATURE

Dostoevski, Feodor — *The Brothers Karamazov*
Shakespeare, William — *A Midsummer Night's Dream*
Silone, Italo — *Bread and Wine*

[Alternates]

Faulkner, William — *Light in August*
Mann, Thomas — *The Magic Mountain*
Tolstoy, Leo — *War and Peace*

HISTORY

Donovan, Robert J. — *The Tumultuous Years*
Kennan, George F. — *Russia and the West under Lenin and Stalin*
Tuchman, Barbara — *Stillwell and the American Experience in China*

[Alternates]

Camus, Albert — *The Rebel*
Malcolm X and Alex Haley — *The Autobiography of Malcolm X*
Tucker, Robert C. — *Stalin as Revolutionary*

University of Tulsa
600 South College Avenue
Tulsa, OK 74104
(918) 592-6000

In the Tulsa Curriculum, students study primary works in six general areas: "Artistic Imagination, study of the products and creative processes of art and literature; Social Inquiry, the laws and practices that shape social, economic, and political life; Cultural Interpretation, the historical record and evolution of a variety of cultures; Scientific Investigation, modern science and technology; Contemporary Experience, issues and ideas of contemporary importance; and Methods of Inquiry, formal and informal logic, reasoning, and theories of learning."

According to the pamphlet that contains the Tulsa Reading List for the curriculum, "whatever their prospective colleges and majors, however specialized their professional interest, students who complete the Tulsa Curriculum carry the hallmark of educated men and women."

Following is the *READING LIST*. Twenty-five professors at the University of Tulsa chose "works that have been of special significance to them and that have helped shape and challenge human life." Each book is annotated by the professor who selected it. The date after the author and title is the first date of the book's publication.

Abbott, Edwin A., *Flatland: A Romance of Many Dimensions* (1884): "Abbott's social satire, *Flatland*, is about intelligent beings who live in a world of two dimensions . . . reminding us that the world may only appear to be what science and society teach, and that discovery of the true world is left to the inquisitive mind." (Janet A. Haggerty, Geosciences)

Arrow, Kenneth J., *Social Choice and Individual Values* (1951): "Arrow's book considers the problem of identifying, from a set of alternatives, that which best serves the interests of society. . . . [It] not only provides one of several important perspectives from which to consider the choice of financial accounting alternatives, but has many additional applications." (Don Vickrey, Accounting)

Beckmann, Petr, *A History of Pi* (1971): "This delightful book offers astute commentary on the development of mathematics, focusing on the contributions of a handful of great mathematicians over the past 2000 years. . . . There is quite a bit of commentary about history, politics, sociology, and science, produced by an author who, although highly opinionated, has a lot to say that won't be found in the standard textbooks. . . ." (John R. Hendrickson, Physics)

Burney, Charles, *Dr. Charles Burney's Continental Travels* (written 1770): "A compilation of journals kept by Charles Burney on his extended tours of Europe's leading musical centers, this book contains Burney's comments not only on music, but on a wide range of artistic and social issues. . ." (Frank Ryan, Music)

Darwin, Charles, *The Voyage of the Beagle: Journal of Researches into the Geology and Natural History of the Various Countries Visited by H.M.S. Beagle* (1839): ". . . The lands Darwin saw, extending millions of years into the past, . . . provided one of the most exciting discoveries in the brief history of the human species." (James R. Stewart, Zoology)

Eliot, T. S., *Four Quartets* (1943): "When I first read them. . .the *Four Quartets*. . .said something to me about the present and my senses. . . . As I became acquainted with Augustine, San Juan de la Cruz, and the Bhagavad-Gita, the writers Eliot loves began to echo in the poems for me. . . . The *Quartets* will say something terribly important to you about how to live in time." (Jane Ackerman, Foreign Languages and Comparative Literature)

Feynman, Richard P., *The Character of Physical Law* (1967): "Pulled out of school to work on the Manhattan Project that built the atom bomb, [Feynman] went on to win the Nobel Prize in 1965. *The Character of Physical Law* contains seven lectures delivered to undergraduates . . . at Cornell University in 1964. . ." (Roger N. Blais, Physics)

Freud, Sigmund, *A General Introduction to Psychoanalysis* (1920, Joan Riviere, tr.): ". . . A series of lively, engaging lectures for a nonacademic audience, the book contains most of the key insights of psychoanalysis . . ." (Robert Hogan, Psychology)

Frost, Robert, *The Poems of Robert Frost* (1946): "Frost's is a poetry that represents the range of literature—nature, lyric, drama, wisdom, and invective—in native terms. . ." (Manly Johnson, English Language and Literature)

Grosser, Maurice, *The Painter's Eye* (c 1951): ". . . This little book is filled with fresh insights and perceptions, revealing the delightful connections between the mundane technical problems of the painter and the elusive nature of the aesthetic experience. . ." (Glenn Godsey, Art)

Hardy, G. H., *A Mathematician's Apology* (1967): "In this essay, a major figure of twentieth-century mathematics explains what mathematicians do and why it is worth doing. . . . For example, number theory— Hardy's specialty—is now essential for national security." (Kevin O'Neil, Mathematical and Computer Sciences)

Hofstadter, Douglas, *Gödel, Escher, Bach: An Eternal Golden Braid* (1979): Professor Clark pretending to speak from the 22nd century writes "Hofstadter's book transmitted with amazing accuracy the fundamental theorems in mathematical logic, philosophy, and computer science that provided the foundation for subsequent breakthroughs." (Austen G. Clark, Philosophy)

Homer, *The Iliad,* (9th century BC Richmond Lattimore or Robert Fitzgerald, tr.): "Of all the literary works that helped shape Western civilization as we know it, Homer's *Iliad* is second in importance only to the Jewish Bible and the Christian New Testament. . ." (Paul A. Rahe, History)

Jefferson, Thomas, *Notes on the State of Virginia* (1787): ". . . Probably no other contemporary document captures so well both the brilliance and limitations of the world Jefferson knew." (Lawrence D. Cress, History)

Kuhn, Thomas S., *The Structure of Scientific Revolutions* (1962): ". . . Kuhn's book altered the way many scientists think about their work. It is among the ten most oft-cited science books of this century." (Robert E. Howard, Chemistry)

Lévi-Strauss, Claude, *Tristes Tropiques* (1955, John Russell, tr.): An account of the author's experiences in Brazil's hinterland searching for untouched native tribes, ". . .this book is a foundational statement of structuralism, the widely influential theory that the vast particularity of life's surface can be reduced to a finite set of deep, universal, mental structures. . ." (Lamont Lindstrom, Anthropology)

Meyrowitz, Joshua, *No Sense of Place* (1985): ". . .How have electronic media changed the situations in which we interact with other people?. . . Meyrowitz answers this important question. . . . To discover the available means of persuasion in this electronic age, this book is essential reading." (Robert J. Doolittle, Communication)

Montaigne, Michel de, *Essays* (1580–92, Donald M. Frame, tr.): ". . . Montaigne. . .in the critical spirit of the French Renaissance, delights in challenging the reader in his reflections on the human condition—on problems in epistemology, morals, and politics. . ." (Elaine Ancekewicz, Foreign Languages and Comparative Literature)

Orwell, George, *Homage to Catalonia* (1938): In a book about the Spanish Civil War, Orwell's "insights on the nature of totalitarianism, whether of the right or the left, are a monument to a man who advocated clear thinking as well as clear writing." (Mary Lee Townsend, History)

Paton, Alan, *Ah, But Your Land Is Beautiful* (1981): A novel about South Africa and apartheid, "it treats all the main parties to the struggle—Afrikaners, English, Blacks, Coloreds, Marxists—and shows how the religious moralities involved have wrought both demonic hypocrisy and true saintliness." (Denise Lardner Carmody, Religion)

Plato, *Republic* (4th century BC, Allan David Bloom, tr.): ". . .Almost any issue (philosophical, literary, scientific, historical, economic, psychological, sociological, etc.) can be discussed within the context of Plato's *Republic*, which treats the broader possibilities of human knowledge and social relationships in a discussion of the ideal political state." (D. Thomas Benediktson, Foreign Languages and Comparative Literature)

Smith, Adam, *An Inquiry into the Nature and Causes of Wealth of Nations* (1776): "Smith's seminal work, written at the beginning of the Industrial Revolution, provided a conduit through which eighteenth-century thought about human nature and the system of 'natural liberty' influenced the study of economies. . . ." (R. Lynn Rittenoure, Economics)

Smith, Adam, *The Theory of Moral Sentiments* (1759): The work "considers the place wealth, and the desire for it, should occupy in our lives. . . . Smith had no great respect for wealth, greatness, or driving ambition. Instead, he recommended "humanity, justice, generosity, and public spirit.'. . ." (Thomas A. Horne, Political Science)

Swift, Jonathan, *Gulliver's Travels* (1726): This book about ". . .the imaginary voyages of an Englishman, Lemuel Gulliver,. . .carries us away with its story while making us think—and laugh—about our own vanities, offering the painful pleasure of self-recognition." (Darcy O'Brien, English Language and Literature)

Whitman, Walt, *Leaves of Grass* (1855, 1891-92): ". . .Written in innovative free verse, Whitman's book celebrates both community and individual, projecting a 'cosmic hero' into an idealized 'America,' where greed, intolerance, and corruption are defeated by transcendental thinking and energetic art. . ." (Winston Weathers, English Language and Literature)

University of Vermont
194 South Prospect Street
Burlington, VT 05401-3596
(802) 656-3370

The reading list prepared by the National Council of Teachers of English is the one the University of Vermont suggests to pre-college students according to Dr. Virginia P. Clark, Chair of the Department of English. It may be obtained from NCTE, 1111 Kenyon Road, Urbana, IL 61801.

University of Virginia
PO Box 9017, University Station
Charlottesville, VA 22903
(804) 924-7751

The University of Virginia Department of English offers students a basic or introductory list of works "generally considered most important for acquiring an educated perspective on Western literature." The department notes that "for works not originally in English, the translation. . .is of real importance. Translation invariably alters an author's creation; bad translation can wholly destroy the quality of a work. Most modern translations are acceptable, particularly those published by Penguin and Signet. When a distinguished translation exists,. . .the translator's name [is] in parenthesis."

Suggested Readings

I. CLASSICAL

Aeschylus	*Oresteia* (Fagles, tr.)
Aristophanes	*Lysistrata*
Aristotle	*Poetics* (Butcher or Else, tr.)
Euripides	*Bacchae*
Homer	*The Iliad* (Lattimore, tr.); *The Odyssey* (Fitzgerald, tr.)
Ovid	*Metamorphoses* (Gregory, tr.)
Plato	*Republic* (Cornford, tr.)
Sophocles	*Antigone* (Lattimore, tr.); *Oedipus Rex* (Grene, tr.)
Vergil	*The Aeneid* (Mandelbaum, tr.)

II. MEDIEVAL

	Beowulf
	Bible (Authorized Version, 1611): Genesis; II Samuel; Psalms 23, 53, 103, 104, 107, 121, 130, 137; Job; Isaiah 40–55; I Corinthians; Revelation
	Everyman
	Sir Gawain and the Green Knight (Boroff, tr.)
	The Song of Roland
Boccaccio, Giovanni	*The Decameron*
Chaucer, Geoffrey	*Canterbury Tales*
Dante	*The Divine Comedy* (Singleton, tr.)
Petrarch, Francesco	Poems
St. Augustine	*Confessions*

III. RENAISSANCE & SEVENTEENTH-CENTURY

Cervantes, Miguel de	*Don Quixote*
Donne, John	*Songs and Sonnets*
Dryden, John	*Absalom and Achitophel*
Jonson, Ben	*Volpone*

Marlowe, Christopher	*Dr. Faustus*
Marvell, Andrew	*Selected Poems* (esp."To His Coy Mistress," "The Garden")
Milton, John	"Lycidas"; *Paradise Lost*
Molière	*The Misanthrope* (Wilbur, tr.)
Montaigne, Michel de	*Essays*
Pascal, Blaise	*Thoughts*
Rabelais, François	*Gargantua and Pantagruel*
Racine, Jean	*Phaedra* (Lowell, tr.)
Sidney, Philip	*Astrophel and Stella*
Spenser, Edmund	*The Faerie Queene*
Shakespeare, William	*Hamlet; Henry IV* Part I; *King Lear; A Midsummer Night's Dream; The Tempest; Sonnets*

IV. EIGHTEENTH-CENTURY

Congreve, William	*The Way of the World*
Defoe, Daniel	*Moll Flanders*
Fielding, Henry	*Tom Jones*
Gay, John	*The Beggar's Opera*
Goethe, J. Wolfgang von	*Faust* (Passage, tr.); *The Sorrows of Young Werther*
Goldsmith, Oliver	*She Stoops to Conquer*
Johnson, Samuel	*Rasselas*
Pope, Alexander	*Selected Poems* (esp. "An Essay on Man," "The Rape of the Lock")
Richardson, Samuel	*Clarissa*
Sheridan, Richard B.	*The School for Scandal*
Sterne, Laurence	*Tristram Shandy*
Swift, Jonathan	*Gulliver's Travels*
Voltaire	*Candide*

V. NINETEENTH-CENTURY

Austen, Jane	*Emma*
Baudelaire, Charles P.	*Flowers of Evil*
Blake, William	*The Marriage of Heaven and Hell; Songs of Innocence and Experience*
Brontë, Charlotte	*Jane Eyre*
Brontë, Emily	*Wuthering Heights*
Browning, Robert	*Selected Poems* (esp. "Fra Lippo Lippi," "My Last Duchess")
Byron, George Gordon	*Don Juan*
Coleridge, Samuel T.	"Dejection: An Ode," "Frost at Midnight," *The Rime of the Ancient Mariner*
Crane, Stephen	*The Red Badge of Courage*
Dickens, Charles	*Bleak House; Great Expectations*
Dickinson, Emily	Poems

Dostoevski, Feodor	*The Brothers Karamazov; Crime and Punishment*
Eliot, George	*Middlemarch*
Emerson, Ralph Waldo	*Essays*
Flaubert, Gustave	*Madame Bovary*
Hardy, Thomas	*Tess of the D'Urbervilles*
Hawthorne, Nathaniel	*The Scarlet Letter*
Ibsen, Henrik	*A Doll's House*
Keats, John	Selected Poems (esp. "The Eve of St. Agnes," "Ode on a Grecian Urn," "Ode to a Nightingale," "To Autumn")
Marx, Karl and Friedrich Engels	*Communist Manifesto*
Melville, Herman	*Moby-Dick*
Pushkin, Alexander	*Eugene Onegin*
Rossetti, Christina	Selected Poems (esp. "Goblin Market")
Stendahl	*The Red and the Black* (Scott Moncrieff, tr.)
Shelley, Percy Bysshe	Selected Poems (esp. "Adonais," "Mont Blanc," "Ode to the West Wind," Prometheus Unbound)
Tennyson, Alfred	*Idylls of the King; In Memoriam*
Thackeray, Wm. Makepeace	*Vanity Fair*
Thoreau, Henry	*Walden*
Tolstoy, Leo	*Anna Karenina* (Maude, tr.); *War and Peace* (Maude, tr.)
Trollope, Anthony	*The Warden*
Turgenev, Ivan	*Fathers and Sons; First Love*
Twain, Mark	*The Adventures of Huckleberry Finn*
Whitman, Walt	*Song of Myself*
Wordsworth, William	Selected Poems (esp. "Ode: Intimations of Mortality," "Tintern Abbey"); *The Prelude*

VI. TWENTIETH-CENTURY

Akhmatova, Anna	Selected Poems
Auden, W. H.	Selected Poems (esp. "In Memory of W. B. Yeats," "Musée des Beaux Arts," "The Sea and the Mirror," "September 1, 1939," "The Shield of Achilles")
Beckett, Samuel	*Waiting for Godot*
Borges, Jorge	*Ficciones*
Brecht, Bertolt	*Mother Courage and her Children*
Brodsky, Joseph	*A Part of Speech*
Camus, Albert	*The Stranger*
Chopin, Kate	*The Awakening*
Conrad, Joseph	*Heart of Darkness*

Ellison, Ralph	*Invisible Man*
Eliot, T. S.	*Four Quartets;* "The Love Song of J. Alfred Prufrock"; "The Waste Land"
Faulkner, William	*Absalom, Absalom!; The Sound and the Fury*
Ford, Ford Madox	*The Good Soldier*
Forster, E. M.	*A Passage to India*
Freud, Sigmund	*Civilization and its Discontents*
García Márquez, Gabriel	*One Hundred Years of Solitude*
Hemingway, Ernest	*The Snows of Kilimanjaro*
James, Henry	*The Portrait of a Lady*
Joyce, James	*Dubliners; A Portrait of the Artist as a Young Man*
Kafka, Franz	*The Metamorphosis; The Trial*
Kundera, Milan	*The Book of Laughter and Forgetting*
Lawrence, D. H.	*The Rainbow; Women in Love*
Lorca, F. G.	*Three Tragedies*
Mandelstam, Osip	Selected Poems
Mann, Thomas	*Death in Venice; The Magic Mountain*
Milosz, Czeslaw	Selected Poems
Montale, Eugenio	Selected Poems
Morrison, Toni	*Sula*
Nabokov, Vladimir	*Lolita*
Pasternak, Boris	*Doctor Zhivago*
Proust, Marcel	*Swann's Way*
Rilke, Rainer Maria	*Letters to a Young Poet; Sonnets to Orpheus*
Sartre, Jean-Paul	*No Exit*
Stevens, Wallace	*Collected Poems* (esp. "The Idea of Order at Key West," "Sunday Morning")
Walker, Alice	*The Color Purple*
Williams, W. C.	"Asphodel, That Greeny Flower," *Paterson*
Woolf, Virginia	*A Room of One's Own; To the Lighthouse*
Wright, Richard	*Native Son*
Yeats, William Butler	Selected Poems (esp. "Among School Children," "The Circus Animals' Desertion," "Easter 1916," "Sailing to Byzantium," "The Second Coming")

Vassar College
Poughkeepsie, NY 12601
(914) 452-7000

According to Dr. Robert DeMaria, Chairman of the Department of English at Vassar, freshman courses are "individually designed and change every year." The following is a representative sampling of literature commonly taught in some of the courses:

AMERICAN DREAMS

Alger, Horatio	*Ragged Dick*
Fitzgerald, F. Scott	*The Great Gatsby*
Hellman, Lillian	*Little Foxes*
Lewis, Sinclair	*Babbitt*
Miller, Arthur	*Death of a Salesman*
Tyler, Anne	*Dinner at the Homesick Restaurant*
Williams, Tennessee	*The Glass Menagerie*

And short fiction by James Baldwin, Ambrose Bierce, Roy Blount, Willa Cather, John Cheever, Stephen Crane, William Faulkner, Ernest Hemingway, Langston Hughes, Ring Lardner, Jane Martin, Louis Nordan, Flannery O'Connor, William Sydney Porter, Philip Roth, Irwin Shaw, James Thurber, Mark Twain, John Updike, Richard Wright

AUTOBIOGRAPHY AND FICTION

Barthelme, Frederick	"Monster Deal" (*Granta* #8)
Carter, Angela	"Sugar Daddy"
Carver, Raymond	"The Bath"; "A Small, Good Thing"; "Where I'm Calling From"; the Carver interview from *Paris Review*
Didion, Joan	*Slouching Towards Bethlehem*
Ephron, Nora	"A Few Words About Breasts"; "On Never Having Been a Prom Queen"
Ford, Richard	"Rock Springs"
Ignatieff, Michael	Essay in *Granta* #14
Joyce, James	*Dubliners*
Kingston, Maxine Hong	*The Woman Warrior*
Lessing, Doris	Essay in *Granta* #14
McEwen, Christian	Essay in *Granta* #14
Mason, Bobbie Ann	"Still Life With Watermelon" (*Granta* #8)
Nabokov, Vladimir	*Lolita*
O'Connor, Flannery	"Everything That Rises Must Converge"; "Greenleaf"

Olsen, Tillie	"I Stand Here Ironing"; *Tell Me A Riddle*
Paley, Grace	"Enormous Changes at the Last Minute"
Phillips, Jayne Anne	"Rayme—A Memoir of the Seventies" (*Granta* #8)
Roth, Philip	*The Ghost Writer*
Wolff, Geoffrey	*Duke of Deception*
Wolff, Tobias	"Barracks Thief" (*Granta* #8)

THE DEVELOPMENT OF ENGLISH LITERATURE

	Sir Gawain and the Green Knight
Chaucer, Geoffrey	*Canterbury Tales* (the general prologue; tales: the Franklin's, the Wife of Bath's, the Merchant's, the Nun's Priest's, the Miller's)
Gardner, Helen, ed.	*The Metaphysical Poets*
Lewis, Matthew	*The Monk*
Milton, John	*Paradise Lost*
Pope, Alexander	"The Rape of the Lock," Selected Poetry
Shakespeare, William	*Antony and Cleopatra; Hamlet; A Midsummer Night's Dream; Romeo and Juliet; The Winter's Tale*
Spenser, Edmund	Selected Poetry (Book I, III)
Walpole, Horace	*The Castle of Otranto*

FORMS OF DRAMA

Baraka, Imamu Amiri (LeRoi Jones)	*Bloodrites*
Jonson, Ben	*Volpone*
Marlowe, Christopher	*Dr. Faustus*
Shakespeare, William	*The Tempest*
Sophocles	*Antigone*
Van Itallie, Jean-Claude	*America Hurrah*
Wycherley, William	*The Country Wife*

And scenes or plays by **Samuel Beckett, Bertolt Brecht, Ed Bullins, Erskine Caldwell, Churchill, Martha Clarke, Hughes, Jackson, Harold Pinter, Oscar Wilde, Robert Wilson**

FORMS OF THE ESSAY

Barthes, Roland	"The Brain of Einstein," "The Face of Garbo," "Strip Tease"
Horkheimer & Adorno	"The Culture Industry: Enlightenment as Mass Deception"
Marcus, Greil	Essay on Elvis Presley

Orwell, George	"Shooting an Elephant"; "The Art of Donald McGill"
Smart, William	*Eight Modern Essayists*
White, E. B.	"The Essayist"
Woolf, Virginia	"Death of the Moth"

And essays by **Ralph Waldo Emerson, Samuel Johnson, Michel de Montaigne, Adrienne Rich, Lewis Thomas, Alice Walker**

FORMS OF NARRATIVE

Austen, Jane	*Pride and Prejudice*
Brontë, Charlotte	*Jane Eyre*
Charters, ed.	*The Story and Its Writer*
Dickens, Charles	*Great Expectations*
Eliot, George	*The Mill on the Floss*
Fielding, Henry	*Joseph Andrews*
Hardy, Thomas	*The Return of the Native*
Joyce, James	*A Portrait of the Artist as a Young Man*
Lawn, ed.	*The Short Story: 30 Masterpieces*
Lessing, Doris	*Martha Quest; A Proper Marriage*

LITERARY KINDS: NARRATIVE

Austen, Jane	*Pride and Prejudice*
Beckett, Samuel	*The Lost Ones*
Hawthorne, Nathaniel	*Hawthorne's Short Stories*
Homer	*The Odyssey* (Robert Fitzgerald, tr.)
James, Henry	*Eight Tales from the Major Phase; The Portrait of a Lady; The Turn of the Screw*
Joyce, James	*Dubliners; A Portrait of the Artist as a Young Man*
Scott, Walter	*Waverley*
Vergil	*The Aeneid* (Robert Fitzgerald, tr.)

LITERARY KINDS: POETRY

	The Norton Anthology of Poetry (3rd Edition)
Agoos, Julie	*Above the Land*
Joyce, James	"The Dead" (compared with the John Huston movie)
Welty, Eudora	"Place in Fiction"
Wright, James	*Two Citizens*

And among others, poems by **Elizabeth Bishop, Robert Browning, John Donne, Langston Hughes, Ted Hughes, Robert Lowell, Ishmael Reed, Walt Whitman**

Major British and American Writers from Pope to Eliot

Austen, Jane	*Emma*
Chopin, Kate	*The Awakening*
Dickens, Charles	*Hard Times*
Dickinson, Emily	*Final Harvest: Emily Dickinson's Poems*
Eliot, T. S.	Selected Poems
Fielding, Henry	*Joseph Andrews*
Hawthorne, Nathaniel	Selected Tales and Sketches
James, Henry	*The Turn of the Screw*
Keats, John	Selected Poems and Letters
Lamb, Charles	Selected Essays
Owen, Wilfred	*Collected Poems*
Pope, Alexander	*Poetry and Prose of Alexander Pope*
Rose, Phyllis	*Parallel Lives*
Tennyson, Alfred Lord	Selected Poems
Whitman, Walt	*Leaves of Grass*
Wilde, Oscar	*The Importance of Being Earnest*

Personal Narratives and Political Identity

Atwood, Margaret	*The Handmaid's Tale; Journals of Susanna Moodie*
Davies, Robertson	*Fifth Business*
Forster, E. M.	*A Passage to India*
Gallant, Mavis	*Home Truths*
Gordimer, Nadine	*July's People*
Jhabvala, Ruth Prawer	*Heat and Dust*
Jolley, Elizabeth	*Woman in a Lampshade*
Joyce, James	*A Portrait of the Artist as a Young Man*
Keneally, Thomas	*The Chant of Jimmy Blacksmith*
MacPherson, Jay	*The Boatman*
Munro, Alice	*The Beggar Main*
Naipaul, V. S.	*A Bend in the River*
Ondaatje, Michael	*Billy the Kid*
Rushdie, Salman	*Shame*
Shakespeare, William	*The Tempest*
Shelley, Mary	*Frankenstein*
Soyinka, Wole	*Ake; The Years of Childhood*
Walcott, Derek	Selection
White, Patrick	*The Aunt's Story*
Yeats, William Butler	Poetry

Self-Discovery: Visions and Revisions

O'Neill, Eugene	*The Iceman Cometh*
Shepard, Sam	*A Lie of the Mind*

Tyler, Anne — *The Accidental Tourist*
Woolf, Virginia — *The Waves*

The Vassar English Department recommends to its students the following magazines and newspapers:

Daedalus
Encounter
London Magazine
New American Review
New York Review of Books
Partisan Review
Poetry
Scientific American

The Manchester Guardian
The New Statesman and *The Nation*
The New Yorker
The New York Times
Times Literary Supplement (London)

Washington University
Campus Box 1089 One Brookings Drive
St. Louis, MO 63130
(314) 889-6000

According to Dr. Robert Wiltenburg, Director of Expository Writing, Washington University has "no reading lists, either required or recommended, either pre-college or year-by-year." Book selections for Washington University's English Composition 100/199 courses change from year to year, and no particular item is ever required. Each year, however, a few books are suggested. Recent lists for these courses have included the following:

AUTOBIOGRAPHY

Adams, Henry — *The Education of Henry Adams*
Dinesen, Isak — *Out of Africa*
Graves, Robert — *Goodbye to All That*
Nabokov, Vladimir — *Speak, Memory*
Welty, Eudora — *One Writer's Beginnings*
Wolff, Geoffrey — *The Duke of Deception*

HISTORY AND SOCIETY

Lawrence, D. H. — *D. H. Lawrence and Italy*
Narayan, R. K. — *The Vendor of Sweets*
Twain, Mark — *Life on the Mississippi*
Williams, William Carlos — *In the American Grain*
Wylie, L. — *Village in the Vaucluse*

NATURE AND SCIENCE

Gould, Stephen Jay	*The Flamingo's Smile*
Leopold, Aldo	*A Sand County Almanac*
Sacks, Oliver	*The Man Who Mistook His Wife for a Hat*
Thomas, Lewis	*Late Night Thoughts on Listening to Mahler's Ninth Symphony*
Thoreau, Henry David	*The Maine Woods*

HUMANITIES

Malamud, Bernard	*The Assistant*
O'Connor, Flannery	*The Complete Stories*
Orwell, George	*Essays*
Paley, Grace	*Enormous Changes at the Last Minute*
Smart, William	*Eight Modern Essayists*
Woolf, Virginia	*Death of the Moth and Other Essays*

HANDBOOKS

Baker, Sheridan	*The Practical Stylist*
Leggett, Glenn H., et al.	*The Prentice-Hall Handbook*

Wheaton College
Norton, MA 02766
(508) 285-7722

Wheaton's First-Year Seminar, according to Dr. Richard Pearce, is "divided into five clusters, which share a set of common meetings and readings." Some of the subjects to be considered in the cluster meetings are environment and the threat of nuclear arms; Freedom Summer and the Democratic Party Convention in 1964 (including the significance of songs and spirituals to the Black Freedom Movement); intelligence testing; Marxism and the Industrial Revolution; optical illusions. The following are books and films considered for tentative cluster assignments:

BOOKS:

Atwood, Margaret	*The Handmaid's Tale*
Orwell, George	*Animal Farm*
Watson, James	*The Double Helix*

FILMS:

	PBS Video: *Human Mind*
	Danton

Eyes on the Prize
Powers of Ten
The Return of Martin Guerre (film re-
flecting medieval family)

Fassbinder, Rainer W.   *The Marriage of Maria Braun*
Eisenstein, Sergei   *Potemkin*

Williams College
PO Box 487
Williamstown, MA 01267
(413) 597-2211

Although Williams College does not have a reading list as such, the following are among the authors and works considered in some of its freshman English classes:

Allison, Alexander W., et al.   *Norton Anthology of Poetry* (Shorter edition)
Arnold, Matthew   "Dover Beach"
Auden, W. H.   "The Unknown Citizen," "In Memory of W. B. Yeats"

Bain, C. E., et al., eds.   *The Norton Introduction to Literature*
Baldwin, James   "Sonny's Blues"
Baraka, Imamu Amiri (LeRoi Jones)   "In Memory of Radio"
Beckett, Samuel   *Waiting for Godot*
Bishop, Elizabeth   "The Fish"
Blake, William   "The Sick Rose"
Brecht, Bertolt   *The Good Woman of Setzuan*
Brooks, Gwendolyn   "We Real Cool"
Browning, Robert   "My Last Duchess"
Carver, Raymond   *Cathedral*
Cassill, R. V., ed.   *The Norton Anthology of Short Fiction*
Chekhov, Anton   "The Bishop," "The Lady with the Pet Dog"
Coleridge, Samuel T.   *The Rime of the Ancient Mariner*
Conrad, Joseph   *Heart of Darkness*
Coover, Robert   "The Babysitter"
Crane, Stephen   "The Blue Hotel"
cummings, e. e.   "in just spring..."
Couto, Nancy   "1958"
DeMott, Benjamine   *Close Imaginings*
Dickey, James   "Cherrylog Road"
Dickinson, Emily   "After great pain," "I heard a Fly buzz," "Because I could not stop for Death"
Digges, Deborah   "The New World"

Donne, John	"Batter my heart . . ."
Doyle, Sir Arthur Conan	"A Scandal in Bohemia"
Dunn, Stephen	*Local Time*
Eliot, T. S.	"The Love Song of J. Alfred Prufrock," "The Journey of the Magi"
Ellison, Ralph	"King of the Bingo Game"
Faulkner, William	"Barn Burning," "A Rose for Emily," "Spotted Horses"
Ferlinghetti, Lawrence	"Dog"
Fitzgerald, F. Scott	"Babylon Revisited"
Frost, Robert	"The Silken Tent," "Design," "In White," "Mending Wall," "Home Burial"
Gaines, Ernest	*Of Love and Dust*
Gilman, Charlotte P.	"The Yellow Wallpaper"
Gluck, Louise	"The Triumph of Achilles"
Hardy, Thomas	"The Convergence of the Twain"
Hemingway, Ernest	"Hills Like White Elephants"
Hempel, Amy	"In the Cemetery Where Al Jolson Is Buried"
Hopkins, Gerard M.	"God's Grandeur," "Spring and Fall"
Hughes, Ted	"The Thought-Fox"
Ibsen, Henrik	*A Doll's House*
Jarrell, Randall	"The Death of the Ball Turret Gunner"
Joyce, James	"Araby," "A Little Cloud," "The Dead"
Kafka, Franz	*The Metamorphosis*, "The Hunger Artist"
Kauffman, Janet	"My Mother Has Me Surrounded"
Keats, John	"Ode on a Grecian Urn," "To Autumn," "Bright Star"
Kennedy, X. J.	*An Introduction to Poetry* (6th ed)
Kinnell, Galway	"Blackberry Eating," "To Christ Our Lord"
Lawrence, D. H.	"Odour of Chrysanthemums"
Levine, Philip	"You Can Have It"
Lowell, Robert	"Skunk Hour"
MacLeish, Archibald	"Ars Poetica"
Malamud, Bernard	*The Magic Barrel*
Mann, Thomas	*Death in Venice*
Marvell, Andrew	"To His Coy Mistress"
Mason, Bobbie A.	*Shiloh* and other stories
Meredith, William	"Parents"
Moore, Marianne	"Poetry"
Morrison, Toni	*The Bluest Eye*; *Song of Solomon*
Nabokov, Vladimir	*Pnin; Lolita; Nabokov's Dozen;* "Signs and Symbols"
Nemerov, Howard	"Boom!"

O'Connor, Flannery	"Everything That Rises Must Converge," "Revelation," "A Good Man Is Hard to Find," "Guests of the Nation"
Oliver, Mary	"The Black Snake"
Paley, Grace	"A Conversation with My Father"
Pinter, Harold	*Betrayal*
Plath, Sylvia	"Daddy," "Metaphors," "Morning Song"
Poe, Edgar Allan	"The Cask of Amontillado"
Porter, Katherine Anne	"Flowering Judas"
Pound, Ezra	"In a Station of the Metro"
Pynchon, Thomas	*The Crying of Lot 49*
Reed, Ishmael	" 'beware' do not read this poem"
Rich, Adrienne	*The Facts of a Door Frame: Selected Poems*
Robinson, Marilynn	*Housekeeping*
Roethke, Theodore	"My Papa's Waltz," "Elegy for Jane"
Schnackenberg, Gjertrud	"Signs"
Shakespeare, William	Sonnets 65, 71, 73, 116
Shelley, Percy Bysshe	"Ozymandias"
Shepard, Sam	*Seven Plays*; *True West*
Singer, Isaac	"Gimpel the Fool"
Snyder, Richard	"A Mongoloid Child Handling Shells on the Beach"
Stafford, William	"Traveling through the Dark"
Stevens, Wallace	"Anecdote of the Jar"
Strunk & White	*The Elements of Style*
Thomas, Dylan	"In My Craft or Sullen Art," "Do Not Go Gentle into That Good Night"
Trimmer and Jennings	*Fictions*
Wakoski, Diane	"Uneasy Rider," "The Photos"
Walcott, Derek	"The camps hold their distance—brown chestnut and grey smoke," "There was one Syrian, with his bicycle, in our town"
Waller, Edmund	"Go Lovely Rose"
Welty, Eudora	"Petrified Man"
Wilbur, Richard	"The Writer," "Merlin Enthralled"
Williams, Tennessee	*The Glass Menagerie*
Williams, William Carlos	"The Use of Force," "Spring and All," "The Red Wheelbarrow," "This is Just to Say"
Wolff, Tobias	"In the Garden of the North American Martyrs"
Yeats, William Butler	"A Dream of Death," "Crazy Jane Talks with the Bishop," "Leda and the Swan," "Sailing to Byzantium," "A Second Coming"
Zagajewski, Adam	"A Polish Dictionary," "Without End," "Song of an Emigre"

Wittenberg University
PO Box 720
Springfield, OH 45501
(513) 327-6314

The English program at Wittenberg has three comprehensive objectives for its students. First, the program "helps the student to be receptive to all literature, to be sensitive to new ideas and feelings, to acquire a sense of cultural identity, to develop a sense of human values pertaining to literature, and lastly, to gain pleasure in reading and rereading." Second, the "program helps the student to share personal responses and perceptions, to participate in new forms of imaginative thinking and expression, to communicate with clarity and style, to gain experience in writing fiction, poetry, and drama, to study avant-garde literature, and to explore the relationship between literature and fine arts." Third, the "program helps the student to know major authors/works in English, American, and world literature, to know Biblical, mythic, and contemporary works, to know how the language of a certain culture reflects a perception of reality, and to know the nuances of the English language, the methodology of literary research, and the development and use of an organizing thesis."

Wittenberg's English majors are expected to be familiar with the following works, and therefore this is literature the department considers especially worthwhile.

	Bible: Genesis, Exodus, Job, Psalms, Matthew
Aeschylus	One play
Aristophanes	One play
Austen, Jane	*Emma* or *Pride and Prejudice*
Bacon, Francis	*Essays* or More's *Utopia*
Blake, William	*Songs of Innocence and Experience*
Browning, Robert	Selections
Bunyan, John	*The Pilgrim's Progress*
Cervantes, Miguel de	*Don Quixote* (selections)
Chaucer, Geoffrey	*Canterbury Tales* (Prologue and selected tales)
Conrad, Joseph	A representative novel
Dante	*Inferno*
Dickens, Charles	One novel, plus one additional novel from a Victorian author
Donne, John	Selected lyrics
Dostoevski, Feodor	A major work
Eliot, T. S.	*The Waste Land*
Ellison, Ralph	*Invisible Man*
Euripides	One play
Faulkner, William	A representative novel

Fielding, Henry	*Tom Jones*
Goethe, J. Wolfgang von	*Faust,* Part 1
Hemingway, Ernest	A representative novel or group of short stories
Homer	*The Iliad* or *The Odyssey*
James, Henry	A representative novel
Jonson, Ben	*The Alchemist* or *Volpone*
Joyce, James	*A Portrait of the Artist as a Young Man* or a major novel by Virginia Woolf
Kafka, Franz	Selected stories
Keats, John	Selected poems and letters
Melville, Herman	*Moby-Dick*
Miller, Arthur	*Death of a Salesman*
Milton, John	*Paradise Lost*
More, Thomas	*Utopia* or selected essays by Bacon
O'Neill, Eugene	*Long Day's Journey into Night* or a play by Miller or Williams
Ovid	*Metamorphoses* or Vergil's *Aeneid,* Bks. 1–6
Pope, Alexander	"Essay on Criticism" or "Essay on Man" or "The Rape of the Lock"
Shakespeare, William	Four plays (tragedy, history, comedy, and romance)
Sophocles	*Oedipus the King*
Spencer, Edmund	Selections from *The Faerie Queene*
Swift, Jonathan	*Gulliver's Travels*
Tennyson, Alfred Lord	Selections
Thoreau, Henry	*Walden*
Tolstoy, Leo	A major work
Twain, Mark	*The Adventures of Huckleberry Finn*
Vergil	*The Aeneid,* Bks. 1–6 or selections from Ovid
Whitman, Walt	Selections
Williams, Tennessee	*The Glass Menagerie* or a play by Miller or O'Neill
Woolf, Virginia	A major novel or Joyce's *A Portrait of the Artist as a Young Man*
Wordsworth and Coleridge	Selections from *Lyrical Ballads*
Yeats, William Butler	Selected lyrics

Wright State University
3640 Colonel Glenn Highway
Dayton, OH 45435
(513) 873-2211

A preface to Wright State's pamphlet "A Fiction Reading List For The General Public" states "the purpose of this list is to guide those seeking recommendations of quality fiction, drama, ... The list does not claim to be exhaustive. Thus it includes only one title for any given author and omits works of substantial reputation considered too esoteric to be of general interest."

The English Department faculty at Wright State compiled the list, which is divided into four sections. Recent fiction is in the first section; classic and contemporary (post World War II) works are in the second and third sections; drama is in the fourth.

The parentheses beside the books contain the nationality of the author and the first date of publication. The key to the abbreviations is at the end of Wright State's listings.

A Fiction Reading List for the General Public

BEST RECENTLY PUBLISHED FICTION

Allende, Isabel	*Eva Luna*
Atwood, Margaret	*Cat's Eye*
Canin, Ethan	*Emperor of the Air* (stories)
Carver, Ray	*Where I'm Calling From* (stories)
Chabon, Michael	*The Mysteries of Pittsburgh*
Dexter, Pete	*Paris Trout*
DeLillo, Don	*Libra*
Erdrich, Louise	*Tracks*
Ford, Richard	*Rock Springs* (stories)
García Márquez, Gabriel	*Love in the Time of Cholera*
Greene, Graham	*The Captain and the Enemy*
Harrison, Jim	*Dalva*
Kennedy, William	*Quinn's Book*
McMurtry, Larry	*Anything for Billy*
Mason, Bobbie Ann	*Spence & Lila*
Oates, Joyce Carol	*The Assignation* (stories)
Tyler, Anne	*Breathing Lessons*
Updike, John	*S*
Winterson, Jeanette	*The Passion*
Wolfe, Tom	*The Bonfire of the Vanities*

CLASSIC FICTION

Acevedo Diaz, Eduardo	*The Cry of Glory* (UR, 1894)
Alegria, Ciro	*Broad and Alien Is the World* (PE, 1941)
Anderson, Sherwood	*Winesburg, Ohio* (AM, 1919)
Austen, Jane	*Pride and Prejudice* (BR, 1813)
Balzac, Honoré de	*Père Goriot* (FR, 1834)
Baroja, Pio	*The Restlessness of Shanti Andia* (SP, 1911)
Bennett, Arnold	*The Old Wives' Tale* (BR, 1908)
Bernanos, Georges	*The Diary of a Country Priest* (FR, 1936)
Bierce, Ambrose	*In the Midst of Life* (AM, 1891)
Bowen, Elizabeth	*The Death of the Heart* (AN-IR, 1939)
Bromfield, Louis	*The Rains Came* (AM, 1937)
Brontë, Charlotte	*Jane Eyre* (BR, 1847)
Brontë, Emily	*Wuthering Heights* (BR, 1848)
Buck, Pearl	*The Good Earth* (AM, 1931)
Bunyan, John	*The Pilgrim's Progress* (BR, 1678)
Burney, Fanny	*Evelina* (BR, 1778)
Butler, Samuel	*The Way of All Flesh* (BR, 1903)
Cable, George Washington	*The Grandissimes* (AM, 1880)
Caldwell, Erskine	*God's Little Acre* (AM, 1933)
Camus, Albert	*The Stranger* (FR, 1942)
Carroll, Lewis	*Alice's Adventures in Wonderland* (BR, 1865)
Cary, Joyce	*The Horse's Mouth* (AN-IR, 1944)
Cather, Willa	*Death Comes for the Archbishop* (AM, 1927)
Cela, Camilo José	*The Family of Pascual Duarte* (SP, 1942)
Céline, Louis-Ferdinand	*Journey to the End of Night* (FR, 1932)
Cervantes, Miguel de	*Don Quixote* (SP, 1606)
Chekhov, Anton	*Short Stories* (RU, 1880s, 1890s)
Chopin, Kate	*The Awakening* (AM, 1899)
Clark, Walter van Tiburg	*The Ox-Bow Incident* (AM, 1940)
Collins, Wilkie	*The Moonstone* (BR, 1868)
Conrad, Joseph	*Heart of Darkness* (BR, 1902)
Cooper, James Fenimore	*The Prairie* (AM, 1827)
Crane, Stephen	*The Red Badge of Courage* (AM, 1895)
cummings, e. e.	*The Enormous Room* (AM, 1922)
Defoe, Daniel	*Robinson Crusoe* (BR, 1719)
Dickens, Charles	*Great Expectations* (BR, 1860–61)
Dinesen, Isak	*Seven Gothic Tales* (DA, 1934)
Dos Passos, John	*U.S.A.* (AM, 1919–36)
Dostoevski, Feodor	*Crime and Punishment* (RU, 1866)
Doyle, Sir Arthur Conan	*The Adventures of Sherlock Holmes* (BR, 1891)
Dreiser, Theodore	*Sister Carrie* (AM, 1900)
Eliot, George	*Middlemarch* (BR, 1872)

Farrell, James T.	*Studs Lonigan* (AM, 1932–34)
Faulkner, William	*Absalom, Absalom!* (AM, 1936)
Fielding, Henry	*Tom Jones* (BR, 1749)
Fitzgerald, F. Scott	*The Great Gatsby* (AM, 1925)
Flaubert, Gustave	*Madame Bovary* (FR, 1857)
Ford, Ford Madox	*The Good Soldier* (BR, 1915)
Forster, E. M.	*Howard's End* (BR, 1910)
Frederic, Harold	*The Damnation of Theron Ware* (AM, 1896)
Gallegos, Romula	*Dona Barbara* (VE, 1939)
Galsworthy, John	*A Man of Property* (BR, 1906)
Garland, Hamlin	*Main-Travelled Roads* (AM, 1891)
Gaskell, Elizabeth	*Cranford* (BR, 1853)
Gide, André	*The Immoralist* (FR, 1902)
Goethe, J. Wolfgang von	*The Sorrows of Young Werther* (GE, 1774)
Gogol, Nicolai	*Dead Souls* (RU, 1842)
Goldsmith, Oliver	*The Vicar of Wakefield* (BR, 1766)
Goncharov, Ivan	*Oblomov* (RU, 1855)
Gorky, Maxim	*Mother* (RU, 1907)
Graves, Robert	*I, Claudius* (BR, 1934)
Güiraldes, Ricardo	*Don Segundo Sombra* (AR, 1926)
Hardy, Thomas	*The Return of the Native* (BR, 1878)
Hawthorne, Nathaniel	*The Scarlet Letter* (AM, 1850)
Hemingway, Ernest	*A Farewell to Arms* (AM, 1929)
Hémon, Louis	*Maria Chapdelaine* (CA, 1914)
Hesse, Herman	*Demian* (GR, 1919)
Howells, William Dean	*The Rise of Silas Lapham* (AM, 1885)
Hughes, Richard	*A High Wind in Jamaica* (BR, 1929)
Hugo, Victor	*Les Misérables* (FR, 1862)
Hurston, Zora Neale	*Their Eyes Were Watching God* (AM, 1937)
Huxley, Aldous	*Brave New World* (BR, 1932)
Irving, Washington	*Short Stories* (AM, 1820s, 1830s)
James, Henry	*The Portrait of a Lady* (AM, 1881)
Joyce, James	*Dubliners* (IR, 1914)
Kafka, Franz	*The Trial* (CZ, 1925)
Koestler, Arthur	*Darkness at Noon* (HU, 1940)
Lawrence, D.H.	*Sons and Lovers* (BR, 1913)
Lewis, Sinclair	*Babbitt* (AM, 1922)
London, Jack	*The Call of the Wild* (AM, 1903)
Malraux, André	*Man's Fate* (FR, 1934)
Mann, Thomas	*Death in Venice* (GR, 1913)
Mansfield, Katherine	*Collected Stories* (NZ, 1945)
Marquand, John P.	*The Late George Apley* (AM, 1937)
Maugham, Somerset	*Of Human Bondage* (BR, 1915)
Maupassant, Guy de	*Short Stories* (FR, 1880s)
Mauriac, François	*The Nest of Vipers* (FR, 1932)
McCullers, Carson	*The Heart Is a Lonely Hunter* (AM, 1940)
Melville, Herman	*Moby-Dick* (AM, 1851)

Meredith, George	*The Egoist* (BR, 1879)
Mitchell, Margaret	*Gone with the Wind* (AM, 1936)
Moore, George	*Esther Waters* (BR, 1894)
Murasaki, Shikibu	*The Tale of Genji* (JA, *c* 1000)
Norris, Frank	*The Octopus* (AM, 1901)
O'Hara, John	*Appointment in Samarra* (AM, 1934)
Poe, Edgar Allan	*Short Stories* (AM, 1840s)
Proust, Marcel	*Swann's Way* (FR, 1913–17)
Pushkin, Alexander	*Short Stories* (RU, 1820s, 30s)
Rabelais, François	*Gargantua and Pantagruel* (FR, 1532–64)
Remarque, Erich Maria	*All Quiet on the Western Front* (GE, 1928)
Richardson, Samuel	*Clarissa* (abridged) (BR, 1747–48)
Rivera, Jose Eustasio	*The Vortex* (CO, 1924)
Rölvaag, O.E.	*Giants in the Earth* (NO-AM, 1927)
Scott, Sir Walter	*Ivanhoe* (BR, 1820)
Shelley, Mary	*Frankenstein* (BR, 1818)
Silone, Ignazio	*Bread and Wine* (IT, 1937)
Sinclair, Upton	*The Jungle* (AM, 1901)
Smollett, Tobias	*Humphry Clinker* (BR, 1771)
Stegner, Wallace	*The Big Rock Candy Mountain* (AM, 1938)
Steinbeck, John	*The Grapes of Wrath* (AM, 1939)
Stendhal	*The Red and the Black* (FR, 1831)
Sterne, Laurence	*Tristram Shandy* (BR, 1760–67)
Stevenson, R. L.	*Dr. Jekyll and Mr. Hyde* (BR, 1886)
Stowe, Harriet Beecher	*Uncle Tom's Cabin* (AM, 1852)
Swift, Jonathan	*Gulliver's Travels* (BR, 1726)
Tate, Allen	*The Fathers* (AM, 1938)
Thackeray, Wm. Makepeace	*Vanity Fair* (BR, 1847–48)
Tolstoy, Leo	*Anna Karenina* (RU, 1873–76)
Toomer, Jean	*Cane* (AM, 1923)
Trollope, Anthony	*Barchester Towers* (BR, 1857)
Turgenev, Ivan	*Fathers and Sons* (RU, 1892)
Twain, Mark	*The Adventures of Huckleberry Finn* (AM, 1885)
Unamuno, Miguel de	*Abel Sanchez & Other Stories* (SP, 1931)
Undset, Sigrid	*Kristin Lavransdatter* (NO, 1920–22)
Voltaire	*Candide* (FR,1759)
Walpole, Horace	*The Castle of Otranto* (BR, 1764)
Waugh, Evelyn	*Brideshead Revisited* (BR, 1944)
Wells, H. G.	*The Time Machine* (BR, 1895)
West, Nathanael	*The Day of the Locust* (AM, 1939)
Wharton, Edith	*The Age of Innocence* (AM, 1920)
Wilde, Oscar	*The Picture of Dorian Gray* (BR, 1891)
Wilder, Thornton	*The Bridge of San Luis Rey* (AM, 1927)
Wister, Owen	*The Virginian* (AM, 1902)
Wolfe, Thomas	*Look Homeward, Angel* (AM, 1929)
Woolf, Virginia	*To the Lighthouse* (BR, 1927)

Wright, Richard	*Native Son* (AM, 1940)
Zola, Émile	*Germinal* (FR, 1885)

CONTEMPORARY FICTION

Abe, Kobo	*The Woman in the Dunes* (JA, 1964)
Achebe, Chinua	*Things Fall Apart* (NI, 1958)
Agee, James	*A Death in the Family* (AM, 1957)
Amis, Kingsley	*Lucky Jim* (BR, 1953)
Asturias, Miguel Angel	*El Señor Presidente* (GU, 1946)
Atwood, Margaret	*Surfacing* (CA, 1972)
Babel, Isaac	*The Collected Stories* (RU, 1955)
Baldwin, James	*Another Country* (AM, 1960)
Barth, John	*The Sot-Weed Factor* (AM, 1960)
Beattie, Ann	*Falling in Place* (AM, 1980)
Bellow, Saul	*Mr. Sammler's Planet* (AM, 1969)
Böll, Heinrich	*Billiards at Half-Past Nine* (GE, 1962)
Borges, Jorge	*Ficciones* (AR, 1965)
Boyle, T. Coraghessan	*World's End* (AM, 1987)
Brown, Claude	*Manchild in the Promised Land* (AM, 1965)
Burgess, Anthony	*A Clockwork Orange* (BR, 1962)
Calvino, Italo	*If on a Winter's Night a Traveler* (IT, 1981)
Carver, Raymond	*Cathedral* (AM, 1983)
Cheever, John	*Collected Short Stories* (AM, 1963)
Connell, Evan S.	*Mrs. Bridge* (AM, 1958)
Coover, Robert	*The Public Burning* (AM, 1977)
Cortazar, Julio	*Hopscotch* (AR, 1963)
Crews, Harry	*Car* (AM, 1972)
Dickey, James	*Deliverance* (AM, 1970)
Didion, Joan	*Play It as It Lays* (AM, 1970)
Doctorow, E.L.	*Ragtime* (AM, 1975)
Drabble, Margaret	*The Garrick Year* (BR, 1964)
Duras, Marguerite	*The Lover* (FR, 1984)
Durrell, Lawrence	*Justine* (BR, 1957)
Ellison, Ralph	*Invisible Man* (AM, 1947)
Findley, Timothy	*Famous Last Words* (CA, 1981)
Fowles, John	*The French Lieutenant's Woman* (BR, 1969)
Friedman, Bruce Jay	*Stern* (AM, 1962)
Fuentes, Carlos	*The Death of Artemio Cruz* (ME, 1961)
García Márquez, Gabriel	*One Hundred Years of Solitude* (CO, 1967)
Gardner, John	*Grendel* (AM, 1971)
Gironella, Jose	*The Cypresses Believe in God* (SP, 1953)
Godwin, Gail	*A Mother and Two Daughters* (AM, 1982)
Golding, William	*Lord of the Flies* (BR, 1954)
Gordimer, Nadine	*Burger's Daughter* (SA, 1979)
Gordon, Mary	*Final Payments* (AM, 1978)

Grass, Günter	*The Tin Drum* (GE, 1959)
Greene, Graham	*The Heart of the Matter* (BR, 1948)
Hanna, Barry	*Hey Jack!* (AM, 1987)
Heller, Joseph	*Catch-22* (AM, 1955)
Helprin, Mark	*A Winter's Tale* (AM, 1983)
Himes, Chester	*Pinktoes* (AM, 1965)
Hoban, Russell	*Riddley Walker* (BR, 1981)
Icaza, Jorges	*The Villagers* (EC, 1951)
Jones, Gayl	*Corregidora* (AM, 1975)
Jones, James	*From Here To Eternity* (AM, 1951)
Kawabata, Yasunari	*Thousand Cranes* (JA, 1959)
Kazantzakis, Nikos	*Zorba the Greek* (GR, 1946)
Kerouac, Jack	*On the Road* (AM, 1955)
Kesey, Ken	*One Flew Over the Cuckoo's Nest* (AM, 1962)
Kim, Richard E.	*The Martyred* (KO-AM, 1964)
Kinsella, W.P.	*Shoeless Joe* (CA, 1982)
Knowles, John	*A Separate Peace* (AM, 1959)
Lagerquist, Par	*The Dwarf* (SW, 1953)
Lampedusa, Giuseppe di	*The Leopard* (IT, 1960)
Lee, Harper	*To Kill a Mockingbird* (AM, 1960)
Le Guin, Ursula	*The Left Hand of Darkness* (AM, 1969)
Lessing, Doris	*The Golden Notebook* (BR, 1962)
Lodge, David	*Souls and Bodies* (BR, 1980)
Lowry, Malcolm	*Under the Volcano* (BR, 1947)
Mailer, Norman	*The Naked and the Dead* (AM, 1948)
Malamud, Bernard	*The Fixer* (AM, 1966)
Marshall, Paule	*Praisesong for the Widow* (AM, 1983)
McPherson, James Allen	*Hue and Cry* (AM, 1969)
Moore, Brian	*The Lonely Passion of Judith Hearne* (IR-CA-AM, 1973)
Moravia, Alberto	*Two Women* (IT, 1958)
Morris, Wright	*Love Among the Cannibals* (AM, 1957)
Morrison, Toni	*Sula* (AM, 1973)
Murdoch, Iris	*Under the Net* (BR, 1954)
Nabokov, Vladimir	*Lolita* (AM, 1953)
Naylor, Gloria	*The Women of Brewster Place* (AM, 1983)
Oates, Joyce Carol	*Them* (AM, 1969)
O'Connor, Edwin	*The Last Hurrah* (AM, 1956)
O'Connor, Flannery	*The Violent Bear It Away* (AM, 1955)
Olsen, Tillie	*Tell Me a Riddle and Other Stories* (AM, 1971)
Orwell, George	*1984* (BR, 1949)
Ozick, Cynthia	*Levitation: Five Fictions* (AM, 1983)
Paley, Grace	*Enormous Changes at the Last Minute* (AM, 1960)
Pasternak, Boris	*Doctor Zhivago* (RU, 1958)
Paton, Alan	*Cry, The Beloved Country* (SA, 1948)
Percy, Walker	*The Moviegoer* (AM, 1960)
Piercy, Marge	*Gone to Soldiers* (AM, 1987)

Plath, Sylvia	*The Bell Jar* (AM, 1971)
Porter, Katherine Anne	*Pale Horse, Pale Rider* (AM, 1939)
Potok, Chaim	*My Name Is Asher Lev* (AM, 1972)
Powers, J. F.	*Morte D'Urban* (AM, 1956)
Powers, John R.	*The Last Catholic in America* (AM, 1973)
Pritchett, V. S.	*Collected Stories* (BR, 1981)
Purdy, James	*Malcolm* (AM, 1959)
Pym, Barbara	*Quartet in Autumn* (BR, 1980)
Quiroga, Horacio	*South American Jungle Tales* (UR, 1959)
Read, Piers Paul	*A Married Man* (BR, 1980)
Rhys, Jean	*Wide Sargasso Sea* (AM, 1966)
Robbe-Grillet, Alain	*Jealousy* (FR, 1987)
Robbins, Tom	*Even Cowgirls Get the Blues* (AM, 1976)
Robinson, Marilynne	*Housekeeping* (AM, 1981)
Roth, Philip	*Goodbye, Columbus* (AM, 1959)
Rulfo, Juan	*Pedro Paramo* (ME, 1955)
Sabato, Ernesto	*The Tunnel* (AR, 1948)
Sagan, Françoise	*Bonjour Tristesse* (FR, 1954)
Salinger, J. D.	*The Catcher in the Rye* (AM, 1951)
Shaara, Michael	*Killer Angels* (AM, 1974)
Sheed, Wilfred	*People Will Always Be Kind* (AM, 1973)
Sillitoe, Alan	*Saturday Night and Sunday Morning* (BR, 1958)
Simon, Claude	*The Grass* (FR, 1958)
Singer, Isaac Bashevis	*The Collected Stories* (AM, 1981)
Solzhenitsyn, Alexander	*One Day in the Life of Ivan Denisovich* (RU, 1963)
Sontag, Susan	*I, Etcetera* (AM, 1978)
Soyinka, Wole	*The Interpreters* (NI, 1965)
Spark, Muriel	*Memento Mori* (BR, 1958)
Stone, Robert	*A Flag for Sunrise* (AM, 1981)
Styron, William	*Lie Down in Darkness* (AM, 1951)
Tanizaki, Junichiro	*Some Prefer Nettles* (JA, 1965)
Thomas, D. M.	*The White Hotel* (BR, 1981)
Tolkien, J. R.	*The Lord of the Rings* (BR, 1954–55)
Toole, John Kennedy	*A Confederacy of Dunces* (AM, 1980)
Tyler, Anne	*Dinner at the Homesick Restaurant* (AM, 1982)
Updike, John	*Rabbit, Run* (AM, 1960)
Valenzuela, Luisa	*Strange Things Happen Here* (AR, 1979)
Vargos Llosa, Mario	*The Green House* (PE, 1965)
Vonnegut, Kurt	*Slaughterhouse-Five* (AM, 1969)
Wain, John	*Hurry on Down* (BR, 1953)
Walker, Alice	*The Color Purple* (AM, 1982)
Wallant, Edward Louis	*The Pawnbroker* (AM, 1962)
Warren, Robert Penn	*All the King's Men* (AM, 1946)

Welty, Eudora	*Collected Stories* (AM, 1980)
White, Patrick	*The Aunt's Story* (AU, 1946)
White, T. H.	*The Once and Future King* (BR, 1958)
Wiesel, Elie	*A Beggar in Jerusalem* (FR, 1968)
Williams, John A.	*The Man Who Cried I Am* (AM, 1967)
Woiwode, Larry	*Beyond the Bedroom Wall* (AM, 1976)
Yourcenar, Marguerite	*Memoirs of Hadrian* (FR, 1951)

Key to abbreviations:

AM,	American	IR-CA-AM,	Irish Canadian-American
AN-IR,	Anglo-Irish	IT,	Italian
AR,	Argentinian	JA,	Japanese
AU,	Australian	KO-AM,	Korean American
BE,	Belgian	ME,	Mexican
BR,	British	NI,	Nigerian
CA,	Canadian	NO,	Norwegian
CO,	Colombian	NO-AM,	Norwegian American
CZ,	Czecholslavakian	NZ,	New Zealand
DA,	Danish	PE,	Peruvian
EC,	Ecuadorian	RO,	Roman
FR,	French	RU,	Russian
GE,	German	SA,	South African
GR,	Greek	SP,	Spanish
GU,	Guatemalan	SW,	Swedish
HU,	Hungarian	SWI,	Swiss
IN,	Indian	UR,	Uruguayan
IR,	Irish	VE,	Venezuelan